Lessons from Mars

How One Global Company Cracked the
Code on High Performance Collaboration
and Teamwork

Lessons from Mars

How One Global Company Cracked the Code on High Performance Collaboration and Teamwork

Carlos Valdes-Dapena

CHANGE
MAKERS
BOOKS

Winchester, UK
Washington, USA

First published by Changemakers Books, 2018
Changemakers Books is an imprint of John Hunt Publishing Ltd., No. 3 East St., Alresford,
Hampshire SO24 9EE, UK
office1@jhpbooks.net
www.johnhuntpublishing.com
www.changemakers-books.com

For distributor details and how to order please visit the 'Ordering' section on our website.

Text copyright: Carlos Valdes-Dapena 2017

ISBN: 978 1 78535 358 1
978 1 78535 359 8 (ebook)
Library of Congress Control Number: 2017930556

A CIP catalogue record for this book is available from the British Library.

Design: Stuart Davies

Printed and bound by CPI Group (UK) Ltd, Croydon, CR0 4YY, UK

We operate a distinctive and ethical publishing philosophy in
all areas of our business, from our global network of authors to
production and worldwide distribution.

Contents

Acknowledgements   xii

Introduction   1

Part I   9

Chapter 1: The "I" in Team, Part 1   10

Chapter 2: Mars and High Performance Teamwork   28

Chapter 3: Research and the First Insights   43

Chapter 4: What Doesn't Work   62

Chapter 5: The "I" in Team, Part 2   82

Part II   101

Chapter 6: Intentional Collaboration and the Three Imperatives   102

Chapter 7: The Practices of High Performance Collaboration   126

Chapter 8: Clarity and Inspire Purpose   151

Chapter 9: Clarity and Crystallize Intent   179

Chapter 10: Intentionality and Cultivate Collaboration   193

Chapter 11: Discipline and Activate Ways-of-Working   226

Chapter 12: Team Learning   263

Chapter 13: Discipline and Sustain & Renew   283

Chapter 14: The Special Practice—Clarify Context   310

Part III   329

Chapter 15: Putting the Framework to Work   330

Using the Appendices   361

Appendix A: Team Purpose   364

Appendix B: Crystallize Intent   379

Appendix C: Cultivate Collaboration   386

Appendix D: Activate Ways-of-Working   392

Appendix E: Sustain & Renew   402

Appendix F: Clarify Context   416

Notes   422

This book is, could only be, dedicated to Janet Aldrich, aka Janet Valdes-Dapena, my wife of almost 30 years. Janet, an accomplished professional in her own right, has been my relentless champion. At the height of her success—she has appeared in five Broadway shows, in regional and international theatrical productions, as well as in soap operas and film—Janet saw something in me. She believed in me more than I believed in myself. She encouraged me, even pushed me, to do and be more than I thought I could. My life unfolded into something I never imagined, thanks to her. This work is the product of her belief, her faith in me, and her blessed impatience with my short-sighted notions of myself.

Acknowledgements

I had always imagined that writing a book was a solitary task. I couldn't have been more wrong. At every stage, it required collective effort. From the initial formulation of our team framework to the first outline of the book and on to the final steps of editing and design, it has taken collaboration to make the Mars Framework for High Performance Collaboration—HPC or just the Framework—and this book about it a reality.

Before there was a Framework or the idea for a book about it, there were people who, without knowing it, were laying the groundwork. In 2008 I was on the verge of leaving Mars as the result of a reorganization. My manager at the time, Zelda Gray, came to me with a suggestion. Over a glass of red wine one evening, Zelda explained that she and another vice president (VP) with whom I had worked, Ulf Hahnemann, had cooked up an idea. They knew I had a passion and a knack for teams and teamwork. They suggested that I create a role as internal team consultant within Mars University, our learning and development function. There was a catch, though. There was no budget to pay for the role. I'd have to earn back the cost of my salary and benefits through charging internally for my services. Knowing that I had support from some of the most respected human resources (HR) leaders in our business, it didn't seem like a big risk. Besides, I liked working at Mars and preferred to stay. So I said, "Yes." Thanks to Zelda and Ulf and to Jim Brodie who was leading Mars University in North America at the time, I stepped into a job and unknowingly stepped into my life's work. Special thanks go to Howard Guttman. Howard equipped me for success by graciously allowing me to work with models and approaches that his firm, Guttman Development Strategies, had been using successfully at Mars for several years. Without him, my new role would never have existed.

A year or so after I began I was struggling to find a way to build team development into one of our leadership programs. Vidula Bal, who led Mars leadership development at the time, suggested that I look at my own cache of team data. That single suggestion triggered a cascade of events that led to this book. Vidula was also the first to lay eyes on early versions of the Framework and the thinking behind it. It was she who said, "Carlos, I think you may be on to something here." My gratitude for her wisdom is beyond my ability to express. My then-teammate, Todd Fryling, got me into a 2011 conference on high performing teams run by the Society for Industrial & Organizational Psychology. While there I spoke with luminaries in the field, including Richard Hackman. Dr Hackman was gracious and generous in allowing me to share some of my early insights and thoughts and then providing feedback and advice on the spot.

Clint Kofford, then a colleague at Mars, and Celia Harmon, a former Mars Associate, worked with me to refine the Framework into something polished enough to be featured in our leadership development programs. Clint's infallible sense of what works, his endless support for my ideas, and his skillfully gentle challenges ensured that the Framework was not only theoretically sound but right for our culture. Celia, with her finely honed trainer's eye and her knowledge of teams and teamwork, helped to finalize the Framework and many of the tools we still use. Phyllis Wallin, another Mars colleague, is an unapologetic perfectionist and an HPC aficionado. Phyllis made sure that whatever we created in relation to the Framework—classroom materials and e-learnings, for instance—was of the highest quality.

Prior to the creation of the Framework there were scores of Mars Associates, Line Managers and functional leaders, who as my clients contributed the data that eventually shaped the Framework. Sylvia Qu thought enough of my skills to bring me to China to work with our Wrigley Leadership Team there. This eventually led to my engagement with the Wrigley Asia Pacific

Leadership Team. Both groups provided valuable experience and information that fed directly into the eventual formulation of the HPC Framework. Mark Andrews, who led our Petcare business in China a few years back, was the first to experience HPC as we know it today. His team served as a living laboratory over three years. Thanks also to Malcolm Armstrong, Carla Lang, Fred Stenou and all my colleagues at the Nutro Company back in the USA who entrusted themselves and their teams to my capabilities and instincts and provided many stories for the book. The inimitable Jen Schulte repeatedly brought me in to work with the teams she supported and led. Craig Hall, who led our Ice Cream business while Jen was there, was wonderful in his willingness to play along. Juliana Saretta is a Mars colleague, a friend, and a client who has called upon me numerous times to support her and her teams. Her faith in me and my practice with teams has been a source of learning and joy and played an important role in proving the value of the Framework. Then there's Rob Moffett, my manager and colleague at Mars, who has for the past six years done all he can to ensure that I had a place to thrive, grow and create, as well as the budget to help pay for it all. Without Rob's support, I wouldn't be writing this today.

As I worked with teams and delivered the earliest versions of the manager-training program that includes HPC, several team members and program participants suggested that I write a book. Once I began the writing process, my league of collaborators expanded. My occasional partner in crime and graphic facilitator extraordinaire, Dana Wright, planned and hosted the writers' retreat that gave the book the kick start it needed. Yvette Huygen and Bea Reilley, two other budding authors who joined us in Tulum, Mexico, provided feedback on the earliest drafts and helped impart and sustain momentum. Dana introduced me to the incomparable Michelle Auerbach, my editor and advisor on all things dealing with writing, publishing and books. Together we created the proposal that was eventually accepted by Changemakers Books. Michelle patiently edited every chapter thereafter, offering feedback, guidance and encouragement. It was Michelle's belief in me that kept me writing when the going was slow and difficult. Michelle introduced me to Tim Ward at Changemakers. Tim, too, took me under his wing, providing superb editorial feedback, reassurance, and gentle pressure to get the damn thing written. Jane Maynard joined the team later and helped shape the graphics in the book, making them more appealing and useful.

Thanks, too, to Vincent Howell, another Mars colleague and friend. As the manuscript came together into something that others could review and comment on, Vincent guided me through the process of bringing senior Mars leaders into the conversation and feedback loop. One of those senior leaders, Debby Hyde, made invaluable contributions as an internal reviewer. This book is better because of her.

I'm fortunate enough to have worked with teams all over the world. Travel, therefore, has been a major feature of my job. My voyages have meant that I missed too many school concerts, field hockey and soccer games, as well as parent–teacher meetings and class holiday parties. My kids, Molly and George, were patient, understanding and supportive through it all. Thanks, guys. I love you.

I've just scratched the surface of those who contributed to making this book possible. I'm profoundly grateful to the hundreds of teams I worked with at Mars and the thousands of Mars Associates who were part of those teams. Without them and the trust they placed in me, there would be no High Performance Collaboration Framework and no book about it.

As you've gathered, I've traveled a lot for work. Business dinners are often a part of those trips. At the end of the first business dinner I attended as a Mars Associate, I learned about a custom that I've come to cherish. As the bill was being paid that night in Boston 16 years ago, and charged to a company credit card, those around the table thanked John, Forrest and Jacquie Mars for making their meal possible. At first I thought they were being sarcastic. I quickly learned that their gratitude, and the gratitude of every Mars Associate I've dined with since then, was and is sincere and deeply felt. I've always found this practice charming, appropriate and a little moving. It's in that spirit of gratitude that I thank John, Forrest, Jacquie and the entire Mars family for making the abundance of my career, and this book, possible.

Introduction

This is a book about collaboration and teams. It's not about chocolate, cat treats or rice, even though Mars makes all these things and more. Mars, Incorporated, is nonetheless an ingredient essential to this account. Our Framework for High Performance Collaboration, the subject of this book, grew directly out of work I did at Mars over 16 years. It's where the ideas that I share in these pages were developed and nurtured. So it's fitting that I set the stage with a story about Mars, its culture, and how that culture led to this book.

For several years global consumption of chocolate has been on the rise. That's good news for a company like Mars. While chocolate isn't our only business, it represents a significant percentage of our revenues. Regrettably, the growing global appetite for chocolate created a years-long chocolate shortage. It's not that the factories couldn't produce enough product. There's simply wasn't enough cacao, the raw material that ends up as chocolate, to go around. This dearth of chocolate began to reverse in 2016 as production picked up. Cacao, though, is a vulnerable tropical crop and future shortages remain a risk. This might seem like the quintessential first-world problem: "What do you mean, I can't have my white chocolate mocha latte supreme?" It's more than that. The crops of around six million small chocolate growers in Africa, South America and Asia remain under threat from climate change, plant disease and comparatively low crop yields. Their livelihoods, the health of their communities, and local economies are all at stake. Companies like Nestlé and Hershey, our competitors, have a lot at stake, too. With so much riding on the health of the ancient but fragile cacao plant, it made sense to act. Fortunately, genetic science provided a way forward. If we could understand more of what goes on inside the cacao plant and the valuable pods it produces, we could act to strengthen the plant, naturally. So we embarked on a project to gain that understanding.

In 2008, leading a consortium that included IBM, the USDA and others, Mars finished sequencing the genome of the cacao plant, yielding what we call the "cocoa genome." Then we did something surprising. As you might know, it's common practice for companies to legally protect the genetic discoveries they make. Drug and medical research companies do this, for better or for worse, regularly. It's a profitable practice. Mars chose to do just the opposite. Along with our consortium partners we published the entire cocoa genome on the internet, making it available to any and all who might be interested. By doing so we massively multiplied the range of research that could be conceived of and conducted, leading to an equivalent increase in the benefits that could be realized. What sort of benefits might, and in fact did, result?

There are three categories of impact that we've seen from the discovery of the cocoa genome: environmental, economic, and social. Knowing the cocoa genome allows for more selective and rapid breeding of the most productive and heartiest cocoa varieties (without relying on GMO technologies, by the way). It's predicted that this capability has the potential to increase cocoa yields by as much as 500% over the long term. Think of what that means for the environment. Cocoa farmers no longer need to raze rainforest lands to increase their output. They can get up to five times the yield from their current holdings. Higher yields have a direct economic impact. They mean more income for the farmers, who then spend that money in their local economies. Some of those expenditures could and do include hiring and paying local employees to work their farms. This leads to the next benefit. No longer do the children of farmers need to stay home to work the land. These children can now attend school and get an education that 10 or 20 years ago would have been unimaginable. Understanding the cocoa genome is a boon for the plant itself, for the farmers, their families and communities, and for every other person, company and country involved in the chocolate supply chain.

Clearly, the deciphering of the cocoa genome is tremendously important to a wide range of stakeholders. It was generous of Mars to share it. This valuable information could have conferred a distinct competitive advantage to our company, at least until someone caught up to us. Why didn't Mars choose this route? And what does it have to do with this book? Both are examples of the Mars Five Principles at work.

The Five Principles are an essential part of what makes Mars Mars, so it's worth taking a moment to summarize them. The Five Principles have been around in one form or another for most of Mars, Incorporated's history. They are the bedrock of the Mars business philosophy. Like a lot of companies' values, the Five Principles are aspirations for how all Mars associates and businesses will conduct themselves. They're more, though, than just nice words on posters in hallways and meeting rooms. The Five Principles are enacted every day throughout the company, guiding near- and long-term decisions and actions. Here they are, in summary:

Quality: The consumer is our boss, quality is our work, and value for money is our goal.

Responsibility: As individuals, we demand total responsibility from ourselves; as Associates, we support the responsibilities of others.

Mutuality: A mutual benefit is a shared benefit; a shared benefit will endure.

Efficiency: We use resources to the full, waste nothing, and do only what we can do best.

Freedom: We need freedom to shape our future; we need profit to remain free.

I won't try to fully educate you about the Five Principles here. For that, I encourage you to visit Mars.com where you will find a thorough explanation of the Five Principles. What's important to understand here is that the Five Principles are an integral part of how Mars operates. In particular, the Mutuality Principle led us to the conclusion that what we'd learned from the cocoa genome research was best shared. The Mutuality Principle states that:

A mutual benefit is a shared benefit; a shared benefit will endure.

We believe the standard by which our business relationships should be measured is the degree to which mutual benefits are created.

These benefits can take many different forms, and need not be strictly financial in nature. Likewise, while we must try to achieve the most competitive terms, the actions of Mars should never be at the expense, economic or otherwise, of others with whom we work.

Every stakeholder in the global cocoa supply chain, Mars included, stood to gain from our publishing the cocoa genome. This is the essence of the Mutuality Principle. So, what does all this have to do with this book? The same spirit of mutuality is behind our decision to publish a book about the Mars Framework for High Performance Collaboration which was developed entirely within Mars.

Effective collaboration and teamwork have always been central to how Mars Associates work. Our Framework for High Performance Collaboration (HPC) is in many ways an expression of who we are as a company. It's also been used successfully outside Mars, though; that's why I've written this book. I'm convinced it can work for you as well as it has for us. The insights from our research are applicable to groups and teams in almost any kind of organization. Our approach will, however, ask that you reconsider some cherished ideas you may have about teams and teamwork. I've structured the book, therefore, to account for both the Mars cultural influences on our Framework and the sometimes contrarian approach we've taken.

In Part I (the first 5 chapters), I present the case for why a new approach to teamwork and collaboration is needed. I'll discuss my background and share information about the Mars culture and the ways our culture shaped our collaborative behaviors. Then, I'll offer an account of the research I conducted. I'll explain what it taught us, not only about what was going on with teams at Mars, but about why traditional approaches to teamwork were falling short. I end Part I by linking the research we did on teams to research done elsewhere on individual motivation. I'll show how group dynamics and individual motivation theories come together for the benefit of collaboration and how this connection between individual and group theories led directly to our Framework.

Part II presents the Framework itself. The Framework has two major components: the Three Imperatives and the Six Practices. The Three Imperatives—Clarity, Intentionality and Discipline—describe three conditions that must be present to consistently unlock collaboration. They are the foundational element of the Framework and are especially useful for diagnosing teams. The Six Practices describe what teams can do to meet the demands of the Imperatives. The Practices are:

- Inspire Purpose
- Crystallize Intent
- Cultivate Collaboration
- Activate Ways-of-working
- Sustain & Renew
- Clarify Context

I provide details about each of the Practices: what they are, what they aren't, plus examples of how they've been applied and lessons we learned doing so.

Part III is dedicated to how others outside Mars can use the Framework. I offer ideas on how to apply and/or adapt the thinking underpinning the Framework to teams and collaboration in other organizations with different cultures.

In the appendices, I share a variety of tools and techniques, organized according to the Six Practices, that you can use as-is or modify for use in your organization to help you deliver better results through collaboration.

No matter where you work or how you use the Three Imperatives and Six Practices, collaboration is more than just a way to get work done and deliver results. It's a way that people in the workplace connect, develop relationships and find meaning in their work. The more productive and positive those relationships are, the better for the individuals, for their relationships, for the work they do and for the enterprise. More effective collaboration makes work better in almost every sense. Since most of us spend a considerable percentage of our lives at work, the better work is, the better off we are.

Our Framework for High Performance Collaboration is one of those things that enriches the experience of working for a living, whether you work for Mars or for one of our suppliers or customers. What's more, our products and brands touch hundreds of millions of consumers every day. Whether it's M&Ms® from the candy aisle, Pedigree® dog food from the pet food section, or Uncle Ben's® rice, what we make puts us into an ongoing relationship with consumers. As the Quality Principle states, "The consumer is our boss." If we can share something that will make life even a little better for the average person, it's good for them and good for us. Sharing the cocoa genome has already touched millions of lives, even if those affected may not be fully aware. While more modest in its impact, the Framework at the heart of this book can do the same. Read this book in that spirit. Take what it offers. Apply it, experiment with it, and share what you learn. Together we'll continue to expand the possibilities of what great collaboration can do.

Direct requests for information to:

collaborationparadox@gmail.com

Part I

Chapter 1

The "I" in Team, Part 1

The Return-on-Investment (ROI) on team building is lousy. I've seen figures that suggest a positive return on investments in things like corporate training programs and employee engagement. I've read about improved business performance based on increases in employee satisfaction. However, I have yet to come across any convincing work linking typical team-building programs to sustained improvement in team performance and outcomes. I feel certain that when, or if, those calculations are ever done, it will suggest a lot of money is being wasted, because the vast majority of the work done in the name of team building isn't creating any value.

I've been either managing teams or working with those who manage teams for almost 30 years. I've experienced or been part of leading hundreds of team-development or team-building exercises. I've taken part in paintball shoot-outs in the woods; I've led others in forming make-believe aircraft companies that designed and then mass-produced paper airplanes which then competed for greatest distance flown; I've sat in circles, and led those sitting in circles, passing a "talking stick" and telling deep, or at least less shallow truths. Some of this work was hugely enjoyable; some was really touching, some embarrassing and some, like my experience with paintball, surprisingly painful. Some of it left me feeling stoked or moved or just plain smiling. Some of it got me down or left me angry. None of these events, however, had a lasting impact on the performance of the group or groups involved.

But why?

Large organizations, run by very smart people, spend significant amounts of money trying to get good at something that you'd think is natural. I mean, humans evolved to collaborate, didn't we? Cave paintings in Europe show bands of early humans working together to bring down prehistoric creatures.

Observations of modern animal behavior suggest that the critters who evolved along with us also work together at things like hunting and child rearing. Birds do it, bees do it, even chimpanzees in the jungle do it. Apparently.

What's more, not only do we appear evolutionarily predisposed to collaborate, we think and act like it's a really good idea. Teamwork is something we hear about endlessly, starting on the playground, in school sports, and then at work. When we aren't hearing about teamwork, we're reading about teamwork in the latest company newsletter, or on motivational posters in the conference room:

Together Everyone Achieves More

When we're told that we're *not* team players, it's a severe criticism. Experts and students in the area of group dynamics devote days and months, even years, to reading about, writing about, and studying groups and teamwork. There are countless books and articles on the subject and who knows how many specific team interventions intended to enhance collaboration in the workplace. Yet, based on my 25 years of professional experience, all this inclination, effort and interest have yielded little in the way of sustained improvements in team effectiveness.

Again, why?

Part of the answer to the "Why?" is that teamwork is almost too sacred to question. Teams and teamwork, like organization charts and bitching around the coffee machine, are an essential part of corporate life for most of us. We may sense that the high we get from those team exercises, along with the bruises, wears off eventually and that things go back to the status quo, but no one is willing to look at that as failure. However, it's in my nature to challenge the status quo and I've become intensely interested in answering this particular "Why" question. I'd like to find some answers so that I, and those I work with, can then develop more effective approaches to enhancing collaboration in the workplace. That's what this book is all about.

The Framework I described in the Introduction arose out of my quest to understand why typical team building is so often a waste of time and what might work better. While this Framework is new, my fascination with groups and how they function is deeply ingrained. I'm the sixth of 11 children: five girls, six boys; five older than me and five younger. I grew up smack dab in the middle of a family whose particular dysfunctions (the subject of another book, perhaps) were magnified by our sheer numbers. Learning how to navigate that sometimes perilous environment instilled in me an intuitive sense of what it takes to survive in a group, and a natural interest in finding new and more effective strategies to do so. In 1994 I was fortunate enough to be hired by Development Dimensions International (DDI), based near Pittsburgh but with offices in New York City, near my home in New Jersey. I spent three years with DDI as an external trainer and consultant. It was during this time that I first encountered many of the concepts that I address in this book. For example, the idea of team dynamics, the stages of team development, and the use of personality types with teams were all part of my DDI experience. After three grueling years on the road for DDI, I was hired by IBM as an internal leadership coach and consultant to senior management at corporate headquarters in Armonk, New York. It was during my tenure in Armonk that I learned about David McClelland's work on motives, a framework that features prominently in the team effectiveness approach I developed. It was also during this period that I decided to go back to school for a second Master's degree, this one in Organizational Development. I attended the American University/NTL program, where our class cohort was also our laboratory for studying and working on group dynamics. I stayed at IBM for three years, leaving in 2000 for Mars, Incorporated, where I remain to this day.

My almost-sole focus on team effectiveness, though, only emerged eight years into my tenure with Mars. The part of the company I was working in at the time was reorganizing and my Organization Development (OD) role was made redundant. Unknown to me, a couple of senior managers who felt I had a talent for working with groups had a plan to keep me around. They proposed to our corporate learning and development organization, Mars University, that they create a role dedicated to supporting high performance teamwork. There was no budget for the role so it would have to self-fund. That is, I would have to charge my internal clients for my work and earn back the cost of my salary, wages and benefits. It was an unusual arrangement but Mars and I agreed to give it a go. I couldn't be more grateful. I was worried at first that I wouldn't find enough interested internal clients to support myself, but within six months it was clear that a role dedicated to team effectiveness could support itself and then some.

I soon realized that I had found my life's work. Ironically, not long after, I began to sense that as rewarding as the work was, and as much demand as there was for it, there was a problem. The role was functioning as designed; I was exceeding the expectations of my Mars University colleagues and my clients. I was earning my keep as clients rushed to fill my calendar, but the results I had expected weren't materializing. Teams were working with me — lots of them — but, more often than not, within a few weeks after my sessions with them, team members weren't working with each other any differently. Something was off. It would be a few years before I would conduct the inquiry that led to this book. As passionate as I was about my work at Mars, and as good as my clients told me I was, cracks in the traditional approaches to team effectiveness that I relied upon were showing years before this. I had always just assumed it was me.

Although I didn't know it then, my first clue to the troubled state of team building came in January of 1994, almost 15 years earlier. I was on my very first assignment as a consultant/trainer working for DDI. I found myself at a small factory in North Carolina, the sole output of which was the fabric, sometimes

called cambric, that covers the bottoms of mattress box springs
and the outsides of disposable diapers. It was a relatively new
plant: clean and airy, sterile feeling, but pleasant for a factory.
Just the week before, I had been certified to deliver DDI's team-
building programs. The curriculum was solid and well-designed
with excellent workbooks and videos, all based on Bruce
Tuckman's 1965 "Forming-Storming-Norming-Performing"
team development model. I was leading a workshop for about
18 employees in a bright classroom full of those one-piece chair-
and-desk units that you see in middle and high schools. The seats
were arranged, as you would expect, in neat columns facing the
front of the room. Welcome back to eighth grade.

I don't recall precisely how long it took, but an hour or two
into the half-day-long training program, things went south. This
was an angry group of employees whose chief gripes were:

- Their managers treated them unfairly
- Management didn't listen to their concerns.

What's more, they deeply resented their bosses for bringing
in this consultant guy from New York with his fancy training
program to "fix" them, when the problem as they saw it was
the bosses. It was a classic situation. Not knowing what else to
do, I chose to depart from the neatly designed leader's guide.
I was going to give them what they were asking for—a fair
hearing. I worked with them to move beyond complaining to
organizing their thoughts into a coherent list of topics they
could discuss with management. The employees were grateful,
if skeptical. Their managers were just plain pissed. They had
paid for a "damned team-training program" and that was what
they expected, not some outside agitator whose listening and list
making only encouraged the sort of moaning they were trying
to extinguish. As I look back on it, my actions were a quaint
combination of rookie mistake and wisdom. Back then, it only

felt horrible. I was fairly certain that my inexperience and lack of smarts, combined with astoundingly poor management at the plant, were to blame. I never suspected that part of the problems was that the approach was flawed.

Over 20 years have passed since my misadventure in North Carolina. In the intervening years, after working with close to a thousand teams using tools and approaches similar to those I had with me in the cambric factory, I have arrived at this conclusion. Whatever model you're working with – Four Stages, Five Dysfunctions, or 16 personality types – team building isn't as straightforward as it seems. Nor does it do what it promises.

Six years ago, I dedicated myself to working with teams at Mars, Incorporated in ways that would make a difference, long term. During that time, there have been two questions rattling around in the back of my mind that were the impetus for this book:

- Why do we spend so much time, money and effort trying to learn how to work in teams, or get better at it, when you'd think it would be second nature to us as social creatures?
- Why does all this effort have little lasting effect?

After all, we're hardwired to eat, to find mates, to play, all of which we humans do with considerable success. So why is collaboration so hard to get right?

It turns out I had been operating from a false assumption; we *aren't* coded to collaborate. For reasons I'll explain shortly, we're coded to do something else that sometimes, if properly directed, ends up as collaboration. The assumption that collaboration is innate leads us to do the wrong things to try to get folks to work together effectively. This in turn leads to processes and programs that end up like my visit to the fabric factory, misguided and not nearly as useful as leaders would like to think.

So what is the problem, exactly?

I think Maslow's Needs Hierarchy gets at the problem nicely.

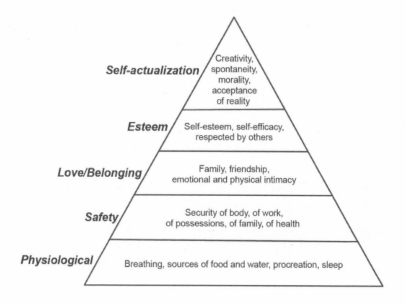

If you're reading this book, I'd guess you're already familiar with this elegant model. If so, bear with me. Our most fundamental needs, those towards the bottom of the hierarchy, deal with physiology and safety and are self-oriented: things like breathing, eating, mating and staying alive. Even though food and sex are usually better when someone else is with us, it's generally true that when things get tough or scary the first thing I'm going to think is, "How am *I* going to deal with this problem and save my butt and the butts of my progeny?", not "How am I going to work with *you* to deal with this?"

Which isn't to suggest that we're never there for each other. What about altruism? There's a lot to be said for altruism and the potentially powerful drive to sacrifice oneself for the benefit of others. We hear with regularity about people putting themselves at risk to save others, in war in particular. From my interviews with veterans and members of the military about their combat training, being there for your comrades, having one another's backs, is literally drilled into recruits for months. This kind of intensive conditioning, though, isn't seen in large, non-military institutions like for-profit corporations.

Then, there is this question: Are altruism and collaboration the same? Is helping others coming from the same mental/ emotional place as working with others? I don't think so. Altruism by definition expects no tangible reward or quid pro quo. Collaboration, on the other hand, is all about shared outcomes and mutual expectations. What is more, in studies of charitable giving, altruism has been shown to be driven in large part by what it provides to the giver, the self. "Warm-glow giving," as it has been called, describes that feeling that the giver gets from his or her act of generosity. Other self-oriented feelings like guilt, social pressure and even social status have also been found to drive altruistic behavior. In other words, it's not about us, not about collaboration. It's about me. I write this not to demean altruism. I only want to make the point that our desire to support others, which is a wonderful and sometimes life-saving human trait, isn't necessarily purely other-focused and isn't sufficient to support—or even the same as—collaboration. If we go back to those prehistoric hunters depicted on cave walls, I feel pretty sure that they collaborated on taking down ancient ungulates not from the goodness of their Paleolithic hearts, but so that they could feed themselves and their families, so that they could survive and propagate their genetic code.

We need to distinguish between collaboration and two other human tendencies: helpfulness and cooperation. I see helpfulness as a sort of lower-order altruism. It may involve dropping a buck in the cup of a homeless woman on the street or helping the guy next door to pull out a tree stump or helping a colleague to figure out how to create a pivot table in her spreadsheet. Helpfulness involves acts of kindness that, at their best, like altruism, seek no reward. When helpfulness does start to involve quid pro quo

18

exchanges, it moves into the space of cooperation. I'll help you so long as helping you helps me. We go along to get along, more or less. Some think of this as collaboration. I don't; at least I don't think of it as effective collaboration. As you will read later in this book, the kind of collaboration I'm interested in involves more commitment and intentionality than either helpfulness or cooperation. Helpful and cooperative people are good to have. For business teams and businesses to succeed, however, genuine, intentional collaboration is what is required. But you wouldn't know that, based on how our businesses are set up.

In the modern, Western world, most of our enterprises are designed to take advantage of our more common, or at least more easily accessed, self-first orientation. For example, the most common organizational structures, hierarchies themselves, play strongly to the bottom of Maslow's pyramid, to our instincts to take care of and work for ourselves first. In a traditional large organization, you will find hundreds, thousands, or hundreds of thousands of generally decent, *me*-centered people laboring away in an environment optimized to take advantage of this perfectly natural human tendency. Things like performance management, pay, recognition and rewards are all typically geared to individuals and they play on this individual survival mechanism. And therein lies the biggest problem with teams and collaboration at work. We preach collaboration, talk and train teamwork, but all the while most organizations are optimized to manage, foster and reward individual effort.

It's not news, right? This glaring contradiction in organizations is another part of what frustrates our efforts to get teamwork and collaboration to stick, and has led to the proliferation of articles, books and consultants focused on these subjects. I owe my career to the many brilliant people who have pioneered the field of group and team dynamics. What they offer can indeed help groups to operate more effectively for a time. Most of what I have tried and used, though, hasn't made the lasting changes for the teams that I or they hoped for. That brings me back to the gap in ROI with which we started this discussion. We do it, and it costs a lot of money, time and effort. We may even enjoy it, but we don't hold on to what we learn after the program is over. It was only a few years back that I began to pay attention to this feeling that something was off, that something was missing from the terrific body of work that I had been schooled in and benefited from. Because even though all those brilliant people studied it, and great minds worked towards it, we seem to keep having to re-learn and re-teach teamwork. Over and over and over.

Since my first feelings of uncertainty about team development, I have come to understand that most approaches to teamwork or team effectiveness aren't designed to directly confront this organizational paradox: Collaboration is second- or third-nature for a large majority of us and this predisposes us to consistently revert to our more selfish ways, especially where we're rewarded and recognized to do so. Those who created the most commonly used team effectiveness approaches may have thought that they were accounting for this reality, but I now believe that most miss the heart of the matter. The preponderance of team effectiveness efforts and tools focus on trying to move groups, en masse, up Maslow's hierarchy, away from protection and survival towards companionship and camaraderie, without effectively addressing the powerful pull of those lower-order drives that are completely aligned to traditional organizational structures and systems. It's an expensive misperception that the Framework I'll offer tackles head on.

Just think about all the work done on trust building—often a core element of team building. Trust-building exercises attempt to elevate us to the third tier of Maslow's hierarchy where we deal with matters of friendship and intimacy. One very common approach to building trust, one that I have used myself, involves personal self-disclosure and the Johari window.

The Johari Window

1 Open	2 Blind
Known to self and others	Not known to self but known to others
3 Hidden	4 Unknown
Known to self but not known to others	Not known to self or others

Like a lot of you, I'm a big fan of the Johari window and how it elegantly illustrates the ways that our knowledge of ourselves and of others can play out in relationships as well as in individual development. Consider box #3 in the window, "Hidden," which is often a focus in trust-building work. The Hidden box describes those things about myself that I have so far kept to myself. My sharing information with you from this private zone is intended by team builders to bring us closer, to build trust based on my willingness to be vulnerable and your opportunity to experience me more fully. The resulting trust enhancement is expected to improve our collaboration. It seems to make sense. In those moments of self-disclosure, when we open our hearts to our colleagues, there can be strong emotional reactions of warmth and empathy that can bond us. I have rarely, however, seen interactions involving box #3, as wonderful as these self-disclosures can end up feeling, make anything more than a transitory difference in work-focused collaboration. Don't get me wrong—trust matters. Later in the book, I'll come back to the role I've found that trust plays in collaboration. For now, I can say that the relationship between trust and collaboration is generally misunderstood. Therefore attempts to address collaboration via trust are misguided. Sure, sometimes, when our disclosure resonates deeply with others there can be a lasting shift in personal relationships. But Maslow's pyramid is a slippery bugger, and when business gets bumpy, as soon as the fecal matter starts to fly, average Joes and Janes toiling in for-profit companies, making genuine efforts to collaborate, will come whooshing back down to the bottom of Maslow's pyramid like Neanderthals caught on a glacier during a thaw.

What's needed is to more fully acknowledge the power of the pull at the bottom of the hierarchy, to provide tools and techniques that account for and can build on this foundation of individualism in ways that eventually lead to cohesiveness. Instead of constantly fighting our nature and our nurture, we can start to work with it. How to do that requires more explanation, and it's the point of this book.

I'll share my research and more of my experiences in order to help you understand what shaped my perspective. All of what follows grew out of my years with Mars, Incorporated, my place of employment, a place for which I have a deep respect and affection. You may find some of it unusual—Mars has a reputation for being different. But if your work has involved leading or developing teams at any large organization, I think that you will find much of it familiar.

Mars Beginnings

I remember standing there facing the small machine on the wall, wondering, "Am I going to hate this—or love it?" That machine was a time clock. It was November 2000. I was beginning my second day at Mars, Incorporated, my first day with an ID badge and an Associate number that would allow me to punch the time clock just like every other Mars Associate all over the world. I was genuinely ambivalent. By punching in on time, I would qualify for the 10% daily punctuality bonus—or as it was known in the USA, "punc." If you've heard anything about Mars and its quirky culture, you have probably heard about this now-defunct practice. Did you also know that when I say "every Associate," I do mean every? From the president of Mars, Incorporated to first line managers to administrators to hourly Associates in our factories, every one of us was required to punch the clock. Unusual, right? I worried that I might find this time clock ritual distasteful. The thought that some functionary in payroll would track the time of someone like *me*, an experienced, mid-career professional with a Master's degree—no, two Master's degrees— as if I were some run-of-the-mill wage-slave! It felt like a ding to my accomplishments and self-esteem.

At the same time, the whole "punc" thing appealed to my sense of egalitarianism, my rebellious, "punk" side. There was, and still is, a part of me that resists corporate norms, especially the privileges of senior leaders. I have an inner rebel who wants to rally the workers to barricades to stand up for themselves. When I worked at IBM my anti-privilege urges were piqued daily. The executive parking spots and dining rooms, the cushy corner offices and the host of other perks that served to signal who was on top, and who was not, had me feeling ready to lead an insurgency on many mornings. This is the part of me that cheered for the Mars time clock that every single one of us punched. I also welcomed the undifferentiated parking lot, the Mars open office (which Mars had employed for five decades by the time I joined) and all the ways that Mars visibly embraced a "one for all, all for one" culture. This philosophy is best expressed in the Mars Associate Concept:

We believe in a relationship between our company and our

Associates that is more meaningful and powerful than what usually exists between employer and employee. Each of us is a stakeholder in our business, and we have a responsibility to uphold our principles and deliver great results. In return, each associate can expect to be respected, supported and valued as an individual, to be treated fairly and equitably, to be rewarded for their performance, and to have opportunities to grow and develop. This is a relationship of mutual trust, dignity and respect, based on the Five Principles, which values people as individuals and allows their great talents to be released.

"This is a place," I thought, "where collaboration—the way I prefer to work—might actually flourish."

The "we're-all-in-this-together" spirit touched and inspired me in my early days at Mars; even as the punc bonus is being phased out, it still does. But I've learned a lot since then, my ambivalence has been validated. Even in an open office, in a company where the Mars family still champions the voice of the lowest-paid Associates, and where the term "Associate" really does mean something different from "employee," there are still barriers to collaboration. The time clock, it turns out, was every bit as paradoxical a symbol as I had experienced it to be. Clock punching (by the time I got there, we pressed keys—punch cards were long gone) is a strictly individual endeavor. This icon of Associate equality was also a reminder that it was individuals who were hired, tracked, measured and rewarded. I punched in to get my 10%, I did my job, I got paid and maybe eventually, I would get promoted. We at Mars were individuals, albeit equal ones, laboring in an environment of goodwill that, just like in most other companies, was designed to make the most out of our individual-ness. Whether it's in a Mars office or an IBM factory or anywhere else, the time clock is just one artifact of many that speaks to the ways in which organizations are ideal places for individual effort to thrive, despite all the good intentions and talk of teamwork.

Mars, though, had more than just good intentions. As I was doing the research that led to the development of the Mars Framework for High Performance Collaboration and to this book, I learned just how unique the Mars commitment to getting teamwork right was and still is. I regularly spoke with academics and consultants, describing the task I had been given: developing a team effectiveness approach specifically based on Mars teams. Time and time again what I got back was a question: "Why would you do that? With all the good work that's been done on teams and group effectiveness, can you honestly expect to learn anything new?" I have to admit that at first, I felt the same way. As my inquiry progressed, and ideas and concepts began to resolve into genuine insights, my view shifted. The central idea emerged: Collaboration in teams was failing to thrive because individual team members neither understood, nor felt compelling, "this-puts-bread-on-the-table" reasons to collaborate. We, and I felt sure others, weren't providing gut-level clarity about why collaboration was vital and indeed a matter of individual survival. What was more, this idea wasn't much discussed, studied or written about by professionals in the field of team effectiveness. It might not be new news, but it became clear to me that it was essential.

Relatively late in the process of developing our team Framework, while attending a conference on high performance teamwork, I shared my methodology and early findings with one well-respected business school professor and author. He asked me, challenged me, saying, "You didn't find anything consistent in all this team data, did you?" In fact, I told him, I had. I described to him the consistent finding that, regardless of level in the organization, irrespective of function or geography, team members admitted to not collaborating because they lacked sufficient understanding about:

- What specifically required collaboration
- Why collaboration mattered—especially to them as individuals.

So team members defaulted to getting things done the best way they knew how—by working harder and longer by themselves. With this explanation, the business school professor warmed to me and my project, and we ended up spending a few hours discussing the findings. He probably doesn't remember me, or our conversations. I, however, will never forget his comment: "Big companies just don't do this sort of thing." Maybe others didn't, but Mars did. I believe we did so based in large part on our willingness, ironically, to stand alone and to be different when it makes business sense to do so. Mars, Incorporated, a 100-year-old family-owned company which had been following its own path through four-plus generations, where the open office was a thing way before it was a thing and where egalitarianism found expression in a time clock, saw that getting real about collaboration required new thinking and real investment.

While Mars may be unique, we aren't alone. Other companies with global footprints, operating in fiercely competitive environments, are confronting issues of sustainability and human rights even as we all strive to remain profitable and grow. Effective collaboration could make an important difference for all of us. For Mars, the decision to invest in building true collaborative capability would have important results that have proven to be useful beyond what any of us expected. In the next chapter I'll talk about the team effectiveness journey that Mars has been on and what it led to.

Summary

- The ROI on team building isn't favorable. While team-building activities have been shown to improve employee engagement and satisfaction, little evidence can be found connecting traditional team building to improvements in how teams collaborate to create greater value.

- Maslow's Hierarchy of Needs helps explain why we aren't natural collaborators. We aren't naturally inclined to collaborate unless it's directly connected to basic human needs.

- Organizations, despite their interest and investments in teams and teamwork, typically incentivize individual effort through pay and bonus structures which ensure that individuals are drawn down towards the bottom of Maslow's Hierarchy of Needs.

- Team-building practices meant to counter this effect don't have lasting effect because they fail to adequately account for our innate individualistic nature or to use it to the team's advantage.

Chapter 2

Mars and High Performance Teamwork

Mars, like a lot of other companies, has a history of investing in team effectiveness workshops and training. We have always believed that a collaborative work environment is a key part of our heritage and essential to our future success. Sure, there were the barriers I talked about in Chapter 1. But we had a few advantages. The Mars Associate Concept and our long-standing use of an open office gave us a leg up on other companies where folks could sequester themselves in offices all day and only engage with others when they felt a need.

The HPC Framework wasn't developed until 2012. Before its creation, the Mars team effectiveness work I was closest to was focused on senior teams in North America. Our president, who would later go on to become the global president of Mars, Inc. and lead the company to unprecedented growth, had become frustrated with the overly polite, often conflict-avoidant way that his leadership team was operating. He believed the key to unlocking high performance teamwork (HPT as we came to call it), and reviving our then stagnating business, lay in creating more candor among leaders. We would address conflict avoidance head on with more open, honest, two-way communication and debate. This would lead to greater speed and innovation, less wasted time and resource, and a greater ability to compete and succeed. Working with consultants we would start at the top and cascade the work with teams to successively lower levels in the organization. Since teams all over Mars and at all levels functioned in this same "faux-friendly," inefficient and ultimately unsustainable way, the cascading approach made sense, at least in theory. We would encounter its limitations as the program expanded.

Conflict aversion is one of those bottom-of-Maslow's-hierarchy, survival-instinct kinds of things. A fear-based behavior that has everything to do with survival, conflict aversion is a pre-emptory triggering of the "flight" part of our "fight, flight or freeze" response. Almost none of the workplace conflict we see is truly life threatening. Despite this, the amygdala, our primitive lizard-brain, may perceive even fairly benign threats as if they were sabre-tooth tigers. The amygdala is non-rational, and yet via the executive centers of our brain we're able to rationalize our responses to fear. For instance, we avoid conflict in the interest of preserving relationships or out of concern that we won't be seen as "team players." As often, we dodge our differences with others so we won't have to deal with the stress of the emotions and the unknown outcomes that may result from conflict-laden encounters. That is, we even fear our own responses to fear. This isn't neurosis—this is fairly typical brain function. Some of us experience it more often and more deeply and others less so. It's all about doing what we perceive will keep us safe and secure. Later in the book I'll tackle this subject again when I delve into my views on trust in teams, trust being the functional opposite of fear. Trust-building exercises, like those I discussed in Chapter 1, may create a small movement where conflict has become fixed. In my experience, though, most such exercises don't get at what underlies most deep-seated conflict avoidance—unacknowledged fear, both of the other and of our own inability to deal with what fear brings up in ourselves. For all these reasons, working with groups in an atmosphere of low trust and fear requires specialized skill. Recognizing this, our president selected a small consultancy of group dynamics experts who skillfully, often forcefully, guided leadership team members to have the uncomfortable conversations that they'd been dodging for years. It was a lot like pulling the bandage off a wound, and sometimes a seriously infected wound, at that. A few leaders loved it, even thrived on it. Other leaders resented it; some even left the company. But it worked — for the most part. An emotional logjam of old resentments and simmering feuds began to be addressed, as honest, direct communications within senior teams became more and more the norm.

At the heart of the approach was Bruce Tuckman's original Four Stages of Team Development model, which had played a role in my first work with teams. Tuckman's model, as you probably recall, predicts that teams move through four nicely rhymed stages — Forming, Storming, Norming, and Performing — by learning either intentionally or simply through trial and error to confront underlying tensions and questions of power and authority within the team. Our consultants facilitated, even provoked, honest, direct conversations about topics that teams and their leaders had been avoiding or unable to resolve. To support these conversations, consultants taught assertion skills and active listening, intervening as necessary to keep things productive and safe. All of this was intended to accelerate senior teams through the Four Stages towards higher performance.

When our president was promoted into the global Office of the President, this approach to high performing teamwork traveled with him. Along with other changes to our business, the enforced candor and the high-quality listening that went along with this approach began to shift our culture, globally, in positive ways, among top teams, at least. Top teams would do their high performing team sessions, then, in line with our cascading approach, they would engage the teams below them in similar work and so the goodness would spread. Scale would become the important limiting factor in taking our approach to team development work more broadly across our business. As I said, we were working with a small firm with a limited number of consultants. What's more, their background and experience was mostly with senior-level teams, and less with frontline managers and those in factories who made up the bulk of our population. When Mars acquired Wrigley in 2008 and we went from 45,000 Associates to over 70,000, our size became the limiting issue. It was at about this time that I got directly involved. My involvement wasn't about scale, though. I was just one guy. My role was more about Mars wanting to build internal capability in team development while at the same time saving money on consulting fees. The business had a need and I had the skills and interest to meet that need, at least in part.

By the time I arrived at Mars in 2000, eight years earlier, I already had over 15 years of experience in working with teams at all levels of organizations, so my interest and aptitude were honestly come by. When they asked me in 2008 to become that less expensive, internal alternative to our external partners, I jumped at the chance. I was immediately captivated and energized by the work. My family-of-origin experience may have predisposed me to an interest in group dynamics and spawned my passion for the healing power of truth telling. Or maybe it was my Master's degree program at American University where for two years, we, the 20 or so students of my cohort, were the subjects of our study of group dynamics. Whatever the inciting factors and aspects of my experience and background, it all fired my passion and became part of my practice working with Mars teams.

You start with what you know. I began by using the team development process our external partners were using. It was pretty straightforward, rooted in the basics of good consulting and time-tested group dynamics theory. The process had as its centerpiece a team feedback hot-seat exercise, usually three to four hours long that was embedded in a longer two-day "team alignment" workshop. The workshop always began with team members introducing themselves to the consultant and sharing their feelings about the process that was about to take place. Next, data from pre-workshop team member interviews would be shared with the team, and findings from that data were discussed and validated in small groups. The open feedback

31

process would usually follow this data-processing exercise. Team feedback was this consultancy's version of opening the Johari window with individuals sharing previously unknown or hidden information about themselves—box #3—and getting blind-spot information from their colleagues—box #2. It was the place in the workshop where truth telling held center stage. I experienced a few variations of this exercise. In one, a team member, the one in the hot seat, would self-disclose to their teammates who were sitting in a circle around them. The "hot-seater" followed a simple protocol that typically included self-disclosure on some version of these two points:

- Things I do that get in the way of our team being high performing
- Things I could do differently to accelerate our team towards higher performance

Following the self-disclosure, the rest of the team would then provide feedback, one by one, to the person in the hot seat about how they saw their teammate either supporting or inhibiting team performance.

Other times, the consultant would have each team member post a piece of paper on the wall with their name at the top and two "1–10" scales on it, one for each of the "cornerstone behaviors" of high performance: candor and receptivity (openness to feedback). Every team member would rate every other team member by placing their initials along the two 1–10 scales based on the level at which they perceived their colleague was demonstrating the behaviors. Each team member would then stand by their chart with the rest of the team gathered around them. They would debrief with the team, noting where they were pleased, surprised, confused or disappointed, and asking for more detail and information where they felt they needed it.

No anonymity was provided in either feedback process.

Sometimes different statements were used in the hot-seat exercise, or other behaviors listed on the flip charts, but the process was always conducted in this open and direct fashion. In a company where even one-to-one, behind-closed-doors performance feedback was typically softened and watered down, and performance ratings were skewed upwards, this kind of public feedback was stunning, unsettling, fear-producing.

I soon began to experiment within the approaches that I've just described. For instance, I continued to conduct data-gathering team interviews, but I also developed a questionnaire for team members to complete that added to the data they would consider during the workshop. Also, our approach used eight characteristics to describe a team at Stage Four of the Tuckman model, and we used these attributes as the working definition of high performance. These attributes talked about, among other things, having a clear strategy, shared goals, clear roles, and so on. It was and is a pretty strong list. It said nothing, though, about a team knowing why they were operating as a team, understanding what the purpose of the team being together was. Nor was there any mention of trust in this list of attributes. I was just beginning to become curious about these two areas in particular and how they played into team effectiveness (both will be discussed at greater length later in this book). So I created a simple in-room survey that I used with teams that included the previously mentioned eight characteristics and added team purpose and trust. Otherwise, I continued to follow the broad outlines of the team alignment process. I conducted feedback sessions using the methodologies I described. As our consultants did, I worked with teams to develop team processes or protocols that their data suggested were absent. Over time, using this hybrid approach, I developed a reputation for my knowledge and skills in team development and for my relatively minor innovations. As I continued to experiment with new techniques and tools, my sense that our team-consulting approach was missing something, potentially something essential, grew. Or, perhaps, it was our assumptions about what was required for high performance that were off the mark. In either case, it was a series of fairly typical team effectiveness interactions with one of our business teams that shed light on the causes of my doubts and that led eventually to the ideas and concepts that form the heart of the Framework I developed.

Before I tell you about the work that led to my "ah-ha" moment, let's revisit the Mars Five Principles that I talked about in the Introduction to the book. People outside of Mars might think of them as just another set of corporate values. They're that and more. The Five Principles are the foundation for how we get our work done. I'll summarize them again here:

Quality: The consumer is our boss, quality is our work, and value for money is our goal.

Responsibility: As individuals, we demand total responsibility from ourselves; as Associates, we support the responsibilities of others.

Mutuality: A mutual benefit is a shared benefit; a shared benefit will endure.

Efficiency: We use resources to the full, waste nothing and do only what we can do best.

Freedom: We need freedom to shape our future; we need profit to remain free.

The Five Principles have been and still are a key to our success. They're even embedded in the thinking that went into our team Framework. The team that was the source of some of my earliest insights, despite its difficulties, had the Five Principles to ground them in what was important. Like all the teams I'll talk about in these pages, they were good people doing a lot of good work. But they needed help. Without knowing it, they would be helping me. What happened as a result of my work with this team triggered my transformation from a knowledgeable, capable traditionalist to a committed collaboration contrarian.

One Room, One Team, Different Purposes

It was early days in my time as an internal team effectiveness consultant at Mars. We were in one of the more peculiar hotel conference rooms I had ever worked in: long and narrow with a low drop-panel ceiling and smoked-glass mirrors along its two long walls. On the floor was a threadbare, reddish carpet, with a royal crest sort of pattern, that smelled of cleaning chemicals and stale cigarette smoke. It looked and felt for all the world like a cheap, cramped New Jersey interpretation of the Hall of Mirrors at Versailles. I was there working with a cross-functional brand team on their team effectiveness and we had reached an impasse. Things had gone uncomfortably quiet in our mirrored cave. Finally, I broke the silence with a flurry of questions that arose out of my frustration, my sense of impending failure, but also from a genuine need to know: "What is it exactly that you're supposed to be doing as a team? I mean, why do you come together? For what purpose?" I wondered how they were supposed to achieve any kind of high performance when they didn't even know why they existed as a collaborative unit, as a team. The silence that followed my questions was telling. It spoke volumes about *their* confusion, *their* lack of clarity and lack of a sense of purpose. In fact, my questions had begun to form just a few weeks earlier when my work with the team began.

I had been asked by the team leader to sit in on a few of his regular team meetings so that I could observe their team dynamic as part of preparing for the off-site workshop at the Hall of Smoke-and-Mirrors just described. I attended two or three of their regular meetings, each on a different topic. What I saw in just one of those meetings was consistent with the others I attended and will sound familiar to many of you.

There were 12 or 13 Associates, men and women, seated

around an oblong conference table in a small meeting room at one end of the Hackettstown, New Jersey offices. One wall of the room had tall south-facing windows. The overhead lights were switched off; the horizontal blinds were lowered and closed, shutting out all but slivers of the low wintertime sun. The brightest sources of light in the room were the spreadsheet projected onto a large screen at one end of the room and the blue glow from five or six laptop computers that team members were working on at their seats around the table. As well, a few Associates were working their Blackberries, which they held just below the level of the tabletop in an attempt to conceal their efforts, like secretive virtuosos of the digital thumb piano. The steady arrhythmic "tap-taptaptap-tap" of fingers on keyboards large and small filled the room as emails were composed and proposals were tightened up, none of which, it appeared, had anything to do with the topic of this particular meeting. In the midst of this dim cacophony, three of the team members were in a heated argument about the rows and columns of tiny, barely visible numbers that were part of the spreadsheet glowing on the screen at one end of the room. Every so often, a head would pop up from one of the computer screens or Blackberries and this person would jump into the spreadsheet debate. Then just as quickly, once her point was made, she would return to the email or PowerPoint® that was otherwise consuming her attention. It was impressive in a way, that ability to jump in and out of the conversation. But it was clear that none of them could be giving their full attention and therefore the full value of their presence to any of what they were doing.

As I watched this disjointed but fairly typical scene playing out, a question occurred to me: What if each of these people had a number scrawled across their foreheads, a dollar amount that represented their salary, wages and benefits on an hourly basis? What if our general manager suddenly walked into this room, and quickly calculated what this day-long meeting was costing the company? I wondered if he would conclude, as I had, that most of these people would be vastly more productive and generate greater value for the company if they were at their desks, or in the factory doing what they were primarily hired to do, instead of sitting in this dimly glowing chamber trying to empty their crammed inboxes or get presentations written while being repeatedly distracted by a debate that didn't involve them?

I have been in some pretty awful meetings in my career— haven't we all? This one was no worse than others I've been subjected to. As I thought about it, it occurred to me that the meeting itself wasn't the problem. Sure, the room was cramped, sub-optimal. The meeting process was a poorly designed "show-and-tell" nightmare of dreadful presentations provoking frustratingly unfocused debates. As it happens, though, this particular meeting, as ridiculous as it was, was a necessary part of a larger, otherwise sound business process that had to continue. New products had to be conceived of, planned for, costed out, tested and launched into the market. Cross-functional collaboration—or at least cross-functional involvement—was and is essential to this complex, multidisciplinary process. As a collaborative effort the meeting was lousy, but work was getting done, albeit much of it unrelated to the topic of the meeting.

The people weren't really the problem, either. Every one of them was a solid Mars Associate. Each of them was committed to working in accordance with the Five Principles. They were there because the Responsibility Principle demanded it, because this is what good Associates, good team players, do: they show up at meetings. Moment by moment as the meeting unfolded, each of them was doing what they thought was most important and valuable to do, whether that was working through their emails, building presentations or debating the projected spreadsheet. The attitudes towards this meeting, and behaviors in it, and in so many others I have observed, were symptoms of overworked individuals thrown together in a badly conceived meeting.

Something else, though, was going on. It struck me that this team didn't know, or had forgotten, *why* they were all in there, *together*. Beyond enacting the Responsibility Principle and their assumptions about the goodness of teamwork, the need for collaboration in a process such as the one at the heart of this meeting was unclear. Each one of them was probably very clear about how they, as individuals, were supposed to contribute. But they didn't, as individuals or as a collective, behave as if they understood how their being together was intended to add value over and above their individual contributions. In fact, their enforced togetherness was getting in the way of individual work, work that was probably just as important as anything they might pay partial attention to in the meeting. They knew their individual jobs and their individual value but were completely unclear about the job and the value of the team *as a team*.

Flash forward a few weeks to our faux-Versailles, where I eventually asked the leader and his team questions that had begun to take shape weeks earlier:

- What is it exactly that you are supposed to be doing as a team?
- Why, for what purpose, do you come together?

The answer I got didn't surprise me: "We haven't really thought about it. We're all supporting this brand and we all just assume that we need to be here for these meetings. Besides, you never know, something may come up that needs input from one of us so we figure we need to be present. Just in case."

OK, a reasonable rationale. But not compelling enough for this group to be able to create any real value through their collaboration.

What's more, I knew that it wasn't just this team that was struggling. Other teams in other functions and in other companies where I had worked and consulted over the years were having similar experiences. Taken in total, what were teams who were operating in this way costing organizations in terms of wasted time and the negative impact on employee morale and engagement? How much money was being ill-spent between these frustratingly unproductive meetings on relatively ineffective team and trust-building exercises that were meant to somehow correct for all this wasted time and effort? What would it be worth to us to turn this situation around, and what would it take?

These were questions I couldn't answer, at least not without digging deeper. Quantifying the costs of the wasted time and effort was beyond my skills. But common sense suggested that the opportunity was big. Once I did the research, the answer to the "What-would-it-take-to-turn-it-around" question was both stunningly obvious and, so far as I could tell, almost completely overlooked by the acknowledged luminaries in the field.

Just as I was arriving at these unsettling notions about how teams were working, or trying to work, my one-man internal consulting practice at Mars was taking off. I was quickly becoming involved with teams at all levels and in countries around the world. Exciting, yes. But I was plying my trade with what was, despite my experiments and enhancements, an inadequate toolkit and with what I was becoming aware were flawed assumptions about what makes collaboration really work. I was experiencing first-hand the cost of the tension between individual effort and teamwork, between:

- The things that drive individual productivity and pull people down Maslow's hierarchy away from collaboration, and
- The potency and potential of, and the corporate need for, value-adding collaboration.

I wouldn't have said it this way at the time—I simply didn't know enough. Regardless of the words I might have used, if this corporate-wide team effectiveness effort was going to work, if it was going to be worth the effort and investment, we needed to explore this tension and address it head on.

At around this time, two other developments within Mars, Incorporated increased my growing sense of unease and put pressure on those of us in the learning and development function to do something more with teams and teamwork.

First, Mars, which had recently acquired Wrigley and a few other businesses, declared that high performance teamwork would be a "Signature Practice." Naming something a Signature Practice connoted that it would be one of the core processes and practices that were so critical to our success that it was to be used across all our businesses, whether recently acquired or otherwise. They ranged from how we manage our finances to things like performance management and Associate engagement. If it was dubbed a Signature Practice, it was something you wanted to be sure you had right. We no longer use the term "Signature Practice," but we still have a set of corporate processes that we expect our businesses to use consistently. In 2009 when "high performance teamwork" was put on our list of Signature Practices, we didn't define specifically what we meant by "high performance teamwork." It wasn't clear whether we were talking about the focus on conflict and feedback that had been used with senior teams or if we were simply reinforcing the generic importance of teamwork done in a high performing way. Regardless, the commitment was made. Someone was going to have to do something to make it real.

Then, a few months later in another part of the business, our leadership development group was revamping our core leadership development offerings to better align with our business priorities and strategy. It was decided, not surprisingly, that high performance teamwork would have to be a major component of one of our new manager development courses.

My colleagues in Mars University looked to me, the "team guy," for answers and content for the program. We didn't own the intellectual property that was used by our external high performance team consultants so that was out. Besides, as I have previously said, I was increasingly certain that the existing approach wasn't what our new managers needed. I had questions at this point, but no answers.

- Was the model for high performance teamwork that our senior teams used truly missing the mark? Or was it the way I was using it?
- How could something as tried and true as Tuckman's Four Stages of Team Development be anything other than "right"?
- Was there really any way to deal effectively with the ever-present tension between individual needs and the ambition for high performing teamwork? Or was I just kidding myself?

I had been working with teams at Mars for two years when I had to face these questions. Those two years of experience, and work with about 120 teams, would provide not only the raw material for answering my questions, but would change forever the way I think about team effectiveness. In the next chapter we'll look at the research I conducted and the initial conclusions that I drew from it. Not only did this work address my concerns, it led to the Framework that is the subject of this book.

Summary

- Team effectiveness efforts relying on time-tested and well-accepted models delivered by external consultants are the gold standard in many companies.
- These efforts cost teams and the companies they're part of time and money, but there's little evidence that they make

a real difference to collaboration.

- The approach based on Tuckman's Four Stages can do some good for teams by promoting healthy conflict and accelerating team development. In our organization, however, these effects didn't seem to last.

- What's more, any consultant-dependent approach has limitations of scope as businesses grow and many teams are beyond the reach of the consultants.

- These shortcomings led us to question our team effectiveness approach and to wonder what else we could do that would be more effective.

Chapter 3

Research and the First Insights

Out with the Old

By 2008 I'd developed a reliable instinct about what works for teams and what doesn't. My gut was telling me that something was off with the most commonly used team development concepts and theories. My instincts didn't crystallize into insights until I took a more disciplined look at what had been going on. Not only did my insights help me understand what wasn't working. They also suggested what might work instead.

A heads-up here: In this book I'm going to suggest that you stop using some of the most widely accepted team effectiveness tools, tools you and tens of thousands of others have been using for years. That's an audacious thing to do given how long these approaches have been around. Then, if that weren't enough, I'll propose what to do instead. I wouldn't blame you for being skeptical. This chapter and the one that follows it address your potential skepticism with information and data from our research process. If you're already bought in and ready to get to work with our new approach, you can skip these two chapters. However, these two chapters might be for you if:

- You're curious about why I decided to move away from typical team effectiveness approaches
- You're skeptical about my take on the usual team effectiveness approaches but willing to be convinced
- You have tried the standard team-building techniques and tools and found yourself wondering why they didn't work out
- You're interested in what lies behind this new approach that I present

- You're a team effectiveness geek like me, and like the more technical stuff.

Now that you know what's coming, let's dig in.

Where Were We?

I closed Chapter 2 with a few questions.

- Was the model for high performance teamwork that our senior teams used truly missing the mark? Or was it the way I was using it?
- How could something as tried and true as Tuckman's Four Stages of Team Development be anything other than "right"?
- Was there really any way to deal effectively with the ever-present tension between individual needs and the ambition for high-performing teamwork? Or was I just kidding myself?

Without knowing it, I had already begun answering the first two questions. In 2008, about a year and a half before I began the inquiry discussed in this chapter, I heard that high performing teams had been declared a Mars "Signature Practice." A Mars Signature Practice, you'll recall from the previous chapter, was one of the processes that Mars, Incorporated leadership decided should be consistent across all of our businesses. While differences between our various businesses needed to be respected, there are efficiencies in consistency and Efficiency is one of Mars's Five Principles.

When I got the news about the team-focused Signature Practice, I asked to lead the search for an external partner to help us define this Signature Practice in a consistent way and then deploy it globally. The external consultancy we had been working with, and with whom we had taken major strides, was small. They numbered about 24 consultants, all based in the USA. What's more, they focused primarily on senior teams using an approach optimized for that level. My gut kept telling me that their Four Stages based approach wasn't applicable at lower levels in our business. I felt we needed a methodology that was accessible to and useful for teams working anywhere in the business. Tuckman's Four Stages probably wasn't it.

There were a lot of well-known team effectiveness processes that came up in our search process and they were all solid. At the end of our lengthy competitive bidding process, though, we ended up dissatisfied with all we had seen. Among others, we had considered Lencioni's Five Dysfunctions material, the Team Performance Model from Drexler-Sibbet, and Situational Leadership for Teams from the Ken Blanchard companies. We even piloted the Blanchard approach with a few teams. It had its merits but in the end it fell flat. Our leaders and Associates weren't responding positively to any of the team effectiveness approaches we thought might work. What we found was that either:

- The organizations behind these offerings hadn't adapted or translated their materials into languages other than English (essential for a global corporation), and/or...
- The material and frameworks just didn't fit with Mars's culture.

While we didn't find the partner we had been seeking, a couple of my questions, as I just mentioned, were partially answered. It wasn't entirely the tools themselves that were the problem. Nor was it the way I had been applying them. Through this process it dawned on me that a lack of cultural fit was at the core of what I had been experiencing in my work with teams. Something in the time-honored thinking that lay behind most team effectiveness models was inconsistent with the needs and character of most teams at Mars. If that was the case for us, then it was probably true for other organizations as well.

At around this time another decision was made that would shape my work on team effectiveness. The intent to take team development more broadly across the organization meant that we'd need to embed team effectiveness in our manager development programs. My learning and development colleagues and I agreed that I, as the acknowledged "team guy," would delve into the literature to see if there was something we could adapt to suit our corporate culture. This was no small task. I took it on with a mix of excitement and trepidation. I was excited about the chance to continue to look for answers and daunted by the nature of what I had agreed to tackle. Corporate culture is a complex thing. A lot has been written about it, much of that contradictory. Even with my Master's degree and organizational consulting experience, I don't claim to have a thorough grasp on corporate culture as a field of study. Nor can I claim to have fully decoded the Mars, Incorporated culture, even though I have studied and lived it for more than 16 years. I did, though, get that when it came to team effectiveness, culture mattered and needed to be taken into account. Whether it's Mars, Incorporated or AT&T or any other company, simply overlaying a generic solution on something as subtle and complex as team effectiveness is a low-odds bet.

Here's what I was sure of when it came to Mars's culture: Mars was and is a place where action, simplicity and practicality are highly valued. Whatever I found and recommended as part of our manager development programs would need to be:

- Theoretically sound
- Profoundly pragmatic
- Usable (without requiring that teams master the underlying theory).

These attributes would make our approach useful and transferable to teams, people, places across the business. As I mentioned in Chapter 2, I had first-hand experience that the Tuckman model wasn't shifting team performance. Nor did anything I came across in our search for an external partner seem likely to work for our culture and purposes. For a time I thought that Will Schutz's work held promise. Schutz's thinking lies behind the well-known FIRO-B instrument.[1] I liked the simplicity of his three-part model built around each person's needs for inclusion, control and intimacy (or openness in his later work). But the more I worked with it, comparing his model to the issues that I had been facing working with Mars teams, the more I realized it, too, was a dead end. At least for us. It was too psychological, too clinical and too easy for a non-consultant to get wrong. It was simple but not practical or easy.

It was now July 2010, about two years since the Signature Process decision and one year since the decision to include team effectiveness in our manager development courses. I felt like I was getting nowhere. At my wits' end, I called a Mars colleague, the wonderful Vidula Bal. Vidula, who was at that time our Director of Leadership Development, holds a PhD and had been a college professor in a past life. After patiently listening to my frustrations, she wisely suggested that I look into all the data I had collected from the roughly 125 teams I had worked with in Mars over the preceding 30 months. "Well, duh," I blurted out. How could I not have thought of that? I got to it immediately, once again excited but also genuinely worried that I would find nothing new, interesting or useful.

The data that Vidula suggested I turn to included:

- Team questionnaires I had devised and used with about 65 teams from various countries, of various organizational levels and from a variety of functions like sales, finance, manufacturing, etc.

- Individual team member interviews from the same number of teams averaging about eight people each, totaling around 520 interviews
- My personal notes and recollections about most of the sessions I had led
- My in-room experiences with all 125 teams.

In addition to my personal data storehouse, I had all the work I had done up to that point while looking for an external consultancy as well as my recent, fruitless literature review. It wasn't going to be dissertation-level research; that's not my style or inclination. But it would be pretty robust.

The first chore was to ensure that I had enough consistency in my data to make it worthwhile. The questionnaire and team member interview protocol I had developed when I began working with teams at Mars had evolved since I started using them. So, I identified 30 teams from a variety of functions and geographies where I had used the identical survey and interview protocol.

Working with my wife—something of an Excel savant—we consolidated all the spreadsheet-based questionnaires. We then dissected the interviews into single-idea snippets, grouped them by theme and then loaded all of these into another spreadsheet. It took about two weeks to bring all the data together and sort it. I spent the next three weeks trying to make sense of it all. As it turned out, I needn't have been worried about not finding anything. The insights that emerged were startlingly simple and profoundly important.

The First Insight: We Just Don't

The interviews

Even though we chose to focus on 30 teams, by the time my research began I had interacted with well over a thousand team members and team leaders. They included Mars Associates in all functions, at every level of the organization and in more than 30 countries. Despite this diversity, what came out of the analysis of the interviews was one very clear but somewhat puzzling message. Coming out of the mouth of a prototypical team client it would sound something like:

> "We're a pretty good—even a very good—team with lots of talented, committed, hard-working individuals that I respect. But I wouldn't say that we actually collaborate all that much, even though I think we should."

I found some variation of this message over and over in my interview data. I asked most of these good folks to tell me what they thought their group or team should be collaborating on. The responses were all over the place: this project or that goal or this other initiative. That is, within the typical team there was relatively low agreement about where collaboration should be happening.

I don't know exactly what I expected but this wasn't it. Smart, hard-working, committed folks who would like to, in fact who knew they should collaborate more than they did – but they simply didn't. I recall at this point in my research wanting to say to my imagined team client, "Well then—you know what you need to do. Just get on with it! How hard could it be?"

In fact, it's very hard. My research finding was an example of the now classic "knowing-doing" paradox (or gap). We know we should eat less, but we keep shoveling it in. We know that we should be exercising several days a week. Instead we keep on working or playing Candy Crush or whatever. People suffer from it, companies suffer from it and apparently so do teams. The causes are numerous: comfort with the status quo, fear of change, and personal defensive routines are a few relevant causes of this sort of stagnation. Simply telling teams to get on with it wasn't going to be adequate as a solution.

What's more, the message I distilled from the interviews threw me by virtue of its un-spectacular-ness. I was supposed to be coming up with deep insights, for crying out loud. I needed big ideas that could be turned into a useful and engaging team development approach. All I got was, "We aren't doing what we know we should be doing." Fat lot of good that was going to do me. I was stalled.

I was once proffered this advice: it's not important to always know what to do. It's only important to know what to do when you don't know what to do. What do I do when I don't know what to do? Confirmed introvert that I am, I get myself to a place where I can be on my own, where I can pace and mutter and think aloud. Searching for something, anything that might help me make sense of this unimpressive message, I shuffled around my tiny office, going back to the books on my shelves, mumbling vague expletives. Eventually I settled down and began to wonder how bright, capable individuals could find themselves stuck this way. Experts tell us that the knowing-doing gap can't be closed by more knowledge; we already have most if not all the relevant information and we still aren't acting appropriately. But what if they didn't have all the relevant information? The first "ah-ha" was dawning on me. What my subjects couldn't see, from their individual vantage points within their teams, quickly became "heel-of-the-hand-to-the-forehead" obvious to me:

> They weren't collaborating in part because they didn't know what they should be collaborating on, what they should be *doing* together.

Part of closing a knowing-doing gap includes knowing what, specifically, needs doing. You can't close these gaps following vague admonitions: eat less, exercise more, etc. What works is specific steps, ideally small ones that are unambiguous. These teams had spent their team development time and dollars on learning each other's types, on taking cooking lessons together, and from time to time having highly facilitated "difficult conversations." What they hadn't done was stop and ask one another, "What, if anything, specifically, should we be working on together?" and "Where should we start?" For these teams, "collaboration" and "teamwork" had served as rallying cries for a generalized way of being together. Instead of focusing on clear, specific team tasks, these teams were settling for what Stephen Colbert might call "teaminess."[2] What they hadn't done was to figure out, to specify what, on the way to their shared goals, vision, etc., required them to collaborate. They needed a combination of knowledge and clear direction.

What the questionnaire revealed

As I mentioned, in addition to interviews that led to the insight I just discussed, I also used a questionnaire with each team I consulted to. It was fairly basic: 20 items using a 1–6 scale from "strongly disagree" to "strongly agree." It wasn't a proper survey; it wasn't statistically bulletproof. I hadn't the budget or the expertise to do that–but it served its intended purpose. When administered to teams, my questionnaire gave me useful information which, when summarized and fed back to teams, got them talking to each other about things that mattered.

When taken in total, these questionnaires, and the discussions they led to, enriched my understanding of why team members were so consistent in their desire to collaborate and yet consistently failed to do so. For our research we combined the questionnaire data from the 200-plus team members in our 30-team data set. This enabled us to isolate the statements that team members most agreed with and those that they most disagreed with. Below, ranked by strength of agreement, are the five items that the team members in our research agreed with most:

- Team members show pride in belonging to this team.
- The team is comprised of Associates with the right skills and abilities, including both functional capabilities and those needed to work in a high performing team.
- Individual team members' objectives are clearly linked to the team's overall mission and strategy.
- Every team member, regardless of function, demonstrates ownership for the business results of the overall team.
- Team members understand their individual roles and responsibilities and those of their teammates.

What struck me when I reviewed these top five items was how individually focused they were. All these statements described individual traits or states of mind (pride, ownership, skills, and clarity of role). The highest ranked item, "Team members show pride in belonging to this team," might suggest that the collection of members share a kind of team spirit. But the interview data made it clear that the source of their pride was primarily the quality and caliber of their colleagues as individuals. It wasn't about the quality of their collaboration or teamwork.

Now consider the five items that team members most disagreed with.

- The team regularly sets aside time to assess its performance as a team and to address team development needs.
- Team members are skilled at surfacing differences and disagreements, and dealing with them in a direct and timely fashion.
- The team has a well-understood process for identifying and making decisions.
- The team assesses its performance on important initiatives to capture lessons learned.
- The working environment within the team is open and generally free from unresolved tensions.

In contrast to the top five, these lowest five dealt with the total team and relationships within it. The collective noun "team" is used as a subject in three of the five items. For example, "The team sets aside time," "the team assesses," and so on. The "working environment" mentioned in one of the remaining two statements is something the whole team creates and experiences. Finally, managing difference and conflict, the subject of the remaining item, is an individual skill. But it's an interpersonal skill that only has meaning in relation to other people in the team.

To summarize, the items that got the strongest agreement all concerned individual attributes, while those with the lowest level of agreement tended to deal with team or relationship matters.

In interviews team members had told me, "I want to collaborate but I don't know what to collaborate on." The questionnaire data reflected how this lack of collaborative clarity affected the focus of their efforts. Skills, roles, and attitudes that dealt with things like individual ownership and personal objectives were easy for individuals to grasp and act on. Understandably then, individual effort and goals is where they were putting their time and energy. The necessarily collaborative activities and mindsets that were by nature more challenging, and higher up Maslow's Hierarchy of Needs, were being neglected. Things like conflict management and group decision-making hadn't been clearly and specifically delineated and so had atrophied. As a result, these behaviors and mindsets had slid to the bottom of the questionnaire rankings.

The questionnaire data led me to this hypothesis about one major barrier to closing the knowing-doing gap identified in the interviews—team members were so clear about their individual goals and tasks, and so competent at attending to them, that this is where they spent most of their working time. As a consequence, they had little time, energy or active interest left to devote to more collaborative efforts.

Observational findings: the levels of collaboration

Another conclusion I reached, based primarily on watching teams in action, was that collaboration has many faces and not all are equal. Some collaboration was almost accidental, arising out of a realization that two people happen to be working on related things. "You're working on that? Wait, so am I. We should join forces." Other times collaboration could be more intentional, where two or more people recognize even before a piece of work begins that they need each other. They may even sit down and contract with each other for what their collaboration will look like. Finally, some forms of work-focused interaction could be downright toxic.

With these distinctions in mind, I began to differentiate between the kinds of collaborative interactions I was seeing. I did this based on a rough calculation of the relative value each type of interaction either created or eroded. What do I mean by value? As I said earlier, collaboration consumes resources: time, energy, money. If collaboration isn't likely to produce a result better than would be achieved if just one person worked alone, then it's probably not worth it; it isn't likely to create any benefits over and above individual effort. Said a bit differently, for collaboration to add value it has to produce a better product, higher profits, dollars saved, time saved or some other clear benefit when compared to individual effort. If it doesn't, everyone is wasting time (and money and energy) and therefore eroding value.

The graph opposite illustrates my take on the relative value of each of the kinds of interactions I identified:

Above the midpoint are the collaborative interactions that tend to create value over and above individual effort. The higher you go, the more payoffs you get for your collaboration. Below the midpoint are the types of interactions and relationships that

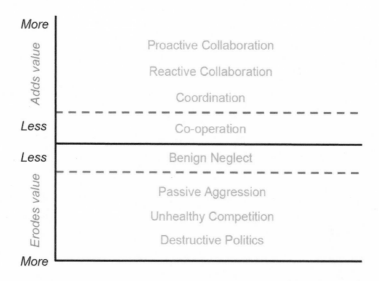

tend to waste time, resources, etc. and therefore erode value. Not surprisingly, the farther down you move, the more value is eroded.

I'll start at the middle of the model, discussing both co-operation and benign neglect. I'll then work my way up explaining each of the levels as I go. Finally, I'll work down, deeper into the "erodes value" zone.

Co-operation—This isn't cooperation as it is commonly understood—hence the hyphen. By co-operating I mean two or more people operating in the same place at the same time, but not necessarily interacting much. It's commonly seen in an open-office environment. Co-operation is like the parallel play I used to see when I took my then two-year older daughter for a playdate in our apartment's playroom. There we were, the other dad and I, he with his little boy and I with my darling daughter. All of us in the same room at the same time so that the adults could talk and enjoy each other's company while the kids played together. Instead, Molly was intently building with the giant red blocks and her intended playdate was obsessed with the toy trucks. Lovely, but not exactly interactive.

Benign neglect—This is just below both co-operating and the midpoint of the graph. It's similar to co-operating but where the physical distance is greater. Benign neglect develops among group members who work for the same boss or in the same function or team but in different offices, sites or countries. These team members generally respect, even like each other, though they aren't part of one another's day-to-day work. When they do get face-to-face, they can be very sociable as teammates reconnect and catch up on all that has happened in their parts of the world. Mars, a truly global company, sees a lot of this type of collaborative relationship. Benign neglect doesn't consume a whole lot of resources but neither does it create much in the way of better outcomes. Because of the tendency for team members to become disconnected and the energy required to reconnect, it sits slightly inside the "erodes value" zone.

Let's move up the model where we find higher orders of collaboration:

Coordination—Once in a while, we run into each other at the coffee machine. There, as a part of our friendly conversation, we have a chance to discuss what we're doing. We may even learn that the work we're doing is related to, but not necessarily overlapping with, each other's. When this happens, we coordinate; we adjust our efforts to the other person's, if needed, and they do the same relative to ours. The payoff is that we have gotten some visibility to what's happening in a related piece of work so that we can respond appropriately. Then, when our moments of coordination over coffee end, we typically go back to our desks and back to our own stuff—back to co-operation.

Reactive collaboration—On some occasions we discover while coordinating at the coffee machine, or in a meeting, that the work we're doing is indeed overlapping or interdependent with someone else's. Out of a desire to be helpful or to ensure that we get what we need, or both, we move up into reactive collaboration; we work closely together for as long as is needed to tend to the overlap or interdependency successfully. There may be a number of benefits in a given bit of reactive collaboration. We might avoid costly duplication of effort. Perhaps we steer clear of arriving at two different proposals for solving the same problem. Whatever the upside, once our reactive collaboration is over we typically drop back down into co-operation, or benign neglect. Starting to see a pattern here?

Intentional collaboration—This level represents planned collaboration (versus reactive), where the shared work is well understood from the start, and the value to be gained via collaboration is clear. Project planning is a kind of intentional collaboration that focuses more on the tasks, the workflow and resourcing. Here, we're talking about less structured kinds of collaboration that often need to happen within a formal project or team. This is the most rarely seen kind of collaborative interaction. In my experience it has the most benefits for the people involved as well as for the teams they may be part of and for the larger organization. With foresight and planning, collaboration can take into account things like the relationships between collaborators, what each of them and their stakeholders require. They can spend time pushing each other's thinking and potentially innovating. Partners who are intentional in their collaboration have more time to think about what might go wrong and to plan for contingencies.

Sure, reactive collaborators could do these things, too. But if you're in reactive mode, you're often involved in putting out fires and trying to make up for lost time, all of which consumes resources that could otherwise be devoted to the work that needs doing.

Now let's consider the interactions well below the midpoint of the graphic, or those interactions that tend to erode significant value. They may not be styles of collaboration as we normally understand that word, but they all rely on individuals interacting, acting together in some fashion, but in counterproductive ways.

Passive aggression—a common dynamic in human relations that occurs when something troubles us and we choose not to deal with it directly. Instead, we take it inside where we stew on it. This happens as much when people are in the same office as it does when teammates are separated geographically. These suppressed conflicts tend to seep out, often in off-hand comments to other teammates. They may also be acted out, as when someone "forgets" a planned meeting or in other forms of supposedly unintentional sabotage. There may not be outright conflict—at least not early on—but you can see how relationships, the climate in a team and ultimately the quality of collaboration can be eroded by passive aggression.

Unhealthy competition is when a person works behind someone else's back with the intent of gaining advantage (e.g. status, recognition) for themselves at the expense of another. This sort of interaction takes its toll on the emotional and mental health of everyone involved, especially those who are its targets. It also role models exactly the sorts of leadership that we claim we don't want to see and that leadership development has been trying to train out of our leaders for the past 40 years. Unhealthy competition crushes collaboration and not just for those involved—an entire team can get caught up in this dynamic, distracting them all from the work that needs doing, which leads to the most corrosive kind of group interaction.

Destructive politics—This is unhealthy competition institutionalized, where striving to advance one's own position at the expense of others has become an organizational norm. I haven't seen a lot of this at Mars. But I have worked elsewhere where this kind of internecine struggle was expected, even encouraged. Destructive politics is one means used by less functional organizations to sort out the leadership wheat from the chaff, forcing those who can't stand the heat to get out of the kitchen. Talk about eroding value for everyone involved, including your business!

Taken together I refer to these last three types of corrosive interactions as dysfunction. What drives dysfunction is an important question for those of us dealing with groups, and I'll return to it later in the book. For now, I'll say that I have found true team dysfunction to be rare. The preponderance of teams that I have worked with spend more of their collaborative energies in the "creates value" zone. I've also found that the majority of Mars Associates are innately helpful, willing to assist their colleagues whenever asked. As I suggested above, there is a pattern, a common dynamic, in the levels of collaboration above the midpoint that plays out like this:

Based on work I did after our Framework was introduced, about 80% of collaborative time in our organization is spent in the cycle represented in the graphic overleaf.

By the way, let's remember that not all work requires collaboration. Sometimes benign neglect and co-operation are perfectly appropriate working styles that will get the job done most efficiently and cost-effectively. The key is knowing how to differentiate between what will benefit from collaboration and

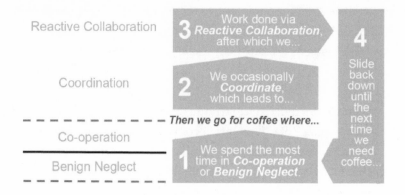

what won't. We'll discuss that in a later chapter.

In my interviews, when I asked team members to describe collaboration, what they talked about, without using the precise words, was this cycle. While they viewed their colleagues as highly competent, they enjoyed being helpful. They were good at it and actually got a buzz from coming to the reactive collaboration rescue. It even made them feel that much more competent. Over time, though, this dynamic takes its toll. Reactive collaboration is basically collaborative fire-fighting. Sure, you get to feel heroic. In reality, reactive collaboration involves doing re-work and correcting errors that were made because people weren't connected with the right other people from the start. Before long the constant acting out of this cycle leads to burnout.

What worried me as I considered this situation was that these team members knew that what they were doing was neither fully satisfying nor sustainable. They were telling me, without having the words for it, that what they wanted, what they needed, was more intentional collaboration with their valued colleagues. They were looking for an answer. So was I.

With only the basic outline of this model in mind, I began to think about what teams and groups could do for themselves. What, beyond the typical team-building and personality tests, could teams do to break their knowing-doing bind, to enhance their collaborative clarity and get more intentional collaboration? What could enable them to do more of what they were telling me they wanted to do and less of the reactive approach that was feeding a sense of burnout? With more thought and some experimentation, I came to understand that it wouldn't just be about what teams could do differently. Any new approach would also have to address what they needed to stop doing, stop focusing on. The concepts and models I had been using had helped teams make limited progress and to feel better about themselves. These same approaches weren't doing much, if anything, to build intentional collaboration. Some, I was guessing, even made intentional collaboration less likely.

In the next chapter we'll explore some of the popular ideas and activities that teams embrace but that don't do much to help intentional collaboration, at least not as they're typically applied. Then we will get into the things that I recommend that teams start doing if they're to move up the charts and start creating real value through intentional collaboration.

Summary

- Mars declared that high performance teamwork was important enough to become a standard practice throughout Mars, Incorporated.
- I had collected data on over a hundred teams from across Mars globally and analyzed this data for insights into what would be required for teams to become more high performing.
- Part of this analysis recognized that there were many levels and kinds of collaboration, some of which created stronger outcomes than others.
- I made a choice to focus my efforts on developing an approach that would help teams to maximize the strongest forms of collaboration, while using the others levels of collaboration as needed.

Chapter 4

What Doesn't Work

Wasted Time, Money and Effort

Collaboration, and the things done to increase and enhance it, requires the investment of people's time and organizations' money and resources. These expenditures hit the bottom line. Many of the most popular teamwork and team-building concepts, though, are a waste of time, money and effort. We can do what the experts suggest and get little if anything in return in terms of our team's effectiveness. For example, a bit later I'll talk about how a concept as popular and intuitively sensible as using shared goals to fortify collaboration in a group actually backfires and drives more individual effort. Other problematic team concepts that need to be examined are more general and more foundational. In this chapter we'll consider:

- The notion of team spirit and the misguided things teams do in pursuit of it
- Why you should be wary when you hear the term "team player"
- What it means to be a "real" team, if it means anything at all
- The concept of dysfunctional teams which, it turns out are rarer than most think

It's important to bring these up now in service of my ultimate goal. By doing so I'm clearing the way for you to consider our alternative approach to thinking about team effectiveness. We have to leave some cherished notions behind in order to get to a better place, to go from knowing to doing.

The Problem with Team Spirit

It's not just what teams do in the name of team building that can be wasteful. There are some widely accepted notions about the nature of effective teams that get in our way. We'll start with the notion of team spirit.

I have had countless leaders tell me how good their teams are. They talk about the wonderful team spirit they have. "Everyone gets along and is feeling good." "We're a strong team." They're usually describing a kind of feel-good team climate that I earlier called "teaminess."

Teaminess, or feel-good team spirit, as lovely as it is, is often a sign that a team isn't challenging itself. These teams are content with that peaceful, easy feeling they have. They aren't insisting on the hard work of collaboration. Nor are they having the tough conversations that genuine collaboration requires. This kind of team spirit blocks a team from becoming high performing.

Let's dig deeper into this prevalent concept. Stop reading, think about team spirit for a minute or two, and jot down a few words that come to mind. Go ahead, do it right there in the box beneath these words.

Let's compare answers. Here are the first five things I came up with when I did the very same exercise:

- Energy
- Goodwill
- Togetherness
- Unity
- Pizzazz

It's my list and probably different from yours. (By the way, I have no idea which part of my brain pizzazz came from.) I have asked others to do this simple exercise. Based on this informal study, team spirit describes the collective buzz that groups get when they experience their sense of connectivity keenly in a positive way. It also contains, I suspect, an element of relief that team members aren't stepping on each other's toes or ticking each other off too much.

What creates the team spirit buzz? Lots of things. Sometimes, it comes out of groups successfully addressing a crisis, of intense reactive collaboration. I had a Marine tell me that "esprit de corps" is built mostly out of shared hardship. Other times, team spirit is the result of a team winning, hitting its numbers or exceeding expectations. Or the vibe of teaminess might follow the group being recognized for their efforts.

I have felt the team spirit buzz and I'd bet you have too. It's sweet and energizing and rewarding—and fleeting. What's more, it's not a reliable indicator of a team's effectiveness or their levels of collaboration. If you find yourselves preparing to spend a few bucks on a ropes course to build team spirit, take a moment. Before you plop down the deposit, ask yourself: What will this activity do, specifically, to enhance the team's ability to create stronger outcomes through collaboration for the enterprise in which you work? Team builders make claims about speeding decision making, improving problem solving, and strengthening innovation. I have rarely, if ever, seen them deliver on these claims.

I don't want to be a killjoy—teams and groups need to have

fun together and they should sometimes do things just for the fun of it. All I'm suggesting is that if you think that a day of zip-lining or stalking each other with paintball guns is going to make your team more effective, then think again. They won't. There is a different sort of team spirit that I do think leads to greater team effectiveness. I discuss this alternative when I talk about team learning in Chapter 12.

Despite my suspicion of it, team spirit is real and worthwhile. I'm suggesting two things. First, find ways for team spirit to arise from the ways in which you and your team connect to do the things that actually need doing. The work will continue whereas the connective high you get from special events is short-lived. Second and most importantly, remember: team spirit doesn't make groups more effective. It's an outcome or indicator and not a predictor, so don't pursue it as an end in itself.

Finally, don't stress yourself if you aren't feeling it. As I said before, team spirit is fleeting and it oughtn't to be a goal in and of itself. It sometimes results from unexpected sources; I've seen groups arrive at a powerful sense of team spirit following intense, uncomfortable debates. Be sure to take a break now and then to let off steam and have a few good laughs—even hit the ropes course. But don't discount that great rush that can come from doing difficult, real work together, even when it gets contentious.

Beware the Team Player

You've heard this before, both in real life and parodied on TV, in shows like *The Office*. "Carlos, we're proud of our team spirit around here. Can we count on you being a team player?" Or, spoken behind our backs where we can't hear it: "Carlos just isn't a team player." The team player dodge is hauled out when false consensus is mistaken for genuine team unity. We invoke the team player when we want everyone lined up behind us, regardless of their actual views.

What if you're the one who won't go along with the mounting, false consensus? What if you're the non-team-player who opposes the view being foisted on the group by its leader or dominant member? In fact, if this were the case, you would be the only true player—team or otherwise. It would be you trying to hold the team to account for considering contrarian views that could strengthen the outcome of whatever they're doing. They don't see this, though. Instead you're set up as the bad guy, as not-a-team-player. As soon as someone utters the words "team player," get quiet. Pay attention, whether it's about you or someone else. It may be a vague compliment. Or it may be a sign that somewhere a healthy, truly spirited debate needs to be had.

What a Team Is, Isn't Important

When I first presented our freshly minted team-effective Framework to my boss at Mars—a wonderful, brilliant and charming British guy—he asked me, "Is this for real teams? Or will it also work for groups?" Being a bit cheeky, I said, "Yes." I had concluded, I explained, that what a team is, or isn't, is irrelevant to effective collaboration. In other words, I have found no practical value in adhering to a strict definition of what makes a team real.

I get the impulse for clarity, though. In the corporate world we use the word "team" so loosely. At Mars and in organization after organization, anytime people convene to discuss the work they have in common they call themselves a team. They may gather face-to-face or virtually. They may be a small group or well into the double digits. The scope of the project may be massive or minute. The time involved varies just as widely. Regardless of size or circumstance, groups like to think of themselves as teams. It isn't worth worrying about.

You, my boss, and others who are smarter than me might say, "Rubbish!" You'd point me to some very sound theoretical definitions of what a team is and isn't. All well and good.

Remember, though, what I said about Mars being a profoundly pragmatic organization? Having the "Are-you-a-real-team-or-not" debate with practically minded managers and leaders, whether they work with groups of 6 or 60, is a waste of everybody's time. I'll bet the same is true where you work. Some levels of coordination and collaboration are required within all of these groups. My job is to help them all figure out what their collaboration needs to look like. They want to know, without using exactly these words, what they can do to optimize collaboration in order to create better results for themselves and their organizations.

But let's not just leave it at that—just because I say it doesn't make it so. It's important to consider others' perspectives on this question. It's what I did when I was formulating the Framework.

Size matters...or does it?

Katzenbach and Smith, the authors of the seminal and still highly relevant *The Wisdom of Teams: Creating the High Performance Organization*, provide us with one definition of a real team. In the pages of my well-worn copy from the 1990s they explained that a real team is:

> A small number of people with complementary skills who are committed to a common purpose, performance goals and approach for which they hold themselves mutually accountable.[1]

Not only is this a well-researched and elegant definition, it makes intuitive sense; it feels right. It provides clarity by drawing lines between what would qualify as a true team and what wouldn't. I agree with all of it, except that size thing. What does "small" mean? It's a bit like the old TV commercial where a consumer in need of extra fiber is worrying about how many prunes (aka dried plums) she should give her kid. Is six enough? Is eight too many? Is three too few? As a team effectiveness consultant, should I refuse to work with a group, or send them elsewhere for help, because with 15 members they aren't "real"? Of course not (and I don't think the authors are saying this either, by the way). Or should I explain, "As not-a-real-team, there is work we could do to help you become a *real* team, or even a high performing team, but again you aren't currently a real team. I'm just saying." I don't think the subsequent discussion would be worthwhile for anyone.

When 80 R&D folks from around the world assemble for their semi-annual meeting, they refer to themselves throughout the three days as the "Global R&D Team." They do this as readily and comfortably as six managers in a single factory in Kansas City call themselves the "Factory Leadership Team." I once tried to explain to a senior global brand manager that his group of 50 managers from around the world who rarely spoke to—let alone saw—each other weren't really a team but rather a community or extended work-group. Do you think he cared to have this academic debate? Not even for a minute. In almost every case the hundreds of teams I have worked with experience themselves as being real, genuine teams sharing some commonness or other, with real work to do for which they were accountable. The brand manager I just mentioned knew that he needed to improve the connectivity and collaboration among his people. He turned to me and my colleagues for help, not for a lesson on what was or wasn't a proper team.

Let's look at one more opinion on what makes a team real. Richard Hackman of Harvard University, something of a team contrarian and a great inspiration to me, wrote the book *Leading Teams: Setting the Stage for Great Performances*. He devotes an entire chapter to what makes for a real team. Towards the end of this chapter he says:

Real teams can be small or large, can have wide-ranging or

restricted authority, can be temporary or long-lived, can have members who are geographically co-located or dispersed and can perform many different kinds of work.[2]

Now we're talking! This understanding of teams is broad and inclusive of all types of groups. What matters is what the group believes, not what I or some other expert thinks. Groups that view themselves as teams, regardless of their size, generally have a sincere desire to improve their levels of effectiveness and collaboration and to experience a stronger sense of cohesiveness and—dare I say it—even team spirit. Helping them understand whether they're a group or a team or a high performing team hasn't been helpful for me or my client teams. What turns out to be helpful for teams like these is:

- Understanding specifically what work is best done collaboratively—and which isn't
- Understanding within their groups who should be collaborating with whom on what
- Figuring out how they and their teams could become collectively more efficient at doing it.

I love a good academic discussion, one I can really sink my teeth into. When I set out to develop this Framework, I was determined to create something practical that could be used by any manager or team member who felt they needed help. I understood that it would have to reflect the best thinking of smart and learned folks like Messrs Katzenbach, Smith and Hackman. At the same time, this Framework needed to account for the quirks and realities of our culture and people.

Our culture was not and is not patient with theoretical debate. I have found the same to be true at other companies. So, when I proposed our Framework, I sidestepped the need to gain agreement on the definition of "real team" by focusing on what

I had come to believe was the powerful, common denominator across all sorts of groups that aim to work better together: value-adding collaboration.

Let's revisit what I mean by "value-adding collaboration." It's when a group or team's collaborative efforts yield better results than could be achieved by an individual or by merely totting up a collection of individual efforts. Remember my chart in the previous chapter that described the levels of collaboration? I have found that maximal collaborative value creation happens at the top of the chart, in what I refer to as proactive or, from this point on, intentional collaboration.

I begin with this hypothesis (influenced by Dr Hackman, by the way):

> An organization creates, or a group forms into, a team because there is a sense that collaboration is needed in order to create or unlock greater value for the organization than can be realized through the simple collection of individual efforts.

The urge to act as a team often begins with organizational structure. "We're all part of marketing. Our boxes all have lines to the same senior marketing person, so we're a team." This can't be enough, though, to expect collaboration. Collaboration when compared to individual effort is time consuming, costly and complex. Expending the effort to act and work as a team had better lead to a stronger bottom line. If a team's collaborative efforts aren't producing incrementally more or better products or results, namely creating value, the larger organization won't—and shouldn't—support that team for very long.

It's not just about what the organization demands. Dr Hackman suggests that there are three criteria by which one can judge successful collaborative groups:

- A team output acceptable to the team's clients, including the broader organization
- Growth in team capability
- An experience that is meaningful and satisfying for each team member[3]

In Mars, we interpret this tripartite gauge of team effectiveness as being about value creation for the organization, for the team and for each individual team member; it is what matters more than any hard-and-fast definition of what a "real team" is or isn't. Most importantly, the teams who are using the approach we developed get this metric. They have embraced this definition and made it their own.

Don't let someone else's definition of "real team" limit your thinking or your collaboration. Whether you're a leader, a team member or a consultant, figure out where value-adding collaboration needs to happen and put your energy and effort into unleashing and enabling it. Furthermore, whether you're working as part of a team, a group or a community, you can apply this fundamental concept. In fact, for these reasons I use the terms "team," "group" and "work-group" interchangeably for the rest of this book.

Dysfunctional Teams—They Ain't What They Used to Be

Dysfunctional teams are where the action is. Or at least that's how I felt when I started working with teams over 25 years ago. I was most worried about—and most fascinated by—dysfunctional teams. Abnormal group dynamics had that whiff of danger about them, and a feeling of familiarity—remember my large family of origin? Makes some sense, right?

You recall that team in the North Carolina cambric factory I talked about earlier? I longed for groups like that with issues I could fix, and in fixing them, feel like a hero. I believed I was at my best in risky team workshops. I shone where all sorts of dirty laundry was being dragged out, where old frustrations and fiercely suppressed resentments came flooding forth under my expert guidance. What a rush. I wish I had known how irresponsible I was being. I can't think of one instance where my efforts with these teams had a lasting, positive effect. In most cases, people left feeling better, feeling a little more teaminess or at least relieved. I can recall, though, several teams that I now wish I hadn't gone near, for their sakes and for mine. I opened wounds that neither I nor the team were equipped to face or to deal with effectively. Sure, no one died. But I feel certain that sessions like these left emotional and/or psychological scars.

It probably goes without saying that as painful as these workshops were, they also taught me some of the most important lessons of my career. I can only hope that my former clients are able to say similar things. As happens with lessons learned from pain, it can take a while for them to become clear. In my case, the lessons began to coalesce about five years ago shortly after I dedicated myself to working with Mars teams. I was beginning a piece of work with a team of leaders and managers who all reported to a VP of Finance. Since the team and I were based in different cities I began by interviewing each team member over the phone. Only minutes into the first interview, I knew I was in for some juicy team dysfunction. There were tears, expressions of fear, anger, and a constant need for reassurance that I would keep the conversation confidential. By the third call, my anticipation morphed into concern and then into an urgent need for caution. I did the smartest thing I had ever done in a situation like this. I stopped the interviews, picked up the phone and called the senior P&O person—we refer to this function as People & Organization, or P&O—supporting the team. I told her, "I can't, in good conscience, continue to work with this team." The problem, I told her, wasn't the team. They might have had their issues, but the bigger, more pressing problem was the boss. I suggested that we talk about how to address that very real issue before we did anything with the team.

As it turned out, they already knew. The VP of P&O, the General Manager who was the Finance VP's boss, and even the VP's peers on the business leadership team knew that this guy was a problem. *The* problem. They were all hoping that in a well-facilitated team workshop, his team of direct reports would set him straight with hard-hitting feedback and requests for him to change. Interesting. His peers and his boss had tried and failed in similar feedback-based workshops to help him see the damage he was doing. If people at his own level and his boss couldn't get through to him, what did they think his direct reports could do? Did they really expect a bunch of junior managers to convince this take-no-prisoners, manipulative, fear-inducing boss that he should change? The VP's peers and boss meant well. They were genuinely hopeful that I could make it work where they had failed. I was an "expert," after all. In my expert opinion it was a dangerous approach with little to no chance of succeeding, and I told them so.

To their credit, P&O agreed to step in and stop the process. They put the Finance VP on a performance improvement plan and got him an external coach. The P&O VP also agreed to meet with the Finance VP and his team. Together they would explain that the team session was being postponed while he, the VP, made a good faith effort to change his ways. Whew. At least for a little while.

Fast forward a few months. The Finance VP's coach was a consultant who spent much of his professional life facilitating team effectiveness workshops. After a few months of coaching he urged the VP to hold a feedback-focused workshop with this team. The intention was to induce and facilitate some honest, direct conversation among them all, to clear the air. In other words, this guy wanted them to do exactly what I had refused to do a few months earlier. The P&O VP, who was understandably nervous about this, called me the week before the workshop asking if I had any advice. Once again, I suggested they not do it. They did it anyway. The process quickly went pear-shaped, as my English boss might say. The team felt pressured to declare, in front of their peers and in a climate of low trust, negative things about their intimidating boss. Their worry was the same as it had been when I was involved with them: that their boss would hold these statements against them later. The workshop got underway but before long members of the team protested and it ended early.

A year or so later during my research, I reflected on this story and others like it that I had been part of. It occurred to me that the vast majority of the teams I was working with were pretty solid. Team dysfunction such as I had experienced with the Finance group was the exception. The vast majority of the teams I worked with were getting business results. Maybe their collaboration wasn't great. But typically they got along with each other, respected one another and were generally engaged. The only time I was seeing problems in teams was when an individual—or two—was behaving badly.

They say that one bad apple spoils the whole bunch. That only happens if you leave that bad apple in the basket long enough to do damage. In the case of the VP of Finance, it was the manager who was disrupting an otherwise pretty good group. The same happens when it's a team member whose behavior is damaging.

No matter how hard we try, we make bad hires. Regardless of how many employment interviews we put a person through or what simulations we have them experience, every so often we employ a person who just isn't going to work out. Maybe it's a skills problem. Maybe it's a cultural mismatch. Whatever the circumstances, bad hires happen. Most companies will make genuine efforts to get mis-hires on track. Others—too many others—will ignore the problem and hope it gets better. But, sooner or later, if this person's struggles continue they will affect those they have to work with, namely the team around them.

Even when it's a team member who's wreaking havoc on a team, it ends up being a leadership problem. Early in my career when I was in the stock photography business I was fortunate enough to work for a gifted and inspiring leader. Henry taught me most of what I know about managing people. His tutelage included one lesson about dealing with performance issues and by extension teams. I was managing a group of photo researchers. Kim, a smart, elegant lady, was in the later stages of her career. She, along with her former manager, had joined our little company from another photo agency. Kim had been put onto my team expressly so that I could address what my boss and his leadership team (which included Kim's former manager) felt were Kim's persistent performance problems. This is more or less what I was told:

> Carlos, here's a woman who is 20 years your senior and has much more experience in our industry than you. She left a longtime, secure job somewhere else to follow her former boss to our firm, only to crash and burn within the first year. We believe in your capabilities, Carlos, junior as you are. We need you to do something about Kim. Let us know how it works out.

Forget that I was managing people for the first time and that I had certainly never fired anyone.

This assignment attested to my boss's confidence in me, for which I was grateful. Talk about being thrown in the deep end, though. I wouldn't have used these words then, but Kim's was a case of cultural mismatch. Our firm was an up-and-comer in the stock photo business. We were moving at light-speed when compared to the older, more staid company from which Kim had come. The change didn't suit her. I did what I could to coach her. I tried to help her see the change that was needed and to help her modify her behaviors accordingly. I also spent a fair amount of time in denial. I was an inexperienced manager faced with an unfamiliar and unsavory task for which I felt wholly unprepared. I was telling myself, "This will all work out," despite the fact that at some level I knew that my coaching efforts would go for naught. Time passed—weeks or months, I don't recall. Kim remained on the team. All the while the air in the office was growing thick with unspoken frustration. Then one day my boss came to me for a chat. While I don't remember his exact words, the gist of his message was this:

> Forget about Kim for a minute. I know you want to do the right thing for her in a difficult situation, as you should. That's one reason I wanted you to handle this. But think about the rest of your team. Kim, whether she means to or not, is letting them down. Repeatedly. As a result your team and numbers are suffering. The team is paying the price for Kim's inability to carry her weight and your apparent failure to do anything about it. Her credibility is already shot and yours is disappearing fast. Your team respects you, Carlos. But you have to do the right thing for them or that respect won't last. Is that what you want?

Man, he was smart. That same day I put the wheels in motion to facilitate a clean exit and soft landing for Kim. It was a bit involved, but it worked. In the end she actually thanked me. That, though, isn't the point. The impact on a team of one person who is struggling or failing is huge. Our team's performance was being dragged down not because we were dysfunctional but because one of our members wasn't in the right job for her. Beyond the erosion of performance, there was the hit to morale and engagement my team was taking. People were talking behind Kim's back and behind mine. The negativity was mounting and adding to our apparent dysfunction. All because her manager—me—wasn't effectively addressing the individual performance problem.

I take three lessons out of this episode and from the story of the Finance VP I told earlier:

Lesson 1: *It's almost always an individual performance problem.* Often the frustrations and issues a team is having arise from a problem individual. So, before you step in to try to help a struggling team, look into the possibility that the issue may lie with an individual. Then involve the right people to address that problem.

Lesson 2: *Don't ever, ever try to fix an individual performance problem with a team intervention.* Whether it's a team member or a team leader who's the nexus of the problems you're seeing, what's called for is solid performance management. Once the individual issue is addressed, a team workshop might be a good idea.

Lesson 3: *In the end, it's always a problem with the manager.* It's the manager, not the underperforming team member, who is on the hook for the performance of the team. Even if a team member is throwing the rest of the team off its game, it's the manager's failure to take effective action that needs to be addressed first and foremost.

In otherwise healthy companies there are few truly dysfunctional teams per se. There are only unskilled or lazy managers who won't or don't take responsibility for the health and performance of their teams. Before you worry about what the team requires, figure out if it's the individuals in the team that need the help and start there.

Real dysfunctional teams

There may be fewer dysfunctional teams than we thought, but

dysfunctional teams are an occasional fact of organizational life. Managers and team members will sometimes do things that disrupt healthy team functioning. In cases like this they create what looks like, and may actually end up as, team dysfunction if not addressed. Refer one more time to the chart I shared earlier:

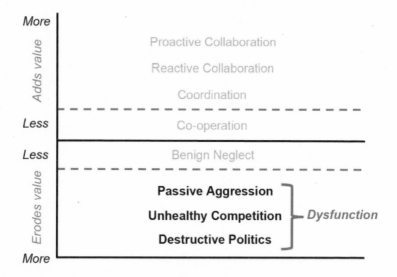

Whenever any of the behaviors at the bottom of the chart become institutionalized within a group, they lead to genuine team dysfunction. For instance, a bit of passive aggression in a group is normal. When passive aggression becomes the way things get done, that's dysfunction. Likewise, competition within a team or group is actually healthy and can be fun. When competition among group members begins to distract them from doing the right thing, and instead each individual focuses on winning as they see it, that's dysfunction. Politics is another standard feature in any organization or team. There are interests that need to be taken into account and agendas that need to be advanced. When politics in a group becomes an end in itself, though, and instead of being used to advance appropriate outcomes and agendas, the politics becomes destructive, a team is dysfunctional. From time to time managers allow or promote these kinds of corrosive behavior, leading to authentic dysfunction.

As I said earlier, true team dysfunction within otherwise healthy organizations is rare. What's more common are individual performance problems that disrupt groups. For any of the behaviors at the bottom of the chart to become a fixture in a team they have to be supported or tolerated by the broader organization. This leads me to the final point about dysfunction.

Dysfunctional organizations

I reached the conclusions in this book during my tenure at Mars. The data, experiences and insights that led to my conclusions came out of 25 years of work with many organizations and groups, both as a manager and as a consultant. Based on that background there is one other cause of so-called team dysfunction that must be acknowledged. Sometimes teams and groups struggle not because of specific individuals but because the organization around them is unhealthy. This can happen in companies that are suffering financially and in companies that are flourishing. They may be old businesses or new ones; they may be in any industry in any country; it doesn't matter. I haven't come across many really rotten companies. When I have, the teams and individuals within them that I came to know struggled. No amount of team building, even of the kind I go on to describe in this book, was going to get at the underlying problem of those genuinely sick organizations.

Yet, I have found that within the sea of negativity that is a dysfunctional organization, teams can be a refuge of sanity, productivity and positive feelings. Great managers find ways to insulate their teams from the corrosive climates that surround them, allowing them to do their best work in a comparatively healthy environment. Leading a highly effective team in a culture or system that seems designed to kill it is exhausting. But it can be done. It's even more important in circumstances like these to do the most effective things to build your group's capability and energy. One part of this is to avoid wasting time on the ineffective measures I've discussed.

A Team of Individuals

I have worked with a few dysfunctional companies, with some scary bad managers and plenty of sub-par team members. But as I've said, the groups themselves were rarely the problem. It was individuals. At the same time, teams require and can only thrive with strong individuals on them. Failure to get such folks on your team, and worse yet, failure to deal with those who aren't making it, is the only certain way I know to doom your team or group.

Much of the accepted wisdom in the realm of team building and generating team spirit doesn't make a real difference to team performance, at least not for long. This is because, no matter how well intentioned or how often used they are, they don't address, head on, the truth that is both the bane of collaboration and its greatest hope: It's all about individuals and what really makes them tick. This is the central paradox of all teamwork in organizations. Consider:

- The majority of work-groups in healthy companies are made up of capable, well-intentioned individuals, many of whom would like to collaborate more.
- It's a minority of groups that can be called "dysfunctional," and those groups can almost always chalk up their failings to individuals or, less often, to the organizations around them.

The individual is the key to addressing the most common types of team dysfunction *and* to unlocking more and more effective collaboration. To quote Katzenbach and Smith, "our need to distinguish ourselves as individuals becomes a powerful engine for team performance."[4] We'll dig deeper into this idea in the next chapter.

Summary

- A great deal of organizational time and money is wasted on notions of team building and effectiveness that, in the end, aren't worth it.
- The ideas of team spirit and of so-called team players are much talked about but are not helpful in creating more and better collaboration.
- Efforts to define what a real team is—or is not—are largely academic and not useful when it comes to improving results-focused collaboration.
- The focus on dysfunctional teams as a subject of team interventions misses the actual causes of most dysfunction in teams: individual managers or team members within the team, or the organization around the team.
- The key to unlocking and enhancing collaboration lies in accounting for the needs and drives of the typical individual team member.

Chapter 5

The "I" in Team, Part 2

The Central Paradox

Teams need lots of things to be successful: effective leadership, some kind of structure, and real work, for example. Effective collaboration is another one of those needs. Teams also rely on skilled, self-motivated individuals as I said at the end of the last chapter. These last two seemingly contradictory needs, collaboration and self-motivated individuals, are at the heart of the paradox that this Framework seeks to make sense of and then capitalize on.

Paradox is a great concept. It comes across as just another business buzzword if it's used carelessly. So I'll clarify how I think of it. A paradox is a statement consisting of two connected, apparently contradictory ideas that, when considered together, can lead to an insight or a deeper truth. The last part of that definition leaves you with a choice. You can look at a statement containing contradictory ideas and be immobilized by the irreconcilable conflict between the two parts of the paradox, resulting in feelings like frustration and stagnation: "What's the point! None of this makes sense, anyway." You can, instead, let the contradiction play on your brain and see where it leads you. "What would it mean to me if both of these ideas were true?" This sort of intellectual examination can reveal something new and interesting. Paradoxes are ancient brain-training technology, used by philosophers and Zen Buddhists alike. Zen Buddhism makes use of paradoxes to help adepts to attain deeper insights. They call them "koans." Probably the most well-known koan is this question: "What is the sound of one hand clapping?" Monks are asked during their training to go off and meditate on koans like this. The idea is that such contradictions temporarily freeze the rational mind, which can't "square the circle." Then, when the rational mind is suspended, things like instinct and intuition kick in, leading eventually to insight.

Business is full of paradoxes. I was in charge of the executive development programs team at IBM for about a year. I was auditing one of our programs once when a koan-like set of contradictions was presented, unintentionally, to our participants. It might have been one of the most productive accidents I've ever seen in a corporate classroom. These were programs lasting five and a half days, conducted at the IBM Learning Center in Armonk, New York. On certain days, we'd close the classroom session with an informal presentation from one of the VPs that reported into Lou Gerstner, then IBM's CEO and Chairman. This was followed by a wine-and-cheese fireplace chat with the VP. The IBM Learning Center didn't have a real fireplace so a couple of my team painted a life-sized, stone fireplace and taped it to the wall in a common area. Our first speaker that week was the VP of R&D, Nick Donofrio, a brilliant, warm and very accessible guy. His brief presentation and the Q&A that followed focused on his people-centric strengths and approach to leadership. The participants were glowing afterwards, inspired and uplifted. Our next fireside chat speaker was Sam Palmisano, who would go on to succeed Lou Gerstner as IBM's CEO. Sam was a funny, sarcastic and tough-as-nails, bottom-line-focused businessman. At about 6 feet 4 inches tall he was also an imposing figure. His message to these budding executives was no-nonsense, clear as a bell and as different from Nick Donofrio's as you could imagine: Expect, as an IBM executive, to be working seven days a week and to relegate your family life to second tier. If you can't deal with it, or if your family isn't up for it, you have a choice to make: hang with this life of leadership or take a different path. It was that simple. Sam's tone could be curt and dismissive which, paired with his message, left jaws hanging in stunned surprise. Afterwards, as the participants sipped Chardonnay and chatted casually around our butcher-paper hearth, I heard more than one of them confide to a peer their despair about the leadership culture they were joining. They wondered how two such different people could sit atop the company. Among this group of about 25 there was a sense that the hard-ass approach to leadership was probably the one they would, in the end, be expected to emulate. I suppose, when a few years later Sam became CEO, it must have seemed that their fears had been realized. But there were others there that day, others who took away a different message. They were the ones who saw past the contradiction and into the paradox. Leadership requires toughness and tenderness, a relentless focus on results and a continuous attention to the people who produce them. The most useful message was contained in the contradiction, the message about leadership as an act of balancing styles, energies and attention.

How does this apply to teams, individuals and team development? As I've said, at the heart of any paradox is a contradiction. Sometimes, a paradox is obscured because the contradictions within it seem out of balance. This clearly was the case for some of those IBM-ers. One leadership style seemed destined to overpower the other. Edgar Schein, one of my favorite business academicians, addresses the imbalance between individualism and collaboration in his book, *Humble Inquiry: The Gentle Art of Asking Instead of Telling*.

> The US culture is strongly built on the tacit assumptions of pragmatism, individualism and status through achievement. These assumptions introduce a strong bias for getting the job done, which combined with individualism leads to a devaluing of relationship building, teamwork and collaboration...[1]

We're going to come back to this quote again later, in an expanded form. Based on this snippet, though, Dr Schein nails it. As I discussed in the first chapter, many companies, like the ones I have worked for, were spawned by this American culture of individualism and achievement. Their corporate cultures and their leadership often reflect these assumptions. Things are out of balance. One half of our paradox—individualism—is, in fact, overpowering the other half. It's not all bad, though. This pervasive bias for individual achievement has produced some amazing business results for companies—Mars, Incorporated, included. At the same time, the unbalanced emphasis on individualism gets in the way of building collaboration that could be:

- Producing even better results
- Consistently creating value over and above the sum of individual achievements
- Driving higher levels of employee engagement
- More proactive than reactive
- Sustainable.

There's an opportunity here but it may be hard to get at. The tension between our deeply ingrained preference for individualism and our desire—or need—for more effective collaboration will persist. We can't give up individual orientation in favor of teamwork, or vice versa. Nor can we simply layer one over the other, veneer-like, and hope for much to change; spread a little teaminess on this collection of individuals and we'll get better teamwork. Yeah, no; it just doesn't work. Remember the story of the disgruntled team at the cambric factory? The tension will go on. The apparent imbalance doesn't have to, though.

I'm not the first person to call out this tension or notice the imbalance in the two sides of this paradox—not by a long shot; every expert on the subject of team effectiveness that I've studied brings it up. For my money, however, most team gurus consistently fail to account for the individual–team paradox adequately in their models and approaches. Katzenbach and Smith, for instance, say it this way:

Teams are not antithetical to individual performance. Real teams always find ways for each individual to contribute and thereby gain distinction.[2]

Essentially they're saying the two aren't necessarily in opposition. Not, at least, when it comes to "real teams." Real teams, we're told, find ways to channel individualism in ways that allow people to "gain distinction." I have two questions about this. First, how do real teams do it? Is it about giving out individual tasks that team members can use to channel and express their individualism? That seems reasonable, so let's assume that's what they mean. That brings me to my second question: How will throwing a team member an individualistic bone to gnaw on do anything to activate or promote collaboration? I support the idea that there is a lot of work that will be best done by individuals. I agree that doing this work will help individuals to feel they're making meaningful contributions. But the assumption that sating the need for individual working will somehow create space for or induce more collaboration doesn't follow logically. It's a bit like assuming that if I offer my kids an ice cream bribe to eat their broccoli, they will end up learning to eat more cruciferous vegetables. They might, I suppose, but there's certainly no guarantee. They're just as likely, if not more so, to fall in love with frozen confections. The collaboration-versus-individual-achievement problem is a bit like broccoli versus ice cream. We know collaboration is a good thing but will nonetheless, if given a choice, go for the tasty treat of individual achievement.

Like other team gurus, Katzenbach and Smith don't adequately acknowledge the awesome pull of individual work and the power of the organizational systems that reinforce it. As an individual, I know that entire pay, performance management and rewards systems are based on compensating and promoting individuals. Taken together, the twin forces of individual achievement and individual incentives easily overshadow and overpower any inclination towards collaboration.

Let's return to Dr Schein's quote from the beginning of the chapter. Here is the last sentence again with the words that follow the ellipses added back and bolded:

> These assumptions [about individualism] introduce a strong bias for getting the job done, which combined with individualism leads to a devaluing of relationship building, teamwork and collaboration **except as means to the end of task accomplishment**.

Look at those last words in boldface type. Dr Schein's book is essentially about asking, listening and the value of relationship at work. In this quote he is suggesting that relationship and collaboration are undermined when individualism and task focus act together. Really? What if task-focused individuals engage in task-focused relationships that end up not only getting results but also creating more productive and effective collaboration? And what if, via these task-focused relationships, people are also able to build deeper and more personal relationships outside of the task? That would be a good thing, right? This is precisely what I have seen happen. To achieve this, though, requires letting go of a dualistic mindset and embracing the power of paradox.

The tension between collaboration and individual achievement is often seen as a necessary evil of organizational life—it's the Jedi versus the Dark Side, the inevitable struggle between opposing forces that we just have to live with. When this conflict, however, is appreciated as a paradox it can help us see how the contradiction can be a source of energy, of creative tension. At least it helped me. Any progress we make in the area of collaboration will be because we have built on, incorporated and/or learned how our preference for individual achievement can exist in a mutually beneficial, dynamic relationship with powerful collaboration. The power of collaboration depends on the power of individualism if we're to make the most of it. This is the central paradox.

Most of the individuals I know through my work are smart and productive. They believe that teamwork and collaboration are worthy endeavors that can produce enhanced outcomes. Most of them, however, work within organizations that are like what Edgar Schein described above. So:

- They seek out and hire the very best individuals they can
- Their HR systems are constructed to track, measure and reward those individuals
- Their training and the instincts of most of their leaders are honed to work with and recognize individual achievement (while using "teamy" language)
- They celebrate, even venerate, individual employees and leaders as heroes.

The people leading our major corporations recognize that in the current complex, rapidly evolving global workplace, effective and efficient collaboration is essential. What do they do to try to unlock more collaboration? They buy the team-building services that are available. They invest in team building that emphasizes and tries to increase teaminess. In doing so they fail to embrace the paradox I've talked about.

Embracing the paradox means moving past what appears to be a conflict between two opposing forces and looking for the energizing insight. Just acknowledging the tension and learning to live with it won't do. In fact, to do so squanders an unparalleled opportunity. Encased in this tension is the seed of the solution to creating more effective teamwork and collaboration. So drop the dualistic, oppositional thinking and adopt the notion that the two truths of individual effort and effective collaboration need each other.

The first practical step in doing this requires that you move away from some cherished approaches to leading and building teams. Team building is useless when it tries to coax and cajole collaboration in the face of powerful, pervasive forces that encourage and reward individual effort. It's even more fruitless when it doesn't acknowledge the tension between the team building itself and those same forces. It sets up an internal conflict in team members that is unresolvable. "I know I'm supposed to be collaborating but, honestly, that's not what I'm good at and not what they pay and recognize me for."

We need a model to understand how individual effort and collaboration can be interdependent, intertwined and good for each other. Once we have that, we can begin to shift how team effectiveness gets done in our organizations. The best part is that this shift can be implemented without screwing around with existing systems, the company's culture or people's heads. It all goes back to a very old idea that, like teamwork, is misunderstood more often than not: motivation.

Tapping into the Achievement Drive: Motives Theory

We need to get real about what makes individual people tick if we're going to tap into their energy for collaboration. The motivation business is massive. There are surely as many if not more people out there making money on motivation as there are people writing and thinking about teams. Some of what professional motivators peddle is rubbish; some of it is based on good social science and really effective. With all the noise in the space of motivation you have to be careful what you choose to work with. That's certainly true when it comes to enhancing collaboration.

There are lots of ways to try to make sense of people, what

they do and why they do it. Like a lot of people in my field I have experience with a range of psychometric instruments. I've worked with the Myers-Briggs Type Indicator™, FIRO-B™, and Kolb's Learning Styles Inventory™, among others. They're all useful. None of them gets at this "what-makes-people-tick" issue better, at least for my purposes, than David McClelland's work on motives or needs states. I learned about McClelland's work during my days at IBM where we worked with Hay-McBer, the consultancy that David McClelland co-founded.

McClelland's work is central to unlocking the paradox, so I'm going to give you some background on him and his work. If you know this already, feel free to skip to the next section. If not, hang with me for a few paragraphs.

McClelland was a giant in the field of human and, in particular, managerial behavior. He laid the groundwork for much of what is done today in the realms of competencies, corporate learning and leadership development. He saw motives as foundational in understanding what made employees, managers and leaders tick. His definition of a motive features the following language:

A recurrent concern for a goal state or condition...which drives, directs and selects the behavior of the individual

He asserted that when it came to work, there were three motives or needs that mattered most:

- Need for achievement (nAch)
- Need for affiliation (nAff)
- Need for power (nPow)

Richard Boyatzis, another giant in the field and a colleague of McClelland's, offered the following thoughts on the three needs states:

Achievement: an unconscious drive to do better toward a standard of excellence. People with strong nAch set goals; strive to take moderate risks; prefer individual activities [among other things].

Affiliation: an unconscious drive to be a part of warm, close relationships, like friendships. People with strong nAff choose to spend time with close friends or significant others; ...prefer to work in groups, etc....

Power: an unconscious drive to have impact on others. People with strong nPow often assert themselves by taking leadership positions; prefer occupations in which they can help or have impact on others, like teachers, ministers or managers.

To illustrate these needs or motives consider the reasons that people play golf. For some golfers it's all about achievement. They thrive on the challenge of competing with themselves and with others for the lowest score in a given game. Getting one's handicap down gives the achievement-driven player a longer-term standard of excellence to work towards. For others, the game is all about affiliation, the foursome (or threesome, or whatever number are playing). Golf provides a healthy shot of relationship—four hours with good friends spent at a leisurely pace, laughing together, talking trash or talking business. Finally, the power motive. There are those for whom membership at the club is the prize. It's about the visible signs of influence. These folks often enjoy the status that comes with country club membership or playing with the CEO or brain surgeon down the street. Or, perhaps, they're the leader and organizer of the golf outing. They get satisfaction from pulling together the group, from seeing to it that the whole event and those required to make it happen—caddies, pro-shop employees—execute it smoothly.

Golfers may be driven by any one of these needs, by all three or by any combination of them. Each of us has a pattern of these three motives with each of the three rated as high, moderate or low. For example, after completing the test for motives known as the Picture Story Exercise (PSE), I was shown to be high in achievement, moderate in affiliation and low in power.[3,4.] Others may be high in power, low in affiliation and moderate in achievement. Being high, medium or low in one need state has no bearing on the others. You could be high in all three, low in two and high in one, etc.

In my days at IBM I was trained to score (at a basic level) and interpret the PSE. This arcane bit of knowledge would come in handy in fashioning my hypothesis while later working at Mars. In the PSE, the subject is shown a series of black-and-white images, copies of paintings or sketches showing people in various settings: two individuals in what appear to be lab coats with beakers and pipettes; an individual seated in front of a window with a glass on a table in front of him, and so forth. The subject is asked to write a story about what is happening in each image. Each story is then scored by a trained PSE scorer.

The person scoring the brief stories is taught to look for words, phrases and expressions in the writing that tend to reveal, without the writer being aware of it, what is important to him or her. It may seem unusual but it's been shown to be a valid and reliable instrument for identifying the three motives. The scoring of the PSE involves learning how to spot the signals for each of the three motives in people's words. This arcane piece of knowledge was indispensable to me as I analyzed the data I had collected from the 30 teams in my Mars research data base. As I pored over hundreds of team member quotes during the research, it became clear to me that:

- These teams were made up mostly of high achievement types.
- Although they weren't highly collaborative, they did value

their relationships with each other as a means to getting their work done.

- They evidenced a comparatively low need for being seen as influential.

On top of this data, I knew and worked with many other Mars Associates whose behaviors and personalities aligned with my read on the Mars team data. I matched this profile myself. Based on this, I sketched what I thought the motive profile of the average Mars Associate looked like.

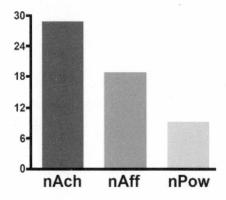

To be clear: I didn't have the resources to conduct a rigorous assessment of the predominant motives in our company. I didn't use the PSE (or the similar TAT, Thematic Apperception Test). I based my hypotheses on my training in McClelland's work and my experience using motives in executive coaching at IBM. I was applying my knowledge, experience and intuition in arriving at this professional hunch—and I would have bet my next year's paychecks that I had it more or less right.

This little graphic created a "eureka" moment for me that almost instantly morphed into an "Oh sh*t" moment. More on the scatological part of my realization later. Notice how in the graphic above the need for achievement stacks up against the other two? It's higher. Remember, high achievement types "drive to do better toward a standard of excellence...They set goals; strive to take moderate risks; prefer individual activities." Let me say that again: they "prefer individual activities." They might enjoy the company of others, but not as much as getting things done themselves—and they don't have a whole lot of interest in influencing others, either.

As I was reflecting on the data and my bar chart, I developed the following working hypothesis:

Mars, Incorporated hired and promoted, without necessarily acknowledging it, people that consistently fit this motives profile, and thus repeatedly reinforced a predominant achievement culture at Mars.

This profile and the culture behind it, I reasoned, contributed significantly to our business success. It also made meaningful collaboration harder than it would otherwise be. When I thought about my time at IBM and at DDI before that, I felt sure their typical employees looked pretty much the same. The same is probably true at lots of other big companies.

I ran my assessment and hypothesis by a few other highly qualified colleagues inside Mars who, to my relief, generally read the data the way I did. They agreed that this picture of our culture and Associates felt intuitively accurate.

One final point. McClelland held that needs/motives were learned (the theory is sometimes called "learned needs theory") through one's life experiences and the environments in which a person was raised or developed. Since motives are learned, McClelland, Boyatzis and others assert that motives can be changed. You might think, "Great! Let's train out some of the high achievement and stoke the affiliation and power and *voilà*—teamwork." The reality is more complicated than that. It turns out that there are a few conditions to making this change happen. Two of those conditions are:

- People will only change if they want to change.
- Change cannot occur without a change in the person's environmental supports.

I'm a practitioner with no claims to the kinds of academic background and achievements of a McClelland or Boyatzis. My experience tells me that changing motives is tough, regardless of the environment. Behavior change is different. I've seen, even been a part of helping, individuals shift their behaviors. It's not easy but it's demonstrably doable. Motives, on the other hand, are "unconscious drives," by definition out of our day-to-day awareness. Let's consider these two conditions in more depth.

People will only change if they want to change. We've all heard this before—"How many psychologists does it take to change a light bulb?" "One, but the light bulb has to want to change." When was the last time *you* succeeded at influencing someone to want to change a subconscious part of themselves? There are people who claim to do it. I've seen them on *Dr Phil*. But my experience pretty much lines up with the advice I was given in my dating years—trying to change someone at a deep, subconscious level is a low-odds endeavor.

Change cannot occur without a change in environmental supports. This one's ambiguous as explained in the literature. It can include things like support groups or online communities. It could also include things like rewards and recognition systems or anything else in the environment that would reinforce the desired change. These sorts of supports will either succeed or fail depending on the culture of the organization. Some corporate cultures might be support-group friendly; others may not. In the achievement-oriented cultures I'm familiar with, social networks, if they exist at all, are focused more on getting the work done. They're less concerned with things like personal or management development. If changing the environment means changing the culture, then addressing environmental supports isn't likely to succeed, either.

So, if we're to change how teams and the individuals within them work, we need to change motives. To change motives, we need to change people and change the culture, neither of which has high odds of success. Great! This is where the "eureka" moment I mentioned earlier transmogrified into something more unsavory, a real "Oh sh*t" moment. At this point, I was:

- Elated by what appeared to be a really useful insight about collaboration and motives
- Feeling trapped having been asked to create something for teams that was a whole lot bigger than I or any of us anticipated or had an appetite for.

It was back to my tiny office to pace and mutter yet again seeking the insight. And, once again, my shuffling self-talk led to a modest but significant breakthrough. Oddly, what popped into my head was an image of a Boeing 747. Not just any 747 but one transporting a space shuttle.

There is something paradoxical about a pair of objects that heavy and that large being able to behave as if they were weightless. On one hand, you have the force of gravity, which, along with the combined weight of a 747 and a space shuttle, would tend to keep this tandem earthbound. Then there are the countervailing laws of aerodynamics. Given the right wing shape and dimensions, and enough speed, the forces of gravity are counteracted strongly enough to generate lift and flight. Two powerful forces, gravity and aerodynamics, are made to interact so as to get 430,000 tons of airplane and spacecraft off the ground and then back down safely. I wondered if there might be an analogous approach to getting collaboration off the ground, so to speak.

The Mars culture and the cultures of other large companies act like gravity. Gravity is a good thing; it keeps us grounded and solid. Without gravity we wouldn't be successful inhabitants of this planet. Mars, Incorporated, without its culture, wouldn't be Mars and likely wouldn't have enjoyed the success it has. It just so happens that a strong aspect of the Mars culture is a widely shared need for individual achievement. That need is essentially weighing down collaboration, making getting it off the ground that much harder.

"What if," I conjectured, "there were a way to make collaboration something more compelling to the typical Mars Associate? Could we make collaboration tangible enough to feel like a thing to be achieved, something that would appeal to an individually motivated, achievement-driven Martian?" In other words, what would it take to tap into that dominant need to achieve so that people would be drawn to working together to get their achievement needs met? I'm guessing that those prehistoric hunters from Chapter 1 felt a compelling need to feed themselves and their families. That need would have played a role in their deciding to work together bringing down, say, a massive mastodon. Their collaboration arose out of basic needs and around a clear, common task. What's more, that collaboration led to relationships, to community and, who knows, maybe to civilization.

Suddenly the stakes seemed high and the potential impact enormous. The challenge sounded daunting: I wanted to do nothing less than reimagine and recast collaboration as achievement. It wasn't as hard as I thought as I'll explain in a moment. It did seem a bit like cheating, however, a little like getting my kids to eat their vegetables by developing ice-cream-flavored broccoli. As I said before, I'm a practitioner and the Mars culture is a pragmatic one. If we could get the collaborative behaviors we wanted, employing only minor psychological sleight of hand, why not?

Within hours of these insights, I had formulated what we would come to call the Three Imperatives for High Performance Collaboration: Clarity, Intentionality and Discipline. These three simple concepts arose from my research and would shape our approach to unlocking collaboration. They wouldn't require us to change anyone's subconscious or to mess with the culture. What's more, the Three Imperatives would form the foundation of an approach to team effectiveness that team leaders and team members could own and drive for themselves. At this point I got my colleagues from Mars University more involved. Clint Kofford, who was the Mars Associate leading the revamping of our manager development programs, and Celia Harmon, a former Mars Associate who was anchoring the design team, became indispensable partners in the development work from this point. Together we forged the Mars Framework for High Performance Collaboration that the balance of this book explains.

Summary

- The key to making sense of the research on Mars teams lay in recognizing a paradox that's at work in most corporate teams.
- The paradox is inherent in the tension between the

prevailing drive for individual achievement and the organizational desire for more and better collaboration.

- Embracing and making the most of this paradox required the application of individual motives theory, in particular the achievement motive as described by David McClelland.

- Once we understand the power of the achievement motive it becomes clear that the path to collaborative success involves making collaboration a thing to be achieved.

Part II

Chapter 6

Intentional Collaboration and the Three Imperatives

I have a brother who works in the metals recycling business. The other day he sent me a text with a link to a video he'd made on his iPhone while he was attending a company meeting in London. Team building was on the agenda. The featured event— and it was an event—began with a demonstration of the Haka by a small group of tribesmen from the southern Pacific. The Haka, as you might know, is a dramatic and stirring traditional war dance done by the Maori people of New Zealand. If you've ever been lucky enough to watch the New Zealand All Blacks, New Zealand's national rugby team, you'll know they begin every match with their rendition of the Haka. Very cool. My brother and his colleagues first watched the Haka demonstration, the one in the video he sent me. Then they worked in small groups to learn the Haka. Each group followed along behind one of the indigenous dancers, mimicking their motions while chanting the war chant that is integral to the dance. Seriously. When it came time to perform, the teams came to the stage two at a time. Each group performed their Haka in front of an audience of their peers. Then, the two groups were judged on the quality of their dances and the level of commitment they seemed to be showing. One team won; the other was eliminated. This is team building, my friends. If what you want is a bit of silly fun, great. If what you want is to encourage and support collaboration, this sort of exercise is a colossal waste of time and money.

To encourage and enable more effective collaboration we have to activate the paradox described in the last chapter. We must face directly into a reality that most team-building approaches don't spend much, if any, time confronting: The power of the individual achievement drive and the systems and attitudes that reinforce it in organizations stymies collaboration. At the same time, the people on the teams we work with really do want to work together more; they crave genuine team spirit and the joys of productive and meaningful collaboration. The organizations, like Mars, where they work say they want the same thing, despite systems and attitudes that favor individualism. We can turn this contradictory set of realities into a force for unlocking collaboration when we embrace the paradox. As my initial research was winding down, I was able to turn my imagination towards the dynamic tension between the forces of individualism and the passion for teamwork. When I did this, a path emerged. I found a way to enable group members to be as intentional about collaborative working as they were enthusiastic about their individual goals and objectives.

Companies, leaders and the consultants they pay have tried all sorts of imaginative ways of maximizing collaboration in the face of rampant individualism, aka team building. There's the Haka, just described. Professional theater troops have been engaged in the effort. There has been a lot of literal building of stuff with everything from Legos® to Tinker Toys® to sets of 2"x6"x12 foot planks. Like I said before, these exercises can be fun. They don't produce lasting improvements in teamwork, though. Before we look at the approach my colleagues and I developed, let's pause to consider one other popular approach that managers and leaders employ in an attempt to motivate team members to collaborate. It involves setting shared goals and priorities. Remember how flummoxed I was during the research when people were telling me that they wanted to collaborate but didn't? I was a believer in those days in the unifying power of shared goals and priorities. All the best minds said it was a key part of a real team. The majority of the team members in my data said they had shared goals and priorities. Still, we weren't seeing a whole lot of intentional collaboration. Consider this purely imaginary discussion between a few Generic Team Members—call them GTM 1, 2 and 3—and an Unfiltered Version of Me (UVM) willing to say what was really on my mind:

> GTM 1: We know we ought to collaborate more, and we really want to, really we do. But we just don't. I wish I knew why!
>
> UVM: Oh, stop your whining and just get on with it. Hey, here's a thought: I'm sure you guys have some shared priorities, right? What are they?
>
> GTM 1: Oh, yeah, that's easy. We have three. Engagement, Talent and Driving Growth.
>
> GTM 2: Hello! That's not what I remember. I don't have our strategy handy but I'm pretty sure our manager told us that we were focusing on up-skilling the team, turning around the business with our one big customer and executional excellence.
>
> GTM 3: No, guys, actually, we all met back in September if you recall and, um, we agreed that it was, um, customer focus and reducing our overheads. I'm pretty, well, very sure about this.
>
> UVM: Never mind, guys. I'm sorry I asked!

There were teams in my study that did have more clarity than these three about their shared priorities—about half of them. In the majority of those cases, though, while they agreed on the buzzwords that represented their priorities, they were operating under different assumptions about what needed to be done in pursuit of those priorities. They were not, as we sometimes say, aligned. Shared priorities just weren't all that shared when it came to what was guiding people's choices and efforts. Therefore, rather than choosing to collaborate, team members reverted to being driven by their achievement needs and to their habit of doing their work individually.

Here's some good news: despite their confusion over shared priorities, team members typically respected and liked each other. They tended to be very helpful when one of their teammates needed a hand. Remember my earlier chart about the levels of collaboration? Being helpful, what I earlier called "reactive collaboration," is a fine, even necessary quality. It often results in problems being solved and fires getting put out. Not only that. Reactive collaboration seemed to energize people, to tap into their innate achievement needs. Reactive collaboration is taxing, though, and can lead to burnout. Nor was it what these team members were asking for based on my interview data. Here's how I would describe what I heard in the data: Team members and their leaders share a desire and a need to cultivate more proactive or intentional collaboration. It was this simple statement that led to the Levels of Collaboration graph I shared in Chapter 3. Here is that graphic again, this time illustrating the desired shift that the data had revealed.

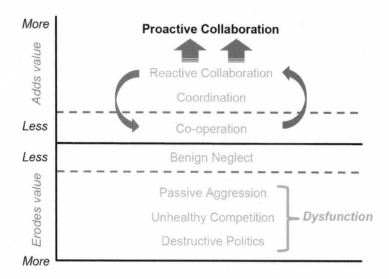

If team members wanted to be more intentional about their collaboration, they would clearly need to do more than focus on shared goals. Let's spend a moment on the word "intentionality."

From Habits to Intentionality

"Intentionality" is yet another business buzzword. In the last 10 or 15 years intentionality has become one of those traits that leadership mavens and self-help authors call us to. It's not quite as common as "authenticity," but it's close. It's probably overused and I wouldn't blame you if you groaned a bit every time I use it. I'd employ a different term if I could find one that fits. Every other word I considered, all of them words that I use and like, can sound just as woo-woo, just as buzzwordy if not more so: purposeful, mindful, choiceful (youch!). Intentionality will have to do.

Being intentional has two parts. It means choosing what you want and then doing what is needed in pursuit of that choice. Intentionality drives our behavior, but it's different from the motives we talked about in the last chapter. Motives, such as the need to achieve, shape our choices by working largely outside of our awareness. Intentionality, while it should inform our choices, is itself a choice. As such it is more conscious. The difference between a motive and intentionality is akin to the difference between our innate hunger and the diet we might choose. Our hunger drives us to eat. Sometimes we select things that are good for us, other times, not so much. A diet, on the other hand, is a choice or set of choices that we make about how we'll manage our drive to eat and the food we consume. Diets fail more often than they succeed. A diet is an attempt to change our habits of eating. Changing a habit is hard for the best of us, especially when that habit is based on an impulse as fundamental as hunger. The same happens with most attempts at team building. They come up against strong motive-based impulses that have hardened into habits of individual behavior. As we've discussed, more often than not, they fail.

Of course, even our habits are to some degree intentional.

You and I, theoretically, always have a choice. I can choose to eat those curly fries that I always eat at this particular restaurant or I can choose to eat the salad. Despite the low-carb diet I've chosen, it's likely I'll cave in to that fried-and-spiced potato goodness. We all get stuck in our habits, especially those based on fundamental urges and appetites, and it's hard to choose otherwise. As a life-coach I was working with once said to me, "You're choosing your stuck-ness." I wanted to punch him for both the made-up word and accusation, but he was right.

The Mars Associates I had worked with and studied were stuck in a behavioral rut. What's more, they were passively choosing to stay stuck in their preference for, and comfort with, being individual contributors. If one of them took on a new work assignment and, out of habit, banged it out herself, quickly, efficiently and with a good result, who could blame her? Her boss was probably in the background yammering on about teamwork and such. All well and good, but she knew how to do what needed doing. Working with someone else might have slowed her down. What's more, she got a lot of satisfaction out of completing the task herself and checking it off her to-do list; it fed her need to achieve and boosted her engagement. Heck, if she did it well, it might eventually have led to a promotion. So, teamwork, schmeam-work. The rut goes on.

During my research I had also taken a look at the cumulative competencies data Mars had gathered through our leadership programs. The data came from the 360-degree feedback surveys that are a part of a few of our courses. There was one theme that had been consistent for years and that further reinforced my achievement hypothesis. The two greatest strengths of Mars leaders were 1) being action oriented and 2) a consistent focus on results. These two sets of skills are considered individual contributor competencies within the Mars competency model. They're closely related to the achievement motive and have become our Associates' go-to choice for getting things done.

Call them habits of performance. These habits have contributed mightily to Mars's business success and they will continue to do so, I imagine. Like most productive habits they have a shadow side. These two competencies had become overused strengths, points of stuck-ness for the culture. Our Associates have become so reliant on these two ways of getting things done that collaboration hardly seems necessary. The problem, though, isn't the competencies. It's that we as Mars Associates have been unmotivated, or at least less motivated, to choose collaboration.

As Mars has become increasingly global, our business environment has gotten more and more complex. The problems we face are more often cross-functional and cross-national. Our Associates need to be able to choose collaboration instead of defaulting to the habit of individual action, as satisfying and effective as that has been in the past. I'm sure this conundrum is familiar to you if you work in a large organization, or work with people who do. Mars is a good example, but definitely not the only one.

Whatever team development approach you choose, if it's going to make a real difference, it will have to help team members break their old habits of performance. One of the big problems with changing old habits and taking new ones on board is a phenomenon called "decision fatigue." Operating out of habit allows us not to have to make choices, not to have to decide. Trying to take new habits on board, like new ways of eating, means we suddenly have to choose what to eat, how much to eat, how often to eat how much of which thing and so on. Something that was once so pleasurable becomes a burden of constant consideration and choosing. Apparently our brains have a finite capacity for decision making. I'm old enough to remember when there was one phone company for most in the United States. Ma Bell, as AT&T came to be known. The rates were fixed and regulated. The monthly bill was easy to read and largely predictable, save for those pricey long-distance calls.

Then, AT&T's legal monopoly was challenged in the courts. Ma Bell was broken up into eight smaller, "Baby Bell" regional phone companies, and competition was off and running. Within a few years we had to choose phone services, both local and long distance. MCI, Sprint and others began aggressively competing for our long-distance business. What was once a no-brainer—use AT&T because that's all there is—became a morass of complex plans and deals and decisions. Sure, the breakup of Ma Bell led to a huge growth in the telephone business and incredible innovation. I never could have dreamed of being able to watch that Haka team-building fiasco via a video shot on a phone and sent across the Atlantic for a fraction of what long distance used to cost. And yet, even today when I'm used to choosing my phone service, part of me yearns for the day when I didn't have to make the choice.

Developing new habits can be exhausting. Before long, we want to succumb to what was customary, to what we know, to our habits. The experts suggest that one of the essential elements of successfully creating different habits involves changing the cues in our environment. You do this by taking away the things that make bad choices easy and replacing those things with cues that help you make better choices. Those curly fries? I know the manager of that restaurant. I could try to have them taken off the menu and replaced with more interesting salads. Simpler still, I could simply stay out of that restaurant and hit the healthier joint down the street.

Mars did this for me, unintentionally, about 10 years ago. My manager had introduced me to the absolute delight of a miniature Dove® Ice Cream bar melted into a cup of hot Flavia® coffee. Both of these are Mars products and both were in seemingly unlimited supply in our coffee-break area. Man, that was good. I had put on around 20 pounds since joining Mars two years prior and this combo of chocolate, ice cream and coffee was a major contributor. Then came cost cutting in our North

American business. No more ice cream case right across from the Flavia® machine. They eventually installed vending machines (that were free to us) but those Dove® miniatures were no longer available. You could only get the full-sized Dove® bars with the sticks. They were delicious, mind you. They just didn't fit into a paper coffee cup. I know. I tried. Within a year, I lost those 20 pounds and more. I knew I needed to lose that extra weight. Not having access to an irresistible treat made all the difference. From then on, I chose simple coffee.

To make the choice of collaboration more feasible and more appealing, we have to address both parts of the intentionality equation. First, collaboration has to be easier to choose. To do that, it has to appeal to our appetite for achievement. Then we have to build into the work environment unmistakable cues that will guide our choices as we proceed in our work together, signposts to clearly guide us and keep us on track.

We've already talked about how shared goals don't do the trick. So, how can we cultivate the habit of collaboration? We have to transform collaboration:

FROM	TO
A high-minded principle	Something concrete: real work with clear outcomes
A generalized approach	A specific way of working
Reactive helpfulness	A proactive choice
Something we might choose to do	A way of working we're held accountable for

That's what it takes for collaboration to become something team members can be more intentional about. Make those changes and you get more intentional collaboration.

Intentional Collaboration

Let's talk a bit more about intentional collaboration and what that looks like. Below is a simple working definition of intentional collaboration:

> Collaboration chosen at the outset of a specific, goal-focused and time-bound piece of work. It is maintained throughout the process of the work by ongoing attention to roles and responsibilities as well as the quality of the relationships of those involved.

Let's analyze this definition. To begin with, this isn't a statement about project management. You'll notice there's nothing in the definition about milestones or deadlines. Those things matter and have to be paid attention to, whether you're collaborating or working alone. That's not what this definition is dealing with, however—it's focused exclusively on the collaborative aspect of the work. Let's look at the major parts of the definition:

Chosen at the outset: Intentional collaboration is planned collaboration. Planning involves choosing (not choicefulness). There are lots of ways to get a given thing done and lots of tools you might choose. If you were writing a proposal, Microsoft Word would be a tool you might choose before you began. If you were planting a garden, it's likely you'd take a spade out of your shed or garage before you began. Collaboration is just another tool. It's not always the right one, for sure. But when it is, if it's chosen in advance of beginning the work it gives us the opportunity to think about how we will use it and get the most out of it.

Maintained throughout the process: The late Stephen Covey, who wrote *The Seven Habits of Highly Effective People*, one of the most successful self-help and business books ever written, talked about "sharpening the saw." He recognized that we need to pause, take a break from our toils every now and again to rest and re-energize, to get back our edge. As a part of our saw sharpening, we might think about how we're feeling about ourselves and our task and even why we're doing it. Individuals burn out if they don't heed Covey's advice. Similarly, collaborative work and relationships benefit from this sort of regular maintenance. If we don't regularly take time to check in with our work partners, to revisit and refresh our collaborative arrangements, our collaboration could go south—and fast.

Roles and responsibilities: When we begin our work together, we will each make agreements about what we expect of each other—who is going to do what and by when, for example. As a great but unknown sage once said, "Sh*t happens." What was true when our collaboration began won't necessarily be true a month, a week or even a day later. The agreements we made about how we will work together will have to be adjusted to take in this natural evolution of the world around us.

Quality of relationships: Collaboration depends on relationship. We won't always like our collaborative partners or feel close to them. We don't need to. What is required is that our relationship be effective in relation to the task we have taken on. It makes sense, therefore, at the beginning to think together about who each of us is, how our preferences, our styles, our strengths and our quirks are likely to affect our collaboration. We can then account for these things in our work. As our work progresses, as our relationship is tested and circumstances evolve, we will want to "sharpen the saw" of our relationship. Pausing occasionally to reflect on how we're holding up as a collaborative unit gives us a chance to talk things out and course correct as needed.

For collaboration to be worth choosing it has to begin as a clear and compelling proposition, one that will engage an achievement-driven person. It then has to stay that way for the duration of the work. Intentional collaboration may seem like a lot, with all of its planning and thinking and checking in. OK, but think about it: Why would you undertake any piece of work without these same mindful behaviors? A bit of caution, though, does make sense. So, I'm going to return to a theme I have touched on a couple of times already. I'm going to put this in boldface type and give it its own space on the page to ensure you don't miss it.

Much of the work you have to do does NOT require any kind of collaboration, including intentional collaboration. Collaboration is more expensive and complex than individual working. You should only use this approach if the payoffs and benefits of collaboration are clear.

This admonition notwithstanding, cultivating intentional collaboration will help teams and their members do more of what they say they want to do and give organizations the results they're looking for. In the fast-moving, complicated, global world many of us are working and living in, we really have no choice. Intentional collaboration isn't easy at first, but it is pretty simple. It requires effort but it's not complex. It has three ingredients that will end up being enacted through six of what we call Practices. Let's start with those three essential ingredients. I introduced them at the end of the last chapter. They're called the Three Imperatives.

The Three Imperatives

The Three Imperatives describe three ingredients required for collaborative success. This description arose from the diagnosis I formulated out of the research. To review: collaboration wasn't flourishing. I found that smart and well-intentioned group members wanted to collaborate more and knew they should. They just didn't. So they focused on what was clear to them and most satisfying: their individual work. This work, usually agreed upon with their manager ahead of time, reliably fed their need to achieve and ensured the team's commitments were met. Collaboration did happen but mostly as a reaction to a problem, to a teammate's unplanned need or to a situation that had become urgent. Collaboration in these reactive cases was easy because the needs and benefits were typically clear—just like their individual work. The clarity and urgency of helping out a teammate tapped into their achievement motives. Once the achievement motive was aroused, collaboration proceeded apace. Because it was unplanned and often layered in on top of lots of other individual work, this habit of reactive collaboration was leading to frustration and eventual burnout.

There was a pattern in all of this. Clear and well-considered individual tasks and goals tapped into team members' achievement instincts with good results. Likewise, accidental or unplanned-for collaboration, with its clarity and/or urgency, consistently lit those same fires of achievement. What would it take, I wondered, for more thoughtful, more planned collaboration to tap into this same source of energy and drive? Could team members take advantage of their innate need to achieve in the service of collaborative outcomes? Of course they could.

It would begin, obviously enough, with clarity. Team members would need to be as clear about what needed collaboration as they were about their individual tasks and responsibilities. Collaboration would have to move from a noble idea to real work. It would have to be as concrete as anything in their individual objectives and feel as significant as an urgent request from a team member in need. Just as importantly, team members would require clarity about what the collaboration would mean for them. Collaboration needs a WIIFM—"What's in it for me?" This sense of having something personal at stake would further ignite the achievement drive. All of this clarity would also enable them to hold one another more accountable for their work together.

Clarity is the first of the Three Imperatives. Clarity is foundational. It is what makes the second Imperative, Intentionality, possible. Clarity and Intentionality are almost inextricably linked, but we treat them separately because it allows us to focus on a few critical distinctions between them. The third imperative, Discipline, is essential if these two are going to be sustained over time. Let's go into each of the three in detail.

Clarity

When it comes to tapping into the energy of an achievement-driven person, clarity is essential and lack of clarity is the enemy. Clarity is fundamental to every aspect of successful collaboration. I think of Clarity as the soil that, when it's prepared and tended to, allows for and promotes the nurturing and flourishing of collaboration.

Remember, the Achiever is a goal-setting go-getter who likes to tick things off their list, who thrives on a sense of accomplishment. The achiever wants to have goals set, and then act on and complete them. If you aren't clear about what you want from him or her, they will default to what *is* clear to them and do that.

For instance, you might say to a team member, "Anne, I'm depending on you and Charles to demonstrate real team spirit on Project Candy Cane." Anne will assure you that she's all about "team" — which she totally believes she is — and get busy doing her thing. What would her "thing" be, given the general tone of the instruction you have given, to "demonstrate real team spirit"? Anne's most likely to get busy with whatever you and Anne agreed were her individual responsibilities and which may or may not have anything to do with Charles. Vague admonitions to act in teamy ways are generally interpreted as, "If your teammate needs you, be helpful." Which of course, most of the folks in your company would do anyway.

Clarity as an Imperative demands that we deconstruct generic buzzword-based commands and get specific about what is needed. Tear down that "Together Everyone Achieves More" poster—you know, the one with the rowing team at sunset—and replace it with several blank pieces of flip-chart paper on which you can begin to create clarity about what your collaboration requires. For instance:

- Clarity about the group's shared and ideally inspiring purpose, an uplifting raison d'être for this group to exist
- Clarity about what needs collaboration within the group
- Clarity about what does *not* require collaboration
- Clarity about who will be working with whom, and on what specifically
- Clarity about the processes the team needs to keep itself operating smoothly
- Clarity about the challenges the team faces and how they will face them together and grow together

It's a pretty long list, but it's hardly exhaustive. I guarantee you, though, just this list would be a great start. It would be way more likely to generate focused, productive collaboration than that poster you tore down or that Haka you were thinking about having the team do.

Just remember this: As soon as you put a group together for any purpose, you complicate things. One of the reasons this is true is because—thank goodness—the people on your team can't read each other's minds. You might read that last sentence and say, "Yeah, I get it. Teams need to communicate, communicate, communicate; maybe even *over*-communicate. It's all about effective communication." Yeah, well…no. Why? Here's a hint: What do you mean by "communicate"? "Communications" when used in reference to a group or team is just another buzzword. Managers come to me all the time, claiming that if their teams would just communicate better, things would improve. Unfortunately, it's a diagnosis that is so vague as to be useless. Worse than useless, in fact. Imagine that you declare that from now on, everyone on your team will over-communicate, with you and with each other. Different people hearing the term "over-communicate" will reach different conclusions about what it means and therefore what needs to be done about it. You might suddenly see more emails and more meetings in an attempt to over-communicate. Ouch. Or, if you're on a team with a talkative boss, she might start talking even more, thinking that this will fix the communications problem. Extra-double ouch. Communications and Clarity are *not* the same thing. Yes, communications will be a part of creating Clarity, and you will need to communicate clearly about important things, like your team's shared work. But if you want truly value-adding collaboration, it's Clarity you need.

Clarity is simple and it's tricky:

Clarity has three important aspects. It's something each team member needs; it's a shared state of mind within a group; it's an ongoing process.

Clarity is organic. Things change. What was useful yesterday may not be useful today. Tactics, plans, roles, priorities, policies all change. What was clear on Monday may be clouded by Friday.

Clarity demands persistence and engagement and yes, communication. Communication as in multidirectional flows of relevant information through conversation (real-time or virtual) and alert, active listening.

Clarity requires testing and questioning assumptions. It requires paying attention, not just plowing ahead. It may even mean slowing down for a time in order to go faster later.

Despite my passion for and knowledge of the topic of collaboration, I fall into the same traps as others who work in large companies where there's a lot to do. For example, I'm a member of a project team that has been working primarily on helping Associates to develop new ways of thinking about holding meetings. This includes using technology for conducting meetings remotely. One of our goals was to reduce corporate travel, thereby improving Associates' quality of life while reducing how much the company spends on airfare and hotels. Our project team is dispersed across two continents and three or four countries. We've been trying to role model remote collaboration by conducting our work using the sorts of collaborative technologies that we recommend. These include Skype for Business™ as well as web-based file sharing and a corporate social media app. I've been a part of this project for two and a half years. Progress has been slow. The first half of this last year has been not only slow but fraught with complications. That all finally began to change when our project leader convinced our project sponsors that the team needed to take time out to sort out our collaborative reasons for being. We all knew what the project was supposed to achieve. We had never, though, taken the time to create clarity for ourselves about how our work together would best serve the project's goals. So, we set up a series of working sessions to do just that. The first one or two we conducted remotely. The third was held face-to-face. What a difference that Clarity made. It was as if a veil had been lifted from our eyes. Suddenly, progress accelerated and results began to come. All it took was all the stakeholders involved appreciating the need for and value of collaborative Clarity.

Clarity underpins truly high-performing collaboration. It

provides your achievement-driven folks with specific targets, things they can act on together and check off their lists so they can feel they're being productive and getting real stuff done. We'll talk more about how to achieve Clarity when we discuss the Practices of "Inspire Purpose" and "Crystallize Intent."

Intentionality

We have talked about intentional collaboration a few times so I'll keep this brief. No over-communication needed here. The Intentionality Imperative represents the seed that gets planted in the rich soil of Clarity and that will one day bear the fruits of your collaboration. For that reason it deserves a few more (well-chosen, I hope) words.

The soil and the seed you plant eventually become intensely interconnected. This is true for Clarity and Intentionality. In some ways, Intentionality is an extension of Clarity with a focus on collaborative agreements and relationships. Our high-achiever types will need clarity about:

• Who, specifically, they need to be working with
• What benefits will be created by the collaboration they signed up for
• What specific agreements among the collaborating parties are needed in order to achieve the expected outcomes
• What the success of the collaboration will look like.

Intentional collaboration flourishes as the outcome of two sets of actions within a group: **contracting for collaboration** and **relationship building**.

When it comes to contracting in typical work-groups (those with a clear leader and well-defined membership) it happens in two dimensions. It begins with contracting vertically—that is, top-down and bottom-up between leaders and team members. Contracting next takes place horizontally, or side-to-side among team members. Contracting in both dimensions involves clarifying specific behavioral expectations for the work that will be shared and then agreeing on how the parties involved will manage their expectations of one another. The idea is to make these collaborative expectations so clear that everyone involved feels their achievement motive kick in.

Contracting between the leader and the team begins with the leader, with input from the team, signing up for a short list of behavioral expectations. The team suggests what they need from their leader in order for them to thrive in a group where collaboration is now a performance expectation and not just a buzzword. A team might ask that the manager, "Seek input from us on budget and resource allocation decisions relative to our projects."

Notice that the request begins with a verb that is followed by words and phrases that clarify the expectation. Action words and specificity are essential if the contracts are going to tap into the achievement motive that thrives on doing and specific outcomes. "Let us help with budgeting," isn't as useful as, "Seek input from us on budget and resource allocation decisions relative to our projects."

Getting to a list of behaviors like this involves conversation and negotiation. In the end, a short behavioral contract is better; five behaviors is my limit.

The leader next develops a similar list of what they expect from the team, overall, in order to support the team's purpose and the work they have agreed to share. A similar process of conversation and negotiation ensues until a final behavioral contract for the team is agreed to. The contracting process is much the same in less structured groups or teams, communities of practice that don't have formal leadership. In these cases the critical contracts will happen only among members. There's more about this contracting process in Chapter 10 on Intentionality and in Appendix C.

These contracts create the clarity and accountability that are the foundation for intentional collaboration. They clarify how team members must act with each other to deliver specific, purpose- and task-focused outcomes. Here's exactly what I need from you and what you need from me to deliver just this piece of work. Now that the collaborative agreements are clear, it's time to address the relationships that are at the core of these commitments. Tasks and behaviors, with a bit of effort, can be readily described. The influence of personalities, of widely variable human traits on how the work will get done, is another story. It's impossible to predict precisely how "the way I am" and "the way you are" will interact as we collaborate on a given task. Precision, however, isn't necessary. Close is good enough, and the right kind of relationship building can have tremendous payoffs if it's done right.

This is different from what most teams are used to. Most traditional team building is aimed at enhancing relationships and trust. It's built around the flawed assumption that "familiarity breeds collaboration." Just because I know the colors or letters that represent your personality, or because I've done the Haka with you, doesn't mean we'll work better together on our big project. It can feel nice, give everyone that teamy buzz we've talked about. Other than that, these exercises are usually a waste of time and money. Remember Maslow's Needs Hierarchy from Chapter 1? When you force people up the hierarchy, even gently and with good intent, they will always come sliding back down to focus on the more fundamental stuff that drives them. The key is to connect the work that matters to high achievers directly to the relationships that will end up getting them the results they crave.

We do this by linking specific shared tasks that were agreed to during contracting to information about how each of you tends to operate, to your styles and preferences. Then team members can talk about where sticking points might arise in their working relationships. They can call out similarities in their styles that could support their collaboration. As grounded as this approach is in tasks and outcomes, it still leads to enhanced trust. I've already suggested that I have a problem with what many call "trust building"; recall my discussion of the venerable Johari window? A bit later, in Chapter 10, I focus on how to do what the Intentionality Imperative requires, including how to work on enhancing trust in even more effective ways.

So far we have talked about the soil—Clarity—and the seeds of Intentionality. They're a great start, but only a start. The final Imperative, the third critical aspect for getting collaboration to flourish, is Discipline.

Discipline

If Clarity is the soil and Intentionality the seed, Discipline is all about the gardening. It's about the routines and good habits you put in place so that your collaboration patch won't just survive but flourish. All the Clarity and Intentionality in the world won't amount to a heap of discarded motivational posters if the group doesn't have the discipline to fulfill its shared intent and collaborative agreements.

Just as with Intentionality, I'm not entirely comfortable with the word "discipline." It has overtones of corporal punishment and Catholic school nuns with wooden rulers. I considered "rigor," but that word is too easily followed by "mortis." I wasn't happy with synonyms like meticulousness, thoroughness or scrupulousness, based solely on how many syllables they have. Diligence was in the running for a while, but diligence wasn't something that the team members I had worked with suffered a lack of. So, Discipline it is. If you have a better word, feel free to substitute it. It's the concept that matters.

What I call Discipline has been written about extensively by other authors who've published books about teamwork and collaboration. "Team process" is another term for it. Our take on it, though, is a little different. Discipline for discipline's sake, while tiresome, can be useful. Discipline becomes powerful when it's thoughtfully aligned with Clarity and Intentionality. When a team knows what requires collaboration and what doesn't, when they have agreed on what their collaboration needs to consist of, they can create disciplines to support and drive these things.

Even with all that, Discipline is probably the least sexy aspect of our collaboration framework. It can be the toughest for individuals with a strong action orientation. It just sounds dull and routine. However, just as routine watering, pruning and weeding are essential for your growing plants to survive and thrive, discipline is indispensable for powerful, sustained collaboration.

We break Discipline into two parts: process and learning. Process involves establishing a few essential team routines and developing—what else?—good team habits. Teams and groups benefit from setting up a cadence of performance, establishing a few norms and ways-of-working for those things that they must do repeatedly and routinely (attending meetings, making decisions, communicating, etc.). These operating habits diminish the likelihood of decision fatigue. They free up mental space and creative energy so that the team can tackle the non-routine, non-standard challenges that driven achievers love and the business depends on. As I've said, what makes this approach different is that we create our routines to align with our clear sense of purpose and our collaborative agreements. In this way, living them is much easier; it feels more natural and less like, well, a discipline.

For example, I'll talk later about a global Supply Chain team in one of our businesses who did terrific work on creating an inspiring purpose and clarifying the work that required them to collaborate. What they didn't do, at least initially, was to alter their approach to meetings. That is, they assumed that their existing meeting discipline—meeting three times a year face-to-face, with video meetings and teleconferences in between—

would suffice in their newly collaborative environment. They even stuck with the same basic agendas focused on business reviews and addressing the hot topics of the day. They found out, though, that this cut-and-paste approach doesn't work. Their meetings were flat and unengaging. People were canceling out and showing a general lack of commitment to their time together. A year after their work on their purpose and shared work, they revisited their discipline of team meetings to bring them into alignment with the commitments they made using our framework. This one adjustment made a vast difference.

Finally, great teams, like accomplished gardeners, never stop learning. They don't just pull up weeds and move on having solved the problem of the moment. They become keen observers of their own processes; they think regularly about what's working and what's not and what they can do about it. They also seek new, improved ways of doing things. This is another way that great teams can tap into the energy of the achievement-driven team members. I'll cover the how-to of Discipline when I talk about the Practices, "Activate Ways-of-Working" and "Sustain & Renew."

In the next chapter I present what the Framework is, and as importantly, what it is NOT, and why. I'll discuss each of the six elements of the Framework—the "Practices"—in the same way. I'll explain what each is intended to accomplish and what cherished ideas about teamwork we have either not included or interpreted differently from what's typical.

Summary
- The Three Imperatives describe three ingredients required for collaborative success.
- Understanding the Imperatives, you can begin to ask basic questions, such as:
  - How do the Imperatives play out in my organization?
  - What will they look like for me and my work-group?

- ◦ What do I do next?
- Clarity is the first imperative. It's an organic, evolving state that requires ongoing attention and communication. You need to keep testing it, refining it and refreshing it.
- Clarity enables and is intertwined with the next Imperative, Intentionality. Intentionality, the key to high-performance collaboration, relies on clear contracting among team members for the work they will share and the ways they will share it.
- Discipline, the third Imperative, supports Intentionality. It's based on establishing a team operating rhythm through creating routines and standardized ways-of-working that allow a team's collaboration to flourish.

Chapter 7

The Practices of High Performance Collaboration

It's time to set out the Framework that I've talked so much about. What makes it distinctive is its application of motives theory to topics like team purpose, team priorities, team processes and even trust. My intention is for you to see into our process and thinking so that you can take the same insights and apply them in ways that will work for your organization. The effort we put into making our Framework resonate with our culture has paid massive dividends. I want you to be able to do the same thing.

There are a couple of things to keep in mind as you begin this chapter. Given its intent to provide an overview of the Mars Framework for High Performance Collaboration, this chapter is more technical and therefore comparatively drier than previous chapters. There are fewer stories and more explanations. Then, if you're familiar with other team effectiveness approaches and tools, you may find yourself thinking as you read this chapter, "Yeah, yeah, I know that." You may be tempted to skip ahead. If you hear that voice in your head, stop and read even more carefully. At Mars we chose to move past the orthodoxy of traditional team building. Orthodoxy literally means "right opinions." It's the generally accepted knowledge applied without question or challenge because it's what we're used to. It's the conventional wisdom. If you think getting your team to perform the Haka is going to get better results, go for it. Try a ropes course, too. Put up some inspirational posters while you're at it. Our Framework moves away from such orthodoxy and instead moves towards ortho*praxy* or "right practices." Our focus is on what groups need to do to get stronger and become more effective. There are some real gems in our approach, ideas and tools that are different in sometimes subtle but always important ways. No matter how much you know about team effectiveness, this will be worth it.

From Imperatives to Practices

The Three Imperatives are valid for teams in all kinds of organizations. They reveal a generally true set of conditions that affect collaboration in large enterprises. What you choose to do with them, though, should come from your company and teams, what they need, and who they are. That's what we did with stunning results. How we got from our Three Imperatives to the Framework that Mars teams use today is a useful tale about how one goes from insights to culturally attuned application. In this chapter I'll share our thinking and process so that you can adapt it to your organization. Even if, in the end, you find that our Practices of High Performance Collaboration work for you "as is," this chapter is worth it. It includes important information about how the various aspects of the Framework work together to create even more impact.

How did we get from Three Imperatives to Six Practices? Recall that the Imperatives describe, in positive language, the three major problems we were seeing in teams at Mars. Those problems being:

- There was a notable lack of intentional collaboration (Intentionality), which was correlated with…
- A broad lack of clarity about what required collaboration (Clarity), aggravated by the fact that…
- Teams generally had no active or effective disciplines to support how they worked together (Discipline).

Just describing conditions, no matter how positive or action-oriented the terms, isn't enough. The Imperatives are and were a useful assessment of what Mars teams needed. We use them today as the basis for one of our team diagnostic approaches; I'll talk more about this in Chapter 13. Teams certainly care about what's not working. They care a lot more about what they need to do to get better. The Practices deliver on that score.

From "What's Wrong" to "What to Do"

To solve the problem of the Imperatives being purely descriptive, and to connect them more to the achievement motive, you could think of them as calls for action.

Clarity—Get clear about collaboration!

Intentionality—Be intentional in your collaboration!

Discipline—Develop and maintain the discipline that collaboration requires!

Even stated this way, the Imperatives are ambiguous calls to action. You could choose to respond to them in a variety of ways. For instance, if the call is to "Get clear about collaboration," that could include any number of things. It could point to your collaborative goals or to general areas that require collaboration. Likewise, the call to develop Discipline could be directed towards a number of things. You could choose to be more disciplined about how you apply project management practices. You might choose to focus your discipline on how team members use communications tools. These are all worthy topics. Some of them might even make sense for the teams in your organization.

We were aiming to translate our theoretical understanding of the Imperatives into a simple, but not simplistic, approach. It would have to:

- Be comprehensive enough to cover a range of possible actions that would help teams, but not so broad that it felt burdensome or complex
- Have innate appeal to our pragmatic, action-oriented

Associates

- Account for a streak of independence and self-sufficiency that is common in our population and in many achievement-driven people
- Be directionally unambiguous without being overly prescriptive.

Our final Framework would be more like Google Maps than a GPS. That is, it would suggest to users various routes they could take to team effectiveness, even indicate commonly used ones. It wouldn't select a single, optimal route for all groups, though. It would allow teams the freedom to choose what was right for them. If our approach didn't meet these criteria, it wasn't likely to take in Mars culture.

Mars teams would do best with a short list of things they could act on that would get them out of the collaborative funk they were in. Less would be more, so the shorter the short list, the better. I'd come across a lot of recommendations during my research for what teams could do to become higher performing. For instance, teams could work on:

- Vision
- Mission
- Purpose
- Trust building
- Meeting practices
- Communications
- Norms.

I sought to include enough elements to cover all Three Imperatives, without overwhelming busy Mars Associates. I thought about Will Schutz and his elegantly simple three basic concerns: Inclusion, Control, and Openness. Like Tuckman's Four Stages and our own Three Imperatives, however, they were descriptive. There's an old saying that weighing the pig doesn't fatten it. Neither does describing it. What we needed would be more prescriptive: actions, behaviors, tasks, or what we came to call Practices.

I went back to the research data. I had been told over and over, "I want to collaborate but I don't know on what or with whom." Behind this desire there was an almost uncontrollable urge to action. This itch to act was most typically satisfied by getting to work on what was clear. More often than not, what was clear for the Associates in the study was individual projects and goals. There is another old saying: What gets measured gets done. (I assume pigs would be included in this advice, but I digress.) If this is true, it's true because to measure something it has to be clear and definable. You could just as well say that "What is clear gets done." This is what the Clarity Imperative is all about. This led me to hypothesize that our Framework for collaboration would have to include:

What: Being explicit and crystal clear about what work needed collaboration

Who: Creating the same kind of clarity about who needed to collaborate with whom and on which specific pieces of work

Why: Developing super-clarity about why collaboration was important, as important as any individual work team members had to do.

Mars so values simplicity that I hoped that these three elements alone would do the trick. It was clear almost immediately that they wouldn't suffice. They were exclusively about Clarity. What about Intentionality? Discipline? Greater collaborative Clarity would kindle more Intentionality, yes. Intentionality, though, needed more to truly catch fire. It would require its own directive(s) to feel real and pragmatic and therefore attractive to achievement-driven individual contributors. Discipline was another story. Associates felt about Discipline much as I feel about my once-every-five-years colonoscopy. It's necessary, even life-saving. I'll be damned, though, if I'm going to get excited about it. Discipline would require its own simple directives or Practices presented in ways that made them palatable.

In the end, we landed on six Practices. They're the heart of the team when it comes to its collaborative ambitions. In the rest of this chapter, I'll provide an overview of the six Practices of High Performance Collaboration, or as we refer to it, HPC. Then, in Chapters 8 through 14, I'll explain each Practice in detail.

Below is a summary of our six Practices. It's organized based on the Imperative that each Practice most closely supports. Clarity appears twice in order to accommodate "Clarify Context," which as I'll explain is known as the "Special Practice."

CLARITY

Inspire Purpose—Addresses clarifying and defining a team's collaborative "Why," its purpose and reason for being. Teams use their purpose in conjunction with the work they've agreed needs collaboration (the next Practice) to guide their efforts and commitments.

Crystallize Intent—Defines the "What," the specific work in a group that is shared as well as the work that is not shared. Teams use their purpose to guide their choices about which work will benefit from collaboration. Together, Inspire Purpose and Crystallize Intent shape everything else teams do in the Framework: their collaborative contracts with each other, their processes—like meetings and decision making and how they go about learning together.

INTENTIONALITY

Cultivate Collaboration—Builds on the work done in the first two Practices. The team's inspiring purpose has implications for how the team will operate, generally. So, the leader and team members come together to agree to the behaviors that will be needed to bring their purpose to life. The output of the previous Practice, Crystallize Intent, is a set of projects and initiatives that require collaboration. Each task will also have been assigned to the team members who will work on it together. In this Practice, team members make task-specific interpersonal commitments for how they will collaborate and for which they will be held accountable. As a part of this, team members share information about themselves, their style and preferences that could be relevant to the collaborative commitments they've made. Based on this, they discuss and agree on how they'll account for these facets of themselves in relationship to their shared work and to each other.

DISCIPLINE

Activate Ways-of-Working—Defining and following a limited set of team processes that are designed to clearly align to the teams' inspiring purpose and to the work that they agreed to share in Crystallize Intent. Where Cultivate Collaboration addresses behavioral commitments between and among team members and the team leader, this Practice focuses on the team as a single operational unit that knows what it's all about.

Sustain & Renew—Practicing ongoing reflection and learning as a group. Intentional collaboration requires that teams be just as intentional about understanding their effectiveness as they are about contracting for specific pieces of work. Teams put in place a discipline of regular inquiry into how their collaboration is functioning. From this inquiry and reflection, they create and maintain an ever-evolving team development plan intended to ensure that they continually enhance collaborative effectiveness.

CLARITY

Clarify Context—This is the "Special Practice," used only during times of significant transition. A team's purpose, its list of collaborative work and the contractual agreements of Cultivate Collaboration are referred to regularly. Clarify Context is only triggered when there is a change in the strategic context that a group is operating in. Changes in corporate strategy, in organizational structure and in leadership are the most common reasons to employ this Practice.

Each of the six Practices is related in some way to all three Imperatives. For each, however, one Imperative is primary. Hence, the organization of the list, above. I'll talk more about the less obvious links in the Practice-specific chapters that follow. For now, we'll focus on a high-level understanding of the six Practices.

The Focus on Action

Why did we choose to call them Practices? Why not "Stages," "Directives," or "Actions"? As I developed the earliest versions of the Framework in 2011, I chose to stay away from using team stages or phases. It was an important, and to some a counterintuitive, choice. It therefore required a lot of explanation in the early days as I shared the Framework with peers and colleagues. Let's tackle the "Practices-not-stages" matter head-on, right now.

Team development stages are orthodoxy when working with business teams—BIG orthodoxy. I used to rely on Tuckman's Four Stages, myself. As you know, I no longer do.

I was in Ohio working with the leadership team of one of our smaller businesses. This was before the creation of our Framework so we were using a version of Tuckman's Four Stages as the basis for diagnosis and discussion. Prior to this workshop, as I generally did, I conducted interviews with each of the team members and administered the previously described survey. We were in yet another dingy-but-clean hotel conference room. At least this one had a window. We were seated in the common U-shaped configuration so everyone could see everyone else. I passed out a summary that covered both the interviews and the survey. I asked my clients to spend 15 minutes reviewing the data individually. I then sent them out in two groups to discuss the data. Each group was to come back with one flip-chart page highlighting their findings. While they worked I created a space for us to discuss their findings, away from the wobbly, burgundy-cloth-covered banquet tables. The seven of them returned in their two clusters and made their way to my makeshift conversation pit. Eight chairs, again in a rough U-shape, facing a section of wall. No tables to separate us or to shield us from one another. It's what good teams do, right? I taped the sheets of paper containing their findings to the wall facing our U. We began talking about what was working, what wasn't, and what was possible. One of the specific questions I asked them to address was, "At what stage in the Four Stages do you think your team is?" "One." "Two." "Two bordering on three," the groups exchanging views back and forth. Then one of them said, "Why is it that when we do team workshops like this we're always either in Stage Two, or close to it? I mean, we may be. But why?" The question caught me up short. He was right. I had noticed the same thing with other teams. They were consistently in Stages One or Two. I had felt it but had never voiced it. I was captive to the orthodoxy. The team in Ohio and I stayed with this question. One of the guys—they were all guys—mentioned that repeatedly being in the first half of the Four Stages didn't feel very good. "It's like we never make progress. It's one of the reasons I hate workshops like this." I understood that. What a downer. What was going on here?

Tuckman's Four Stages model is probably the best known, but by no means the only one of the "phasic" approaches to team diagnosis.

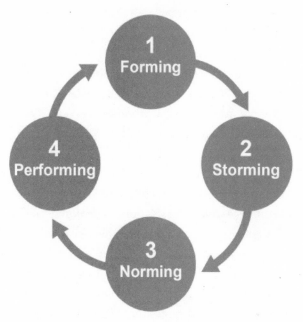

I started working with teams almost 30 years ago. Back in the day, the teams I was working with, like the one at the cambric factory in North Carolina, typically sat on the same floor, in the same building, in the same city, in the same country. I found Tuckman's model useful for groups like these. It helped me describe and make some sense of what I was seeing. It also gave teams a way to understand and talk about themselves.

As time has passed, the nature of what a business team is and how teams are constructed has changed massively. So have the enterprises that they're part of. I continued using a version of the Four Stages model until about five years ago. It formed the basis of my practice when I began focusing on teams at Mars. By the time I ended up with the leadership team in Ohio, I was already having serious doubts about it. It wasn't describing in a helpful way what I was seeing and working with.

Those of us who are interested in and make our living from working with teams owe a lot to Bruce Tuckman and his work on team development. It was a breakthrough in his day and made the work I do today, including this book, possible. It's time to get real about Tuckman's work, though; his Four Stages (eventually five and for some even six) aren't based on research into work teams as I currently experience them and understand them. Tuckman's model was based on his review of 50 academic articles, most of them psychoanalytical studies of therapy groups.

Got that? The Four Stages model is based on a meta-analysis of scholarly articles. It's not based on in-person work with living, breathing teams. What's more, a majority of the articles were about therapy groups, not teams working within complex businesses. Therapy groups do a lot of good; I have nothing against them. Heck, I've even been part of one or two. (They were less uncomfortable than a colonoscopy, but not by much.) For all the good they do, though, therapy groups don't have a lot in common with present-day business teams. They don't have to deliver business objectives. They don't have strategies or work plans or have to respond in a competitive marketplace. As far as I know, it's pretty hard to get fired from a therapy group, though I'm told it can happen. Finally, I feel certain that the members of the therapy groups that Tuckman studied were largely operating in physical proximity to each other. Odds are they were all in the same city, in the same building in the same room at the same time. Tuckman's research was based on an entirely different reality from the one most of us face when working with teams in large organizations. It's no wonder the Four Stages model wasn't working for me.

There's one other challenge in using the Four Stages model. The theory suggests that when team membership changes, the team is returned to Stage One of the model, Forming. That assertion made sense to me 10 or 15 years ago, but...

> by concentrating on stages, such theories imply a mechanical predictability that is out of keeping with the dynamics of change, the extent of the flux over time and the degree of individual variability that seems to be the case.[1]

I can't argue that teams tend to move backwards in their development when a change occurs. When a new leader or new members come on board the team itself changes. The problem is that this sort of change happens every three or four months to teams at Mars. I'll bet the same is true where you work. When it comes to teams, as with so much else in our lives, things aren't as stable or predictable as they were in the 1950s when Tuckman was doing his work.

Given the world I was working in, following the logic of the Four Stages began to seem futile, even damaging. How could I responsibly suggest that a team go back and repeat everything they had done three months earlier before Bill, their new manager, joined? Would I ask the same when two months later Claus, a new team member, joined? Then one more time when three months after that, David left to pursue "other professional opportunities"? Since joining Mars, I've worked with hundreds of teams that have faced the kinds of changes I just described. According to the stages orthodoxy, these teams would all be at either Stage One or Stage Two *all of the time*. While this may be true according to the theory, knowing that they're Forming or Norming isn't useful for them. In fact, it was frustrating and discouraging, as the discussion in Ohio made clear. It felt as if they were going nowhere except maybe backwards. I came to believe that teams have only an academic interest in what stage they are in. They prefer to know what they can *do* regardless of their stage of development. They wanted to move ahead, feel productive and grow.

As I said, I owe Bruce Tuckman a deep debt of gratitude. I don't completely dismiss his model, or others that suggest a linear, stage-wise development process. These models make sense and can still be valuable in some circumstances. We have to at least question their applicability in the current workplace. What matters to work-groups and teams is finding practical enhancements to their levels of collaboration in ways that feel valuable. They want to understand and act so that they can grow their effectiveness consistently, regardless of how new or mature they may be as a team.

The word "Practice," while it's not about stages, suggests more than mere actions or team to-dos. I'm a yoga student and instructor. I've been practicing yoga for about 15 years. I keep on practicing and I keep on learning. Yoga has become a part of my daily life. If it hadn't I wouldn't be benefiting from it the way I do. Teams, if they honestly commit to enhancing and sustaining their collaboration, would do well to think of the work they do on their team as a set of ongoing, ever-useful and growth-promoting practices. That's how and why I landed on the word and why my colleagues agreed to stick with it. We developed the HPC Framework in late 2011 and early 2012. Since then I've learned of one or two other team approaches that have adopted the word. You can understand why.

Our Practices are calls to action. The name of each Practice begins with an action word, a verb. When our action-addicted Associates first look at the Framework, they immediately get the message that it is about doing. "Inspire Purpose!" "Crystallize Intent!" and so on. That was the intent, and it has worked.

Are our Practices the "right" Practices? For Mars Associates they are. I can tell you with certainty that these Practices have made a significant and lasting difference to hundreds of Mars groups and teams, and thousands of our Associates. What's more, I have spoken to a number of colleagues working outside Mars, some in large companies and others who work with not-for-profits and community groups. Those who have either adopted or adapted our Framework have told me that the Practices are making a difference for the groups they work with, too.

Dynamic Relationships among the Practices

Let's talk about how the Framework and its Practices come together as a whole. Here is the graphic we use to illustrate our Framework.

In a moment I'll discuss the thinking behind the graphic—it tells a story and it has a story. Before I do that, I want to give you a more thorough summary of the Practices. For now, we'll focus on understanding enough about each Practice so that you can best appreciate how the Framework and its parts work together.

INSPIRE PURPOSE

Related Imperative: Clarity
What it addresses: Clarifying the meaning, importance and value of the collaborative work of the group.
Core question: Why?
Questions that drive the Practice:

- Why do we exist as a collaborative group?
- How might we create unique value through our collaboration?

Why it works: Study after study has shown that people are drawn to meaningful work that delivers more than just a paycheck. This is especially true for those entering the workforce now, in the mid-to-late 2010s. Lots of companies have compelling visions, missions, or purpose statements. The real work, though, happens at the level of the individual and the team. So, Inspire Purpose aims to create a clarity of meaning relative to a group's collaborative work. It's not just achievement-driven individuals who will find this Practice compelling, but it may be more important for them than others.

At the same time, of all the Practices, this is perhaps the most challenging for pragmatically minded, achievement-driven people. "Why are we talking about his fluffy stuff when we have real work to do?" I hear this kind of thing about half the time I work with teams on their purpose. After guiding teams through the deep, often moving conversations required when developing a purpose statement, they invariably report that it was among the most important and useful conversation they have ever had at work. I'll share a few examples of purpose statements Mars teams developed in the next chapter.

CRYSTALLIZE INTENT

Related Imperative: Clarity

What it addresses: Creating and maintaining clarity about the specific tasks and initiatives that require collaboration among team members, and those which don't require it.

Core question: What?

Questions that drive the Practice:

- What is the work that must be shared—and what work will not be shared?
- Who will be working with whom, and on what specifically?

Why it works: Through the research, team members told me over and over that they'd love to collaborate more. They just weren't clear about what they should be collaborating on, or with whom. This Practice tackles that problem head on.

This Practice has been a game changer at Mars and it will be for your teams, too. No matter how good your organization may be at developing strategies and deploying business plans, I'd wager that Crystallize Intent will be new for you. When was the last time you and your team stopped and asked yourselves, "Of all the work we have to do, which work will benefit from collaboration and which won't?" And then, "Of all the work that *will* benefit from collaboration, what's the right level of collaboration—how many of us ought to be involved?" If you have had these conversations, congratulations. You're in a productive minority. They're simple questions that don't get asked often enough. Without this kind of Clarity, collaboration is going to be less intentional. With it, the achievement drive can be awakened and then directed towards the right collaboration at the right level.

CULTIVATE COLLABORATION

Related Imperative: Intentionality

What it addresses: Creating clear accountability for collaborative work. It includes contracting for specific collaborative tasks among team members and contracting the expectations for collaborative behaviors between the leader and each team member. Also, this Practice addresses trust among team members focused on the tasks that require collaboration.

Core Question: Who?

Questions that drive the Practice:

- Who are you, who am I, and how will this factor into our relationship and collaboration?
- What commitments will we make to each other about the work we'll share?
- What commitments will we make to our leader about how we will collaborate?
- What do we need from the team leader to support our collaboration?
- How will we build strong relationships in service of our shared work and the team?

Why it works: This Practice builds directly on the two Clarity-based Practices just discussed: Inspire Purpose and Crystallize Intent. Once everyone is clear about the importance and value of their collaboration, once they've agreed what work requires collaboration, the flames of achievement are ignited. When team members see their names against specific tasks, they respond with action. When they see their names paired not just with actions but also with the name of a teammate, they'll follow their impulse to act and channel it towards joint accomplishment.

It's essential that, as a part of this Practice, group leaders clarify how they'll hold team members accountable for both the work *and* their collaborative behaviors. Paradoxically the best way to implement this accountability is via existing individual performance management systems. Team members agree with their leader to include in their annual performance plans at least some of their collaborative commitments. Come review time, these commitments are subject to review just as any individual task would be. With this Clarity and heightened accountability, everyone can buckle down and figure out what their collaboration needs to look like and make solid commitments to each other.

ACTIVATE WAYS-OF-WORKING

Related Imperative: Discipline

What it addresses: Creating and maintaining a few simple team processes and norms for how the team as a whole will operate in line with its purpose and collaborative commitments. This Practice and the previous one, Cultivate Collaboration, both deal with ways of working. Cultivate Collaboration focuses on collaborative relationships and behaviors between specific subsets of team members. Activate Ways-of-Working, by contrast, is about team-level discipline and agreements around things like meetings, decision making and communications that the entire team commits to.

Core question: How?

Questions that drive the Practice:

- How will we operate our group most efficiently and effectively to deliver on our collaborative promises?
- What simple processes and routines will we follow to function most efficiently as a team?
- What are the ways-of-working, aligned with our purpose and shared work, that we must put in place if we're to establish a reliable cadence and strong collaborative habits?

Why it works: All team models worth their salt include something about team processes. What's different in this Framework? Clear links to a team's purpose and to their specific collaborative agreements. These links make this version of team discipline more likely to take. Teams aren't being asked to adopt random "best practices." Instead, they put in place a few bespoke routines around things like meetings and team communications that are tailored to *their* purpose and the work they have all agreed requires collaboration. For instance, if a team has declared in its purpose that they will act as "architects of the future" of their business, they'll drop any tactical topics from their meeting agendas. Instead, they'll only make time for issues that are likely to be part of shaping the longer-term future.

SUSTAIN & RENEW

Related Imperative: Discipline
What it addresses: Establishes a discipline of ongoing reflection and learning about how the team is or is not functioning. Creates and maintains a team development and growth plan.
Core question: What now and what next?
Questions that drive the Practice:

- What is going on within our team now and what do we need to do next to take our collaboration to the next level?
- How will we keep learning and growing?
- How are we doing now and what else could we do to get even better?

Why it works: This Practice is about continuous learning. Like the previous Practice, some version of this Practice can be found in other team effectiveness and organization effectiveness approaches. In fact, this is one place where I agree with what has become orthodoxy in the field of organization and team development. High performance and excellence require ongoing reflection and learning. Sustain & Renew expresses the nature and spirit of "Practices," more generally.

CLARIFY CONTEXT

Related Imperative: Clarity

What it addresses: Clarifies how a team fits into the larger organization and the dynamics that drive it. Only activated during periods of change or transition that affect the environment in which a team is working. Similar to Sustain & Renew but focused outwards instead of on the team.

Core question: What's the broader context we must pay attention to?

Questions that drive the Practice:

- What has changed in our environment and circumstances that we need to respond to?
- How should we respond and how will it affect our collaboration?
- How do we need to change and adapt to what's going on around us?

Why it works: Clarify Context ensures that teams keep it 100% real. It is the most existential of all the Practices, even more than Inspire Purpose. A business team's existence depends on the organization's needs. This Practice ensures that a team stays connected to the external realities that created it and make it relevant. It isn't for every day or every occasion. Every so often, things change, sometimes in a big way. Once a year or every 18 months a team can and should assess the conditions and circumstances they're working in. This enables them to make smart, adaptive choices that serve their collective intent and the needs of the organization that created them.

Why the Framework Looks the Way It Does

There you have the Framework and its Practices. Each Practice has a logic that connects it back to the Three Imperatives. The overall Framework has a logic, too. It's reflected in the graphic we created. The HPC Wheel suggests how the six Practices work together. You could take these same basic elements and depict them in other ways. We did. My colleagues and I played with the six Practices like puzzle pieces until they came together in a way that worked for us. Your culture and company are unique. Your version of this Framework should reflect that. Chapter 15 provides several ways to help you think about how to either adopt it or adapt it to suit your organization.

We placed the Practices within the circle in a particular order. Through applying the Framework with teams, we found the optimal sequence for a team working through the Practices for the first time in a relatively stable environment. This is how they're arranged in our graphic. Earlier I said we didn't want our Framework to be overly prescriptive. That's true. However, for first-time users this sequence makes best use of the relationships among the Practices and the ways in which they build on one another.

The process of working through the Practices for a first-time team that is clear about its context, its organizational reason-for-being, begins with Inspire Purpose. It then proceeds in a clockwise direction, ending up in the center. It's the relationships among the Practices that make this sequence effective. Here's how that works.

- Inspire Purpose addresses a team's collaborative "Why?" A team's "Why" strongly influences its "What."
- The "What" is the focus of Crystallize Intent, which deals with the collaborative tasks and projects within a group. The work done in Crystallize Intent significantly shapes a group's approach to the next Practice to the right, Cultivate Collaboration.
- Cultivate Collaboration deals with "Who" and with working relationships based on having completed the work of Crystallize Intent. Once this Practice has been established, teams move on to the "How" of Activate Ways-of-Working.
- Activate Ways-of-Working focuses on establishing team processes aligned to the team's purpose and shared work. With this done, teams move into the center of the circle, Sustain & Renew.
- Sustain & Renew, with its "emphasis" on learning, engages teams in planning for how they will sustain their team effectiveness efforts going forward.

Remember, what I just described is for teams just starting to use the Framework. For these teams, Inspire Purpose is foundational and will influence many of the choices they make from that point on.

Of course, there are lots of times when working outside of this sequence makes sense, especially for experienced users. For each of the Practices, there are times when it may be the best place to start. We'll look at reasons for choosing different starting points in the later chapters that go more deeply into each Practice. There is one exception to the "purpose-first" sequencing that I'll discuss now, though. It involves the outermost element of the Framework: Clarify Context.

Clarify Context is about the big picture, about fundamental and existential issues for teams. Why wouldn't you always start with it? For the same reason I don't climb out of bed every morning and contemplate the meaning and value of my life. Sure, every day is a new beginning (though my knees don't always agree, despite my yoga). As I said earlier, I love big ideas and pondering consequential things. I can navel-gaze with the best of them. Like a lot of my fellow Mars Associates, though, I have a need to just get on with it. Starting with Inspire Purpose is tough enough for hard-charging people who are anxious to get down to cases and produce tangible results. Stepping back and contemplating the bigger, more existential questions, at least in our culture, can be a bridge too far. We've chosen to save Clarify Context for those times when it's plainly necessary, when the value of doing so is readily evident. As already stated, it's most appropriate for times when a team is facing major change. Perhaps the broader business strategy has changed significantly. Maybe there's been a reorganization. Maybe a new leader has taken the helm and wants to completely reorient the group and the work it does. Whatever the case may be, Clarify Context is the place to start when things around a team are shifting and their direction may need to change.

Speaking of direction, you'll have noticed arrows in the graphic sitting at the edges of each of the Practices. They aren't all pointing in a clockwise direction as you might expect. They point to the left, to the right, and outwards from the center. The implied flow for novices that I just discussed is valid. Ultimately, though, each of the Practices interacts with those around it. These vital interconnections are among the subtleties explored in upcoming chapters.

Finally, let's talk about Sustain & Renew and where it sits in our Framework. It occupies a central and therefore prominent position. You've been paying attention so you'll recall my saying ad nauseam that what we needed more than anything else at Mars was more intentional collaboration. Why isn't Cultivate Collaboration, which deals specifically with Intentionality, in the center, then? The short answer is, "It used to be." In earlier, alternate renderings of our Framework, Cultivate Collaboration sat in the middle like Da Vinci's Vitruvian Man reaching out and touching what encircled it. If you were to adapt our HPC Framework for teams in your organization, you might choose this approach (which is illustrated in Chapter 15.) At Mars, though, the data was unequivocal; the thing our teams were worst at and seemed to have the least excitement for was pausing to reflect and learn. Remember that among the teams we studied there was and is a genuine interest in and even passion for collaboration, albeit in a general teamy sort of way. We felt we could harness that energy easily because it was there already. On the other hand, generating focus on learning and continuous adaptation was going to take more effort, more clarity, more discipline. Hence its central position. Besides, Sustain & Renew is the Practice that touches all of the others most directly. Every Practice is subject to reflection, study and improvement. Only a central position illustrates that connectedness accurately. Again, you may see it differently. I'm explaining all this so that you can take what we have learned and make it work for your organization.

Having completed this chapter, you have a solid, high-level grasp of the Mars HPC Framework and where it came from. It's time to delve more deeply into how each of the six Practices of HPC is meant to work. The next chapter begins this deeper dive with a focus on the HPC Practice, Inspire Purpose.

Summary

- The HPC Framework seems intuitive and similar to other team effectiveness models. Important differences lie beneath its surface so it's worth taking the time to become familiar with all its parts.

- The six Practices grow out of the Imperatives and bring them to life. The Imperatives describe what's needed for more intentional, effective collaboration, whereas the six Practices specify what teams do to address those needs.

- This focus on action and doing makes HPC different from a model like Tuckman's Four Stages which only describes stages of development.

- The HPC Framework is pictured as a circle with arrows connecting the six Practices to suggest that teams can move within and through it as they need to.

- There is, however, a suggested sequence for teams using the Framework for the first time, beginning with Inspire Purpose and moving clockwise, ending in the center.

Chapter 8

Clarity and Inspire Purpose

Think back to a certain musty, mirror-lined conference room. The same one from all the way back in Chapter 2. I was working with a cross-functional brand team when I had my first major "ah-ha": There was a significant difference between why a group was created and that team's collaborative purpose. In this case, the team knew why they had been assembled into a team — they all worked on one big and important chocolate brand. Each one of them was a professional in his or her field, each an outstanding Mars Associate. Despite the obvious connections and potential synergies, they lacked clarity about what benefits their being a team would actually create. Yes, they all worked on the same iconic brand. Each played a crucial role in the ongoing and future success of the brand. Each one knew why they were there. One was from the Finance function. There were a couple from the manufacturing side who could make sure that the factories could deliver what was expected. Commercial, which houses our procurement function, also had a seat at the table. There was a Sales representative — or two — and at least one person from every other major function. Each one was focused on doing their functional bit. Being in the room together, as they were on a regular basis, was meant in part to ensure the right level of coordination among these intertwining specialties. If you recall, there were about 13 members of this team. They all had interdependencies, but the level of coordination required among the functions varied a great deal. Sales and Marketing had an understandably high level of interdependence. So did R&D and Supply (manufacturing). If a conversation needed to take place between, for example, Finance and Supply, it was typically happening in the room with all 13 people present. So were the conversations between Sales and Marketing, and R&D and Supply, and so forth. Meetings were convenient times for these function-to-function catchups and information exchanges because everyone was on hand. Convenient, but not efficient or effective. Was having 11 other people sitting through a discussion between one Sales and one Finance person the best use of everyone's time? No. With 13 members on the team and all major functions represented, the number of possible function-to-function conversations quickly multiplies. So does the opportunity to consume outrageous amounts of time unproductively.

If you added it all up, person by person, this group was spending hundreds of hours per month together. They were doing this without a clear sense of why their coming together mattered beyond maintaining a low level of cross-functional coordination. Clearly, this was a team that needed to stay connected, that needed to collaborate on some vital things. But which vital things? Why did these things require collaboration and not some other things? How often, and for how long, should they be meeting? These questions weren't answered in their business strategy. Their organization charts didn't help. What they needed was clarity about their collaborative team purpose and the specific work that would fulfill that purpose.

Clarity is the fertile soil into which you plant the seeds of intentional collaboration. The soil of Clarity has two essential elements: the why and the what. I'll talk about the first element in detail in this chapter. We'll discuss the big "Why," the concept of team purpose and, in particular, our Practice, Inspire Purpose. In the next chapter we'll consider the second element of Clarity: the big "What," what we call "Crystallize Intent," which focuses on the shared work of a team.

Inspire Purpose—the "Why"

Purpose is a bear; it's tough work. It forms a vital part of our

Framework, but getting to it is often hard work. It's worth it. The time we spend in this chapter understanding team purpose, why it's important, what works and what doesn't when it comes to purpose will be time well spent.

A major part of the difficulty with purpose is that it's a big, juicy topic that can be approached in a lot of ways and applied at various levels. Just enter the word "purpose" into the search field at Amazon.com. Scads of titles will come up. I've read a number of them. There are several good ones about finding and living according to one's individual purpose; *The Purpose Driven Life* by Rick Warren is one well-known example. *The Why of Work* by Dave and Wendy Ulrich deals with why it's important for corporations and the leaders who run them to cultivate and share a larger sense of purpose. There are a few great TED talks on the subject, like the one by Simon Sinek—again about corporations. There's even the odd Broadway show tune that deals with purpose: "Purpose" from the hysterical *Avenue Q*.

What Do *We* Mean by Purpose?

We'll need to distinguish among these various types and levels of purpose so we can apply the concept specifically to teams. Most authors and pundits would agree that purpose, regardless of the level, is about meaning and meaningfulness. It's about understanding "why" in a deep sense: why we're here, why we do what we do and what difference we hope to make by doing what we do. Steve Jobs declared that it was important to "Make a dent in the universe." He was driven by an awesome sense of purpose, as are many other well-known leaders. Most of the authors, thinkers, and creators who address purpose do so at either an individual or a corporate level. They focus on either living a purpose-full life or on getting companies to understand how important it is to have a corporate purpose, a "Why", that goes beyond shareholder value and the bottom line. At Mars, we understand the value of having a larger purpose at the corporate level. We have our Mars Five Principles. We have a clear vision, an ambition for what we want to be to the world and to the people in it. We've also learned that teams, to be at their best, need clarity of their collaborative purpose.

A team's purpose, as I suggested in the previous chapter, answers these questions:

- Why do we exist as a collaborative group beyond our obvious functional responsibilities?
- How might we create unique value through our collaboration?

A team purpose statement is the best way we've found to capture and record the answers to these questions. At its best, a team's purpose statement describes the value that the team intends to add to the organization and its stakeholders through its work together as a total team. It's a fairly narrow application of the idea of purpose. That's another reason it's hard. A team's most powerful purpose is often not obvious, but in the end it has to be clear and specific.

The typical business team is what I call a "de facto team." It's a team because the organization chart says it is. All of its members report to the same person or are part of the same function or project. The majority of de facto teams I work with, like the 13-person chocolate brand team I talked about earlier, are collections of strong individuals with equally strong individual achievement needs. They meet these needs by working hard, mostly by themselves, at what they know and do best. They find value and get a sense of personal purpose primarily through their individual efforts and achievements. Yes, they're often helpful to each other—they turn on reactive collaboration when needed. They get value from this. Helpfulness provides a jolt of personal connection and from time to time even meaning. Beyond helpfulness and reactive support, though, lies the possibility of planned and intentional collaboration. That's what a team purpose seeks to clarify and unlock. We build strategies and create clarity for our people about how to enact them. We create detailed budgets so we'll know how we'll pay for what we plan to do, and how much return we'll expect from those efforts. The leaders and managers I know are superb at planning for and being intentional about so very much. Why wouldn't we do the same for the investment of ourselves, and our time, that we make in collaboration?

A team purpose statement ought to make plain to team members the value that they *could* create by acting as a collaborative whole. This isn't to say they can't or shouldn't each add individual value to the enterprise. In fact, that's got to continue or careers and the business will suffer. The point of a team purpose is to make super-clear a group's collaborative reason for being. Teams need to know how their collective efforts could deliver bigger and better results than they would get if everyone was working on his or her own and simply coordinating as necessary.

Trying to suss out a team purpose is as challenging as working on purpose at any other level. It may be harder. Trying to get at the essence of anything is painstaking. You're striving to get past the obvious and into the realm of the possible, the aspirational, all the while trying to keep it real. It's easy to lose your way.

This chapter addresses some of what makes it hard, without trying to resolve unresolvable tensions, like the one between aspiration and practicality. Even in the face of paradoxes like these, this is about Clarity. Clarity of team purpose is a vital step in tapping into the achievement need that is otherwise primarily met by individual tasks. With a clear, powerful purpose, collaboration feels like real, tangible work, as real as anything written into an individual's annual performance plan.

Another challenge in working with team purpose is that purpose as a concept is often confused or conflated with two other common concepts: vision and mission. You may think that what I'm about to do is splitting hairs. It may be, but these are hairs that need to be teased apart. There are two reasons. Doing so will allow us to focus on purpose as it applies specifically to teams. Once we've done that, we can go on to discuss how these three distinct concepts can work together in a mutually reinforcing way.

Vision, Mission, or Purpose?

Vision, mission, and purpose—let's call them "VM&P" for simplicity's sake—can be defined any way you like. This definitional ambiguity, though, doesn't help when you're creating clarity for a team. In fact, it makes things more difficult than they should be. Understanding how we apply the term "purpose" within our Framework requires that we understand all three words and how we use them at Mars when working with groups.

First there is the levels problem. VM&P can be applied at multiple levels. All three, or some subset of them, can be used by large enterprises, small businesses, groups and individuals. For example, I use vision and mission in the context of strategy development and deployment. I tend to use purpose at the individual and group level. Below are the working definitions of VM&P we use in our work with teams at Mars:

Vision: A compelling picture of a desired future state that will be shaped by the direct result of your choices and actions. A vision is best stated in the present tense to convey a sense of possibility. It could be described as what you want to achieve, long term. For example, this is from the not-for-profit Oxfam: "A just world without poverty."

Mission: The course of action or actions that you choose to bring your strategy and vision to life. It also suggests an emphasis. "We could do a hundred different things. We're going to focus on X and Y." A mission describes a "how." For example, "Sell our product at or below our competitor's prices in grocery and drug stores in every region of the country."

Purpose: A statement of why something matters: why a person, group or company believes they exist beyond the results they might create. It conveys the deeper meaning and impact of a life or a group's efforts.

Many people I work with assume that VM&P are interchangeable. "Vision, mission, whatever." The distinctions matter, though, especially when it comes to creating more effective teams. I see great value in both vision and mission statements, but we don't include them in our team effectiveness Framework. Team-level visions and missions can inspire or add focus, but they don't, by themselves, trigger more proactive collaboration. Team purpose does. Why? Because it's specifically about the value and importance of collaboration right here, right now. It's not a statement of what will be true years from now. It's about how collaboration in the present can create that ideal future. It's a compelling statement about why and how a group's collaborative efforts matter to them and the business they serve.

The process of developing purpose is easier, though, if your team's business context is clear. As I said above, vision, mission, and team purpose are distinct concepts. VM&P can and should be mutually reinforcing concepts. In fact, a group does best when it's operating from all three. This was brought home forcefully to me about a year ago when I was working with a group of P&O leaders in one of our businesses.

There had been a reorganization that brought together two previously separate parts of this large business. Two, once separate P&O functions, along with all the other duplicated functions in those two businesses, were to be joined. On top of that, the recently merged P&O team had a relatively new leader. The new VP of P&O asked me to help her team to think through her function's strategy as well as her leadership team's approach to collaborating using our HPC Framework. Given the degree of organizational change, we would begin with Clarify Context, focusing on the broader business and their functional strategy within it. We would then work through the other five HPC Practices in the sequence for first-time teams discussed in Chapter 7.

We planned to work on the function's vision first. Once we had that, we'd do an assessment of the current state, compare that to the vision, and think about how to close the gap between the two. I created some pre-work, gathered their responses, and brought this with me to our first workshop, where we intended to focus on their three-to-five-year vision. It was a good plan. We couldn't get much traction on their picture of the future, though. The current state kept getting in the way.

The conversations among the team members were honest and deeply self-searching as they considered the climate within the overall business at that moment. It had been a rough few years. Associates they sensed were feeling discouraged and disconnected. The business was asking a lot of them. These typical Mars Associates had responded with hard work, creativity and sacrifices. They kept the business running and profitable. The sense of progress just wasn't there; it felt like a struggle to many. Not only that; there was a feeling that their leaders didn't understand what they were going through.

The P&O function wasn't primarily responsible for the climate in their business, obviously. The business's leaders and the managers who worked for them had the lion's share of accountability for levels of engagement and Associate satisfaction. P&O, though, in its role as "co-pilot" was a vital partner to Mars leaders and managers in these areas. Like most HR functions, P&O owns the processes and mechanisms for things like hiring, learning & development, leadership development, and Associate engagement. Clearly the P&O

function had a responsibility and the means to affect how Associates in their part of the world were experiencing their workplace. The conversation about the lack of Associate confidence and disconnection from leadership came out of what I had designed as a discussion about the team's vision. It appeared that my carefully planned conversation had gone off the rails. In the team-consulting business, though, we like to say that a discussion is "going where it needs to go." By digging through the muck of the moment, the group eventually came to understand what they wished for, their vision for the future. Their vision took some time to evolve, but here is where it landed:

An enterprise of confident Associates, focused on growth, who state, "I believe in our business, my Line Manager and myself."

It may sound like a modest vision to you. To them, it was an ambitious and motivating picture of a future they would be proud to co-create with the leaders, managers, and Associates they supported. We then went on to outline a mission for them, a description of how they'd make this future happen. Through focusing on line manager skills and abilities and simultaneously reenergizing the Mars Associate Concept that I talked about in Chapter 1, they would create this enterprise of confident Associates. This work on vision and mission required a one-day workshop, followed by a period of drafting and commenting on drafts done via email after the workshop.

With a clear picture of what their function sought to accomplish (vision) and how they'd go about it (mission), they were then able to settle in for a conversation about their purpose, how their collaboration could bring their vision to life. We scheduled a second workshop devoted to working on their purpose and defining what work they would actually share. It was one of the easiest purpose conversations I have ever been a part of. Using a process I spell out in Appendix A, they agreed that together, they needed to be:

Insightful and provocative leaders inspiring confidence.

I'm wary of groups that declare that their role is to inspire others. The general intent to inspire others lacks clarity. In their case inspiration would be the consequence of being both insightful and provocative P&O leaders. The team would go on to clarify, post-workshop, what it would look like to be "insightful," and "provocative." They defined the behaviors associated with these two attributes so that they could know when they were being "on purpose," and when they were not.

Teams that are familiar with the broader business context they're working in have a consistently easier time discovering their inspiring purpose. Understand what a vision is all about. Be clear about what a mission conveys. If you and the team you're working with need to develop a vision or mission, go right ahead. Then, ask yourselves, "How will we, acting as a team, need to *be* together to make our vision and mission come to life?" When you answer this last question, dig deep. Make it personal. Think about the gifts that each of you brings and what fires each person's passion. Remember, it's all about making it meaningful.

There's one final distinction to make about team purpose statements; they often don't translate easily outside the team. As I did with the P&O team just discussed, I encourage teams to think about the long-term results they dream of creating—their vision. I suggest they develop a mission, a story about the high-level path to reach their vision. These two artifacts create the context for creating a relevant purpose statement. They're also helpful when explaining to others outside the team what your group is about. The team's purpose is less useful in this way. Much of the power of collaborative purpose statements comes from how specific they are to a given team and how personally meaningful they are for team members. This doesn't always translate outside the team. For instance, consider another Mars example:

We are entrepreneurial stewards of the brands and people entrusted to us.

Someone without an understanding of the particular pressures, issues, and opportunities facing this leadership team might dismiss this statement as just so much jargon. For this team, though, the statement resonated strongly. Our Ice Cream & Substantial Snacks (ICSS) business was a collection of smaller brands within our larger North American chocolate portfolio. They were broken out from much larger brands like Snickers® and M&Ms® so that they could be focused on and grown. What's more, this small business-within-a-business was seen as an incubator of future talent. Here, a person could be a first-time Chief Financial Officer (CFO) or Supply Chain leader without the risks they would face if they were put into a similar leadership role in a business ten times the size. The words they chose for their purpose captured the idea that their role, together, was to grow both brands and people. More than that, they felt that theirs was a precious trust. Mars is deeply committed to its brands, even smaller ones. Mars is also very much dedicated to its people; the Associate concept I've talked about is just one example of this dedication. This purpose statement acted as a reminder to this team of the important role they had to play as custodians committed to growth. It was more than just a reminder, though. It acted as a beacon, guiding them on their way until the day a few years later when their brand portfolio was again restructured. I'll talk more about this team again when I discuss how teams adapt to change.

A strong team purpose is grounded in the realities of the

business or organization that a team works within. Clarify Context, the last Practice we'll discuss, is about ensuring that teams have clarity about the strategic and business context in which they operate. The purpose statement itself, however, need only be meaningful to those who created it.

Do We Need a Collaborative Purpose?

What if your group doesn't have any work that requires that they collaborate as a group? This is an important question with two possible answers. The first answer is, "Then you probably don't need this Practice as a part of your team's development." No definable collaboration, no collaborative purpose needed. That's not going to give you and your team the "warm-and-fuzzies" but it's true. When we were first launching the Framework, I was talking to a Finance manager in one of our offices. He was getting ready to bring the Framework back to his team but he was struggling. He wanted to help them understand the value of team purpose to get them excited about working on it. To do this, he was trying to come up with some sense of what his team's purpose might be. His "team" consisted of the financial people at his site as well as the administrative staff that supported the senior executives at the same site. Once he explained this to me, the reason for his struggle was clear: there was no single purpose that the two groups within his team shared. The two groups didn't work together and had no need to do so. In fact, we agreed, he was leading not one but two different teams. Each of his two teams might be able to develop their own purpose statement, but probably not the two of them together. This sort of hybrid group crops up all the time, especially in large organizations. Sometimes there just isn't a natural place for this group or that team to fit in. So, you plug them in to a convenient line on your "org charts" while offering a plausible rationale. That's just reality. If you find yourself in this situation, I urge you not to force a single purpose on the whole group for the sake of teaminess. It won't be authentic or helpful. It will confuse team members, whether they admit it or not. It will certainly lead to hours, days, and weeks of time wasted on phony collaboration, costing your organization a lot of money.

Kevan Hall, author, consultant and former Mars Associate, has a simple way of thinking about the difference between teams that have a collaborative purpose and those that don't. He talks about "spaghetti teams" and "star teams." Spaghetti teams are highly interdependent and connected like so many strands of angel-hair pasta in a bowl. Star teams have a leader at the center with each team member operating independently, as a point of the star, and connecting through the leader. Spaghetti teams with all their connectedness are more likely to have a clear, collaborative purpose. For star teams, it's less clear. Some star teams, like the one I'm a part of, define their purpose as learning together, using their team as a hothouse for generating insights. Others may see their team's role as keeping people connected and engaged. For star teams that do declare a purpose, their ways-of-working should reflect the group's true nature. For instance, purpose-driven star teams will probably make fewer business-related group decisions together than will more intertwined spaghetti teams. Their meetings won't need to be all that frequent or long since they're comparatively less interdependent. Let your Inspiring Purpose help you make sense of how you work. What's more, if you don't have a common purpose, don't force it.

Another response answer to the "no-collaborative-work" question is: Maybe you haven't looked thoroughly enough. There are often hidden or less obvious opportunities for your group's collaboration to create benefits. The example I gave of the team I'm on and how we've declared our purpose as generating insight together is one instance of this. Or let's say you lead a procurement function where each team member is a buyer focused on one or another class of raw materials. One person buys sugar, another buys rice, yet another buys oils, and so forth. Each works with different suppliers and deals with different market dynamics. There's no apparent place for collaboration to play a role. Let's go on to say that this team of professionals each leads their own team. Their teams include the future leaders of the function. You may see where this is headed. Who better to think about and work on the development of these future leaders than the team that includes their bosses? This group of leaders could choose to dedicate at least some of their time together to discussing their people, their next moves, who among their Associates are obvious successors to roles on the leadership team, and so forth.

That second answer, about looking harder for collaborative opportunities, has gotten me in trouble. Some of my colleagues think that it amounts to forcing collaboration. I get that. We're meaning-making creatures—we can find meaning in all sorts of circumstances. This is especially clear following awful, seemingly random, or senseless deaths. Loved ones and friends who experienced the loss seek to make meaning of it by having donations made in the departed loved-one's name or starting foundations, again bearing the deceased's name, "so that this never happens again." It's a beautifully human and life-affirming instinct. It can be taken too far, at least where teams are concerned. I'll be unequivocal on this: Teams without genuine collaborative opportunities should *not* bother with purpose, at least not as we use it in our Framework. I'm not a believer in collaboration for collaboration's sake. On the other hand, I've seen the kind of exploration done by the procurement team pay off. If it's feeling like your group lacks the grounds for shared purpose, ask yourselves, "Are we missing anything? Is there some role we could or should be playing as a team that would amplify the value we each create individually?" Or, better still, turn the question around: "What wouldn't get done or would be at risk if we didn't do it collectively?"

When the Obvious Isn't Enough

There are times when a group's collaborative opportunities are obvious, but insufficient to the challenges at hand. A leadership team I was working with in India was grappling with just this problem. They wrangled for hours with the question of an inspiring shared purpose. This was the top team in this business, mind you. Together, they owned the business strategy, business planning, resource allocation, and the like. They had a lot of real and pragmatic reasons to collaborate and they were already doing so. Their business hadn't grown in three or four years, unfortunately. Their Associates, they told me, had fallen into a state of torpor. These leaders felt there had to be something beyond what they were already doing that could turn things around. Several hours into the discussion, one brave team member provided a provocation that came from ancient Hindu mythology and stories of the god Shiva. There are thousands of such stories, and each story has many variants depending on which part of the vast Indian nation you're in. This particular story involved Shiva in human form, rallying his troops before a great battle with the cry *"Har har mahadev!"* The translations from ancient Sanskrit, like the stories themselves, vary. This team's understanding was that Shiva was inciting and energizing his soldiers by telling them, "We are all the Mahadev," the Great or Auspicious One. The conversation brought this team alive. They agreed that the greatest thing they could do as a group was to reawaken their people. Together they would engage all their Associates in the work of making the next business breakthrough. They decided to jointly commit to helping every other Associate in their business to see themselves as a part of the make-or-break transformation that needed to take place. They needed more than a communications campaign or a series of engagement workshops. It was essential that they come together as a group to role model the behaviors they wanted to see in everyone in their business. If they didn't play this role, no other person or group in their business could.

My friends in India were declaring their intention to collaboratively inspire their Associates. There's that "inspire" word again. So I asked them, repeatedly, "How will you do that?" and "What does inspiring behavior look like?" I reminded them that what's inspiring for one person won't be inspiring to everyone. In response to my provocations, they, like the P&O team earlier in this chapter, created a short list of behaviors that they all committed to and that would embody the spirit of "*Har har mahadev.*" They took a slightly different approach and framed their list as a set of "From–To" statements. They would go "from" acting one way "to" acting another:

From	To
Diffident	**Confident**
Working from fear / Trepidation	Boldness
Fragmented	**Cohesive**
Silos	Enterprise responsible
Circular, beating around bush	**Direct, to the point**
Polite	Candid
Taking it personally	Depersonalizing
Holding back	Constructive challenges / Pushing back
Under the carpet	On the table
Passive	**Full on**
Disengaged	Active listening
Formal/Flat	**Fun loving**

They would use this list as a scorecard each time they met,

scoring themselves on the "To" behaviors. If they weren't living up to these behavioral commitments, they'd talk about how to change that. What they were doing well, they would celebrate, and discuss how to get even better.

We didn't land on a final purpose statement that day; teams often don't. A purpose frequently emerges only after weeks of patient thought combined with intermittent conversations. They eventually shared with me what they ended up with:

OUR TEAM PURPOSE:
We are courageous leaders creating the vision for change and building a winning legacy.
Har har mahadev!

While it may not resonate for you, it had great meaning for them. In combination with their behaviors, this team's purpose provided a sense of team identity that they had lacked. It also served as a prompt to lift them out of their habitual ways of working and towards something greater.

The Practicality of an Inspiring Purpose

Despite my skepticism, inspiration matters. Why else would we name a Practice "Inspire Purpose"? What's inspiration got to do with the Clarity Imperative and tapping into the achievement motive? Study after study has shown that even the most achievement driven of us prefers to find meaning in our work. Work isn't primarily about the tasks and the paycheck. In our own, sometimes humble ways, each of us wants to make a dent in the universe. A team purpose statement seeks to tap into and make the most of this very real human urge.

We can get all warm, fuzzy and teamy when we think about purpose. Like vision and mission, it seems so profound, so existential. It can be. A team's purpose, though, has to be a pragmatic thing, too. Your purpose statement is stronger when it is both inspirational and practical. It should speak to the best in your team, the greatest they're capable of, while at the same time making plain just what, specifically, will benefit from your collaboration. What's more, a really useful purpose statement also plays the role of reminding you what won't get collaborated on. A purpose statement will get you out of bed in the morning because it connects you to an aspiration, directs your efforts, and helps you and your team decide what you won't be spending your time on. This kind of clarity hooks into hearts, minds, and motives.

I'm making pretty bold claims about what an effective purpose statement does. I want to be just as clear about what a purpose statement doesn't do:

- It doesn't explain what your function does. "We are a world class engineering & maintenance team." That's more of a mission statement.
- It doesn't include the words "world class," "best in class," or "state of the art." These are so overused as to be meaningless and may even evoke cynicism.
- It doesn't take up a full page. One sentence is best. Maybe two.
- It does not describe what you will achieve—leave that to a vision statement.

A purpose statement describes what your team wants to be as a collaborative whole to the business or to the world. It isn't about explaining how you will go about your work (that would be the mission of a mission) or exactly what the outcome of your collaboration will be (that would be a vision.)

What Makes a Great Purpose Statement?
Not all team purpose statements are created equal. Mind you, I tend to be hypercritical in this area. I have colleagues who aren't.

They believe that if a purpose statement is meaningful to the team, that's all that counts. I agree with them, up to a point. At the same time, Clarity is organic. What was clear today may not be clear next week or next month. What feels meaningful today may feel differently in a few weeks. Purpose is foundational to this Framework. It's worth thinking hard and working patiently on ways to make it as effective and lasting as possible.

As I said before, much of the work on purpose has been focused on organizations. I'll borrow from that realm to further clarify what I look for in a strong purpose when it comes to teams. Life is Good® may be the most overtly purpose-driven company I know of. Their purpose, "Spreading the power of optimism," is evident in their company name, Life is Good®. Their purpose statement is just that, a purpose. It's not a vision for the future. Nor is it a mission; it doesn't describe how they'll spread optimism. It's short—one sentence, it's dead simple, and it describes how they want to be and act in this world, here and now. The other thing to notice is how it meets the criteria of being both practical and aspirational. The ambition to make their business all about spreading optimism is itself the height of optimism. At the same time, it's completely feasible. Go into one of their stores and you'll experience their purpose in action as you shop and interact with their pleasant, helpful, but not overly fawning staff. Their products with simple, cheerful graphics and positive slogans embody their purpose. On top of all this is their commitment to donate 10% of all their proceeds to kids in need. Life is Good® as a brand isn't for everyone. You can't argue, though, with the way in which they have expressed their purpose and striven to live into it. "Spreading the power of optimism" works as a purpose statement. Can you arrive at a similar purpose statement for your group or team?

Let's get even more specific. To help teams understand what makes for a great purpose statement we use an acronym that we developed: BeCAUSE. It stands for:

Be: What and how will our team "be"?

It's about how you want to be with each other, and what you want the team to be to your people and to the business. It's not about your functional goals, tasks, or outcomes.

C: CATCHY — sticky, clever, memorable

The purpose statement should catch your attention and the elements should stick with you because they're memorable.

A: ASPIRATIONAL — hopeful, appreciative, future-focused

The purpose statement inspires the team to move forward with hope. It does not describe the current state but the future ways of being that the team wants to attain.

U: UNIQUE — original, differentiating, distinctive

The purpose statement communicates the unique contribution of this team. The statement is an original creation unlike any other team's. It isn't a replica from the level above but differentiates the team from others.

S: SHORT — concise, brief, crisp, simple

The purpose statement should be easy to remember and share because it is brief and concise. Refine the statement to the simplest form while retaining all the attributes listed above. Team members should be able to remember and repeat it easily.

E: EVERYDAY — useful, practical, consistent

A purpose statement must be easy to understand and have practical everyday application. It provides direction for meeting agendas, directs decisions, and guides thinking about how the team spends its time and resources.

We give this tool to teams so that they can assess their draft purpose statements against it. It's a tool that gets a lot of use.

To bring BeCAUSE to life, let's talk about what is probably the best team purpose statement that I have seen in Mars. I referred to it earlier in this chapter. It was created by our Global Petcare Leadership Team several years ago, at around the same time we were developing this Framework. It meets all the criteria for what a powerful purpose statement is and does. It was created, however, independently of this project. Before I get to it, though, let's zoom out and consider some of the context. Here is the Global Petcare segment's vision statement:

A Better World for Pets

Our petcare business isn't merely about selling more cans of dogfood or x% more Greenies®. Yes, Mars Petcare includes the manufacture and sales of pet foods and treats for dogs, cats, fish and even birds. We make Pedigree®, Whiskas®, all-natural brands like Nutro®, and the veterinary brand Royal Canin®. Did you know, though, that Mars owns chains of veterinary clinics as well as two state-of-the-art pet nutrition and health research facilities? Mars Petcare is committed to changing the world that our pets live in for the good of animals and their owners.

The Global Petcare Leadership Team considered their ambition of "A Better World for Pets" and asked itself, "What's our role in leading this change?" This is what they came up with:

Together we are courageous architects of the future of Petcare.

This is how they saw their job as a team. Let's dissect the statement to get at what makes it work as a team purpose statement.

Together—Simple enough. This is clearly going to be a statement about what this group intends to do and be collectively.

we are—Present tense, "are." This isn't about a wish for the future. It's about who they're going to be together in the here-and-now, every time they meet and interact.

courageous architects—Others will lead R&D efforts, make the products, work with customers, etc. This team sees themselves as designers and planners, architecting boldly and bravely. These words, much like those in the India team's list of behaviors, express an aspiration for how they want to behave as leaders every day.

of the future—Purpose statements are about the here-and-now. As a leadership team the future is something this team has to pay attention to as part of its regular routine. They won't be meeting to discuss the latest crisis at a factory. They have good people working for them who can do this. They will focus their agendas on creating what's coming, the major trends they need to watch, and their long-range intentions. They'll discuss what sort of talent and capabilities will be needed for the coming future. This commitment to the future shapes what they will spend their precious agenda time on today.

of Petcare—They aren't architecting just their business. Rather their concern is how they can shape the entire category of pet food and care including consumers, customers like the big store chains, even competitors. This is an aspiration that at the same time suggests something as practical as what will make it onto their meeting agendas. They want to tackle only the big stuff that could change the very markets they compete in.

Let's compare this statement to the criteria set forth in our BeCAUSE acronym:

- It expresses who this team wants to be, as individuals and as a collective.
- It is simple and catchy but not overly simplistic.
- It is both aspirational and practical/everyday.
- It's short—ten words—and therefore easy to remember.

I've talked to members of this team who have told me that they apply their purpose in real time to keep themselves on track and operating at the right level. It does just what a good purpose statement is meant to.

I've shared a few examples of purpose statements from senior teams. But you don't have to be a leadership team to create an inspiring team purpose. Factory teams, sales teams, and others have the opportunity to use their collaborative intentions to magnify their impact on others and on the businesses they are part of. The question, "How great can we be, together?" can be answered by anyone at any level. I offer specific ideas and tools for how to create team purpose statements in Appendix A.

The Challenges of Creating a Team Purpose

As I said at the beginning, purpose is a bear. There are some general watch-outs that we should talk about.

Most teams I work with start down the path of creating a purpose statement and end up with something more like a mission. For instance, here are elements of a few draft purpose statements from within Mars:

- Continuously deliver the best confectionery solutions...
- Deliver breakthrough solutions...
- Transforming ideas into tangible quality solutions...
- Delivering customer excellence...

These phrases either focus on outcomes—"the best solutions," "breakthrough solutions"—or they refer to actions such as "transforming ideas," or "delivering excellence." There's a place in the Framework that focuses on tasks and deliverables— Crystallize Intent. I'll cover that in the next chapter. Furthermore, these snippets of purpose statements tend towards business jargon. If your purpose statement contains the words "breakthrough," or—heaven forbid—"world class," you're probably missing the mark.

All of the sample phrases I just provided express worthy intentions and sentiments. They shouldn't be dismissed outright. I'm pretty sure that each of them meant a lot to the groups that created them. At the same time, they miss the point when it comes to purpose within our HPC Framework because they focus on the "what" and "how," and miss the "why."

From doing to being

Team conversations about purpose can be tough because we want to express big ideas that can be hard to pin down. Here's a bit of good news: It's OK to begin with something tangible. This can include exploring what a team produces or does. Go ahead, talk about your mission. Craft a vision. These can lead you to your team's inspiring purpose so long as you don't stop with them.

To help steer clear of the "our-purpose-is-what-we-do" trap, focus on *being* instead of *doing*, as our BeCAUSE acronym suggests. Take a look back at the Global Petcare Leadership Team purpose statement. It begins with a statement of being: "Together we are..." They don't proclaim, "Together we will create..." or "Together we will achieve..." They declared that together they would BE "courageous architects of the future." They chose a metaphorical, almost archetypal, role that each team member will play individually and that the team will embody collectively. It's more than a role, though. It suggests a state of mind or self-image. Like any state of mind it can be summoned at a moment's notice. A great purpose statement expresses who we need to be, at our collaborative best, to get the results we hope for.

The idea of being-not-doing is also expressed in this purpose statement that I shared earlier:

We are entrepreneurial stewards of the brands and people entrusted to us.

Whether you intend to be "courageous architects" or "entrepreneurial stewards," you will want to clarify your desired way of being by "behaviorial-izing" (talk about a buzzword!) it. As I did with the India team, be sure to ask yourselves, "What are the behaviors that go with or embody that way of being?" You won't include these behaviors in your purpose statement. Record them elsewhere so you have them to refer back to as needed. This will enable you to assess how well you're living into your purpose when it comes time to assess your team's health and progress as part of the Sustain & Renew Practice.

Getting to an inspiring purpose

As I said earlier, when it comes to purpose statements, I'm tough to please. I'll look at a team's purpose statement and get all judgey. I've frequently been surprised and delighted, though, when I sit down with a team member and they explain their purpose to me. The words they put on paper often don't reflect the nuance or the passion of the conversations that went into them. This has more to do with writing ability than it does with the authenticity of the emotions and concepts they were trying to express. Purpose statements, especially hastily written ones, can easily miss the mark. It's one of the reasons I find it helpful to allow time when creating a purpose statement, to make it an iterative process covering days, if not weeks. As the conversations continue, as the big ideas simmer, it's helpful to break out a thesaurus, even a book of quotations. In fact, a purpose statement is as close as a team may ever come to co-creating poetry. It's just how it is when working with something like purpose. Here is a simplified version of the steps I follow when working with a team on their purpose:

- Gather all the relevant documents that explain the strategy, vision and mission that are guiding the group's work.

If they don't have a vision or mission, consider working with them to create them as a starting point.

- Gather the group and explain the overall Framework and this process.
- Break the team into small groups and ask them, "Who must you be, together, in service of your commitments to the business/organization?" I often have them answer this question not with words but with images, pictures cut from magazines, or using prepared picture-card decks such as those available from The Center for Creative Leadership. This helps them get out of their heads. You can even have them draw the answer to this question.
- Bring the small groups back together for some show-and-tell about their discussions. If you use images, have them share those. Capture the big ideas on flip charts or on screen.
- Ask them to look for common themes across the group. Capture these themes using words and phrases.
- Break them out again, but into different small groups. Ask them to translate the collected themes into short, bullet-point statements, perhaps even into a single draft purpose statement.
- Bring the groups back together to share their bullet points and statements. Discuss and explore ideas. Capture any new ideas that arise.
- Stop here and agree to a pause in the process, of at least a week and as long as a month. This pause allows for intuition and subtle mental processes to work. Charter a small group to take this raw material away and to craft a few variations of the purpose statement for the team to consider at their next gathering.
- At a subsequent meeting, reveal and discuss the small group's work. If appropriate, agree to a final purpose statement.

- Revisit the statement 60–90 days later to see if it still resonates.

In Appendix A, I provide a more detailed explanation of this approach and one other that teams have used.

Not matter how you get to it, a powerful purpose statement is like a haiku. These three-line poems use a few words—17 syllables to be exact—to paint rich pictures for the reader. With so few words to work with, choosing which words to include is often easier than choosing which words or ideas to remove. Both choices are essential to making your haiku—or purpose statement—potent and practical. So, be patient. Crafting your purpose statement may take time and many iterations. It will be worth it for its ability to keep your team focused and collaborating on those things that really matter.

Clarity of team purpose is only part of the Clarity that teams need to focus their efforts and engage the achievement drive of team members. It addresses the "Why" of their collaboration. Teams also have to clarify their collaborative "What." They have to determine precisely which work requires their collaboration and which doesn't. The next chapter discusses Crystallize Intent, the Practice that takes this next step.

Summary
- Inspire Purpose addresses the "Why" of collaboration. It's about finding meaning in a team's collaboration and identifying how a team's collaboration will create value.
- A purpose statement is different in important ways from both a vision and a mission. A team purpose is more about being than doing or achieving.
- A team's purpose connects it to the larger strategy and functional goals, while at the same time connecting to team members' personal values and aspirations.
- Your purpose statement is meant primarily for your team;

there's no need to share it. Mission statements are usually better for communicating your team's intent outside of the team.

- Take your time developing your team purpose statement; allow your purpose to reveal itself over days, or even weeks.

Chapter 9

Clarity and Crystallize Intent

In 2012 I went on the road with an early version of the Framework. I traveled to work with a team of R&D leaders. We gathered in a corner conference room in one of those "rent-an-office-space-for-the-day" places. We were three floors up in a modern space with windows all around, bean bag chairs, and digital whiteboards. The clean lines and sense of space of our rented room stood in contrast to the mood of this group of accomplished R&D leaders. They were, a bit like the P&O team in the previous chapter, distracted and uneasy. Among the many projects and processes they were responsible for, one was especially troubling for them. Their function was tasked with changing the culture and attitudes of hundreds of factory-based Associates who had come into Mars as part of one of our acquisitions. As you know, Quality is one of the Mars Five Principles. Our standards for product quality and food safety are something we don't compromise on. Associates at a couple of the sites that had joined our factory network hadn't yet internalized our commitment to quality, and some were actively resisting it. This cool late-winter day, as the R&D team and I explored their purpose, this source of complication kept coming up. This issue wasn't one, though, that the entire team had to face into every day. Only those Associates and Line Managers concerned with product quality encountered it regularly. It was, arguably, not this team's problem to deal with. This didn't feel right to them. It was a matter of inculcating the Mars culture into this new Mars business. "Leaders lead culture change," they were telling me, "regardless of their specific functional responsibilities." They felt they had to share accountability for addressing this thorny problem.

I had to agree with them. There were certainly tasks or projects that they should all share. This problem at the plants was probably one. At the same time, there was a lot more work that they didn't all need to collaborate on. I was wrestling with how to bring this distinction to life so that they didn't take on more collaborative work than was appropriate and realistic for them. This was when I hit on a model that has proven pivotal in the application of this Practice. The Radar Screen, which I'll describe later in this chapter, is the way that we now help teams to create clarity for themselves about where their collaborative efforts will be best spent. It's straightforward and easy to use. As with other concepts I've discussed, though, there are prized notions that teams have to let go of or rethink before the Radar Screen can work as intended.

The "What" of Shared Work

Clarifying a team's collaborative work is simple, especially when compared to working on a team's purpose. It's so simple, in fact, that a lot of users of the Framework miss the point, thinking they get it before they do.

The most common misapprehension is that Crystallize Intent is about shared goals. Hear me loud and clear: This Practice is *not* about shared goals or common objectives. Other approaches to team effectiveness will tell you how important shared goals and objectives are. Yes, they're important. At Mars, we're experienced at crafting goals and objectives as part of our strategies and then cascading them into the various places they need to go, including to teams. Our shared goals and objectives ensure we know what we're aiming for and what we need to be successful. What they don't do, in and of themselves, is ignite collaboration.

The Fallacy of Additive Collaboration

Just because a group of competent—even high performing—individuals report into the same person and share a set of objectives does not make them a high performing team. I guarantee you that the R&D team I just discussed had a clear set of shared goals including the one that involved the intransigent Associates at the plants. They were stuck nonetheless. I'm not a fan of sports analogies. I'm more of a haiku guy. In this case, though, I'll use a sports analogy because it brings home the point so clearly. Duane Wade, LeBron James and Chris Bosh, three superstar basketball players, came together on the Miami Heat in 2010. They were dreadful, at first. Their abilities were unquestionable. Their goals and objectives couldn't have been clearer: Score more points than the other guys, in a majority of the games they play. That's how you win a championship. As simple and clear as this objective was, they spent a month floundering. Talented individuals merged into a group, no matter how clear the goals they may have, do not equal a great team. LeBron and his guys managed to turn it around eventually. They became a team by figuring out who they were, as a collective and to each other, and what they could be together. Their goal, to win the NBA championship, was operating in the background. It wasn't, however, what finally made them a winning team. Great teams aren't all about great individuals with clear goals. In fact, I submit that shared goals and objectives will, in and of themselves, tend to diminish collaboration, not enhance it. I call the belief in the collaboration-enhancing powers of shared goals "The Fallacy of Additive Collaboration."

The idea of clear goals and metrics that are established at the top and then cascaded down into the organization is well established and not likely to go away soon—nor should it. It exists for good reasons that I can't argue with. At least at the organizational level. However, high performing teams need more than goals and success metrics. They have to articulate a shared team purpose. Then they identify the resource-consuming work that they will share accountability for and let this unlock their collaborative energies. They don't subscribe to the Fallacy of Additive Collaboration.

At the heart of the Fallacy is the mistaken idea that we have achieved collaboration nirvana when we add up everyone's individual results and they equal the shared goal we set. The best example of how the Fallacy plays out is in a Sales organization. Let's say I'm leading a Sales team dedicated to one large customer. My team and I share a top-line revenue growth target for the year. Let's say we're aiming for 10% growth compared to last year. There are five salespeople working for me; each one represents one of the major brands my company produces. Each of them has a different growth target for their brand or product. Some of their targets are higher than 10%, some lower. When they're all added up, though, they will equal our overall 10% sales goal target for the year. So, we have our shared number and everyone knows how they'll contribute to it. We even have incentives, so that if we exceed our shared growth target we'll all get a bigger bonus. Is this going to drive awesome teamwork or what? Maybe. If you're one of my salespeople, how are you likely to respond to these goals and incentives?

You're most likely to do what you know best and focus on the brand and products you sell to ensure that you make your contribution to the overall target. You're NOT more likely to collaborate with our fellow salespeople, to help them hit their targets. Heck, they know their brands, they know how to sell. They'll do their thing, you'll do yours, and in the end it will all add to and maybe even exceed that 10% overall number. "Woohoo! Go team, go! Thank goodness we all did the Haka at our off-site last year!"

You can see why I call it the "Fallacy of Additive Collaboration." Not only is this approach *not* teamwork, it reinforces individual effort at the expense of collaboration. The truth is that shared goals and many incentives drive more, not less, individually focused behavior. We'll feel all warm and teamy when we make our shared numbers. We associate that good feeling with what we're calling "teamwork," when in fact those feelings were the result of our individual exertions and the individual efforts of our colleagues. That's not teamwork, and confusing it with teamwork obscures the most powerful aspects and the promise of true, intentional teamwork and collaboration.

Granted, sometimes what's required is a collection of great individual efforts. In fact, some level of individual effort is always required. Once again, please, don't force collaboration where it won't add value. In cases where an orchestrated collection of individual efforts is called for, as in my Sales example, then shared goals are essential. Even in teams with high levels of required collaboration, you want to know what the overarching goals are. If you have decided that collaboration really is appropriate, you need to be clear about how you will support and drive it. Shared goals, while necessary, aren't the way to do that. What drives collaboration, what taps into the achievement motive and engages people's collaborative attention, is shared accountability for real work.

The Essence of Crystallize Intent

The essential ingredient of this Practice is working with a group to identify which work requires collaboration and which work doesn't. All work within a group can be sorted into one of three buckets: individual work, small-group work, and work that will be owned by the total group.

At Mars we illustrate the levels of collaboration using the Collaboration Radar Screen that came out of my work with the R&D leadership team.

Notice how this simple diagram, overleaf, turns how most people think about teamwork inside out? The center of attention for most of us is our individual work. It's what gets our attention, not teamwork. Usually, some vague notion of teamwork and feelings of teaminess lie at the outer edges of our awareness. In our approach, we clarify collaboration and put it smack in the

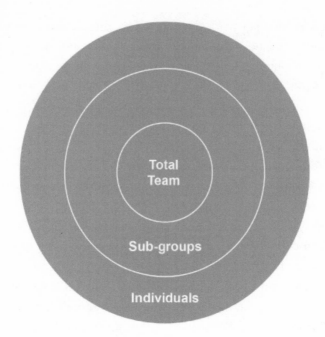

middle. Small-group collaboration lives in that space in-between total team collaboration and individual work. In a non-HPC world of teaminess, being helpful and reactive when needed roughly equates to the middle ring. The difference is that in HPC, it's about thinking ahead and planning for collaboration.

In Appendix B I provide detailed directions on how to use this tool with your team. Here are the basics:

- The few initiatives or projects—not more than three, ideally—that the total team will share accountability for and that are most closely aligned with your team's purpose, go at the center.
- The work that will be shared by sub-groups within the team go in the next ring out.
- The outermost ring is where you place the projects and initiatives that will be handled by individuals.

The discussion about where all the various tasks belong is fascinating and engaging. The question for the moment is, "How do you decide what tasks go where?" I'll start with the outer ring and the role and importance of individual work within teams.

As I mentioned in the previous section, most of the work in a team gets done by individuals. Yes, they interact with their colleagues as necessary. They aren't relying, however, on proactive collaboration to get these individual tasks done. Given the way we structure and populate companies, looking for and hiring the best, most capable individuals we can find, this makes sense. I've said it before—you wouldn't want to undo this effective reality even in the name of collaboration. Therefore, this outer circle often contains the greatest number of tasks within the team. This work is typically least related to your team's collaborative purpose for obvious reasons. The tasks in the outer ring will be related to getting done what the business needs your function or group to get done in support of its mission and/or strategy. Collaboration isn't required, so your team's collaborative purpose isn't relevant. How many projects or initiatives end up here depends on all sorts of factors like who's on the team, the kind of work you do, the business you're working in, and so on. Don't shy away from filling up this outer ring. If you and your team determine a job is best done by an individual, then put it there proudly. Now, let's move inwards on the graphic.

Where collaboration is likely to pay off, that is, where you expect it:

- to increase the likelihood of success, or
- to improve speed or efficiency, or
- to enhance the quality of outcomes…

…then it makes sense to plan for it. In these cases, tasks will go in either the second ring or the center.

When it comes to collaboration, size counts and smaller is better. This much Messrs Katzenbach and Smith got right when in their definition of "team" they refer to a "small number." Collaboration by a small group within a larger group is the most efficient and effective way to realize the benefits of collaboration. Why? Because the more people you get involved in anything, the more complex it becomes to do. If you have a team of seven, having two team members collaborate on a given project is simpler and likely to go more smoothly than involving all seven, no matter how compelling your team purpose.

If your group or organization is anything like ours, then this second ring of the Radar Screen process can be tricky. Mars tends to be an egalitarian, high-involvement culture. Many of us feel we have a right to be heard and to have our views valued on almost anything. This has its upsides. It's a culture where ideas are freely exchanged. Its downsides are clear: too many people involved in too many things. For this part of the process to work, you have to have a mindset of involve-only-the-most-necessary-people. Those who think they should be involved in lots of stuff have to get used to the idea that they might not get to be. For instance, I was working with a team recently where the Finance head felt she needed to "collaborate" on almost every project. To be sure, every piece of work within this Mars business had a financial component to it; money was being spent and had to be accounted for, regardless of the work being done. In fact, this is always true and this tendency to want to be involved is common for Finance and sometimes for HR. In this case, we spent 30 minutes creating clarity for the Finance head and the team about the difference between needing-to-be-aware and intentional collaboration. (The Levels of Collaboration graphic from Chapter 3 is helpful in these conversations.) Where teams decide to draw the lines will vary. The important thing is to have the conversation and to make the distinctions.

We've found that the Radar Screen helps to smooth and even

accelerate this transition to less involvement. Perhaps it's the visibility the process provides that helps to calm the control urges of those who tend to over-involve themselves. In some cases, to help people to make this shift, you may want to provide opportunities for them to feel that their voice has been heard on projects where their active collaboration isn't required. This is what the team I described above did to help their Finance person begin to let go. At some point, though, your team members need to trust that their colleagues can deliver on the work that's been given to them and just get on with their own responsibilities.

There are cases where having the entire team share accountability for a project or initiative makes sense. This is especially true when a piece of work is strongly aligned to your purpose statement. This brings us to the center of the Radar Screen. For instance, if your team's inspiring purpose is centered on your role as talent developers, a major project dealing with talent development may well end up at the center of your Radar Screen. Just as with small-group collaboration, full-group collaboration is only appropriate when it can be shown to add or create definable value like speed or efficiency. In the case of total team collaboration, a team has to be even more selective. Remember, size counts. Larger groups, for all their diversity of thought and style, are less efficient and often more frustrating for achievement-driven individuals. Recall that 13-person team I've talked about a few times. What person wants to sit through a meeting where a few other individuals are slogging through the details of a project that only they care about? If the work at the center of your Radar Screen doesn't clearly benefit from having everyone's intellect and creativity focused on it, then move it to another ring.

Here are some examples of categories of work where total group involvement often makes sense:

- Strategy development

- Financial planning and/or budgeting
- Talent management within an organization or function
- Deployment of organization-wide programs like engagement efforts
- Projects of great strategic importance or complexity, or that are high risk

The last bullet is important and a bit tricky. Collaboration on such projects may be of a different sort. For the first four bullets, you can imagine everyone at the table having a say, providing input and owning parts of the work. The last bullet, though, calls for the group to act in a different way, almost like a board of directors. In these cases, not everyone at the table will have a clearly definable task or deliverable within the project. Instead, their task is to contribute energy, creativity, and critical thinking to a vitally important piece of work. When might a team want to operate this way? The R&D team is the perfect example.

The R&D leadership team agreed, in the end, that shifting the culture and behavior at the plants was something they had to lead together. Not every discipline in R&D and not every person on this team had a direct role in making this change happen. Nonetheless, they would share accountability for it as a total team. This initiative ended up on a sticky note in the center of the crude Radar Screen I had sketched on the whiteboard.

What did this choice mean in terms of how they would work? At every team meeting, once a month, this project would be reviewed and discussed. Problems would be flagged and if possible solved. If necessary, resources would be shifted within the function to ensure success. This wasn't just about updating and informing—that could be done via email. This was real work on a real project that benefited greatly from the team's collective intellect and problem-solving capabilities. In this case, the two people leading the project were required to let down their guard, to allow their teammates complete visibility into what they were doing, what was going well as well as what wasn't. It required these two to trust their colleagues and to risk being vulnerable with them. This approach turned the project around for R&D and for the overall business. The benefits that this kind of collaboration created were worth it, to them, to their colleagues, and to the entire enterprise.

When discussing what goes at the center of your Radar Screen, your team purpose is the primary filter. You'll refer back to it repeatedly. If a task or project isn't clearly aligned with your stated purpose, one of two things could be off. Perhaps the work doesn't belong at the center of your Radar Screen. Or, less conveniently, it might be that your purpose is somehow missing the mark. Don't make the mistake of treating your purpose statement as sacred. If it needs to be rethought, do it. Inspire Purpose and Crystallize Intent need to work with each other, and they have to serve the collaborative needs and intent of the team.

Radar Screen Recap

The process of completing the Radar Screen is highly engaging and worth every minute spent on it. It forces that conversation about "What needs collaboration and what doesn't," in a way no other technique does. So that you can appreciate what I mean, I'll say a bit about the process here. We typically do this exercise using small sticky notes on a large sheet of white paper with three concentric circles drawn on it. One piece of work per sticky note. This allows us the freedom to move things around based on the conversation. Every sticky note is read aloud and then placed in a tentative position on the Radar Screen. We ask people to start with the work they think is most important. Discussion ensues until agreement is reached about where that sticky note should go. The same approach can be approximated in virtual meetings using presentation software and screen sharing. One key to this is to be sure that each sticky note, real or virtual, includes the name or names of those leading the work. This enables the team to see who will be collaborating on what and with whom. Including names also enables us to move smoothly into the next Practice, Cultivate Collaboration. I provide much more detail on the Radar Screen process in Appendix B.

When you have completed your Radar Screen exercise, you end up with what I sometimes call your "collaboration map." It's a graphical representation of where your collaborative energies should go, and where they shouldn't. It has tremendous power to make collaboration feel real and something that team members can feel genuinely accountable for.

Inspiring Purpose and Crystallized Collaborative Intent Together

If you've had a chance to apply the ideas and precepts offered in this chapter, by now your team will have articulated a clear and ideally inspiring purpose. You will have mapped out what work specifically requires collaboration in ways that will bring the team's purpose to life. Taken together, your purpose and shared work create a tangible sense of team identity. "This is who we are. This is why we exist to collaborate and what we do to fulfill our purpose." Team members and leaders have told me repeatedly that engaging in these two Practices provides a clear sense of meaning for them, individually and within the context of the group. It helps them to connect more personally with, not just the team and the work they have to do, but also the larger business.

Completing your purpose and Radar Screen, though, are just the beginning. Remember, we call them "Practices" for a reason. You have to practice them. Every meeting agenda and every meeting will be at its best when it is consistent with your team purpose and with the work on your Radar Screen. Use your team purpose and Radar Screen to guide the creation of your agendas and again as a scorecard at the end of your meetings. Ask yourselves, "Were we entirely 'on-purpose' in this meeting?" "Did we focus our collaborative efforts on the work we agreed should be at the center of our Radar Screen?" As work is completed and new work comes in, the Radar Screen is revisited and updated. Every so often or when there are significant changes, your purpose, too, will require a revisit. This is the nature of Practices. They become part of your everyday ways of working and being. This is when they really deliver on the effort you put into them.

These two Practices create the Clarity that sets the stage for the rest of the Framework.

- Knowing what work requires your collaboration and with whom you have to collaborate, you will begin the process of making intentional collaborative agreements.
- With a clear purpose and collaborative agreements, the team can then decide on essential team processes, like how and when to meet, in ways that align clearly with the work that needs to happen collaboratively.
- Finally, since the team knows what it wants to be and how it prefers to collaborate, they can focus their learning and improvement towards those specific ends.

In the next chapter I'll get more specific about how intentional collaboration can be cultivated and nurtured, now that the soil has been prepared.

Summary

- Crystallize Intent is about clarifying the "What" for the team, the work that requires collaboration. It also identifies the work that won't require collaborative effort.
- Crystallize Intent is not about shared goals. Shared goals are necessary for measuring progress, but our research revealed that they tend to drive more individual than

collective effort.

- The Radar Screen is the essential tool for practicing Crystallize Intent.
- Crystallize Intent, together with Inspire Purpose, creates a sense of meaning and identity for the team and its collaboration.

Chapter 10

Intentionality and Cultivate Collaboration

Remember the first insight from Chapter 3 about collaboration? When people were asked about it they said: "We just don't." People were telling me that they knew they should be collaborating, at least on some things. Despite this, they weren't collaborating. They weren't acting on what they knew or on their sense that teamwork was important. In other words, they weren't being intentional. Why? Their need for individual achievement was overpowering a vague, and therefore weak, concept of what it meant to collaborate.

The achievement motive eats vague for breakfast. Give me specifics, give me targets and objectives, things I can check off my list. The people in my study were unclear about what specific work required collaboration and why it mattered. Nothing about the general idea of teamwork could compete with their intense drive for personal achievement. Everything in the previous two chapters was meant to address this imbalance. Inspire Purpose tackled the "Why" of the group's collaborative efforts. Crystallize Intent focused on the "What," the specific tasks and projects that required collaborative working. Clarity in both these areas is only a first step.

Clarity is indispensable, but Intentional collaboration is the point. Work done on Clarity, on purpose and shared work, only prepares the soil. It's still necessary to both plant and nurture the seeds. That's the object of the Practice we call Cultivate Collaboration. As we practice it at Mars, Cultivate Collaboration has three aspects that roughly align with the Radar Screen from the previous chapter. The first deals with the total team. It aligns with the work at the center of the Radar Screen and how the team commits to address that work, together. The second addresses the work and team members involved with work in the middle ring. It emphasizes building accountability among these collaborators. The third aspect is all-encompassing. It focuses on building strong relationships throughout the team. It's not directly aligned to the outer ring but includes it. This chapter is more or less structured according to these three aspects of cultivating collaboration.

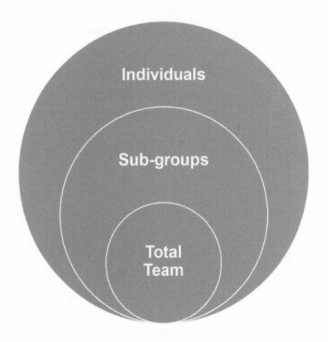

Note: I picture the Radar Screen here as I sometimes create it, since it creates broader areas for my sticky notes.

Before we dive in, though, there are a couple of points to cover based on our experience with this Practice.

Why Clarity Isn't Enough

Not long ago I spent the better part of two days with a group of Supply Chain senior leaders within our global Drinks business.

Several months earlier, we had worked on their inspiring purpose and mapped their collaboration using the Radar Screen. Things weren't shifting much, though. We reconvened to try to understand what the matter was. Their purpose, which the team agreed on, seemed right. It was the Radar Screen they felt was off. They didn't feel they'd identified the right work at the center. The good news was that they quickly had an insight into what needed to change in that part of the Radar Screen, where they had placed the work the entire team agreed to share responsibility for. After some hearty discussion, they made the required changes. Following this, I agreed to lead some exploratory work on the strength of one-to-one relationships in the team. All good, right? Going from Clarity to Intentionality and relationships. There's a catch that I missed at the time, though. The exercise I set up was one I had used for years and it wasn't explicitly tied to the team's Radar Screen. It had every team member assessing all the relationships they had in the team, regardless of whether or not these pairings included collaboration on specific work. The exercise and the conversations it generated felt good to them, regardless. We identified a few relationships that needed attention and asked that those individuals connect with each other. Running low on time, we moved on to planning their next steps, including how they'd handled the unfinished relationship conversations. We wrapped it up and went our separate ways.

Four months later, during a conversation with the team leader, I heard that once again little had changed in terms of the quality of her team's collaboration. The improved clarity about the "What" of their shared work that had come from the Radar Screen update hadn't been enough to unlock their latent collaborative intent. Not only that, the work we had done on identifying relationships that needed work hadn't made much of a difference. It was immediately clear why: that clever piece of work that I had concocted was too generic. As I said, it wasn't linked to the Clarity work that had come before it. The soil was prepared; the seeds were ready, but they never quite got into the ground.

As obvious as this is, I have to say it: There is a difference between creating and having an intention, and acting with intention. In my research, hundreds of team members told me that they intended to collaborate more—they just didn't. It's fair to say that the road to teaminess is paved with good intentions. The team I just described had the same genuine intentions. They weren't acting on them. Why? They had done a lot right. They had figured out why their collaboration mattered, what work required collaboration, and even how to start. What's more, through this process they had identified who needed to be working with whom. They then examined their relationships. This exercise, despite my experience and my own good intentions, came up short. It lacked what's required to draw the focus of achievement-driven individuals towards collaboration. It didn't help them to create accountability for collaboration on specific pieces of work. It didn't give them a way to forge agreements with each other about how their focused collaboration would play out. I, the expert, had forgotten one of my, until now, unwritten rules: Work on relationships in the absence of clear accountabilities leads, at best, to teaminess. Before we get into how we apply Cultivate Collaboration to the work done on the Radar Screen, let's talk about how three key elements come together to make this work: individuals, their work, and relationships.

Embracing Relationship Management

I frequently tell managers who are just starting with the Framework that they have a mental and behavioral shift to make. They will go from managing individuals and tasks, to managing individuals, tasks *and* relationships. Relationships are one of the three foundational elements of collaboration.

By suggesting that team leaders "manage" relationships, I'm not asking them to play the part of counselors or relationship

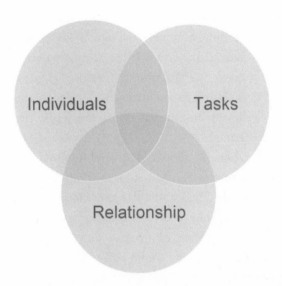

advisors. Nor am I recommending they attend to relationships in a general way, making sure that everyone is getting along. I'm saying that relationships, just like your people and the work they do, are essential to delivering on your group's commitments. This is especially true where a team has committed to make the most of their collaboration. Why wouldn't you want to pay attention to important relationships, what's working, what's not, and provide support in appropriate ways? The three—the work, the individuals, and the relationships—interact to produce the results you planned for.

This advice is true not just for managers, by the way. Every team member has to think the same way and attend to the same three things. The Practice of Cultivating Collaboration relies on this tripartite formula for collaborative success.

Back to the Radar Screen

Cultivate Collaboration begins by looking back to the previous Practice and the Radar Screen. Remember that any sticky notes in the center of the Radar Screen and the sticky notes in the middle ring contain multiple names.

Based on those names, and the work that each sticky note describes, the group now moves into a series of structured conversations based on who will be doing what with whom. We call this process "behavioral contracting." The goal of these conversations is setting expectations for how team members will collaborate with one another based on the work identified and who each of them is.

These are not—I repeat *not*—open-ended "let's-get-to-know-each-other-better" interactions. These are conversations built around specific tasks and the specific people who will be performing them. They will serve and support relationships, but relationship isn't their first focus. The primary focus at this point is—here's that word again—Clarity. Even in the midst of creating Intentionality we rely on Clarity about the work and Clarity about who each person is and how they prefer to work. Once these are established, you'll seek to deepen the relationships among collaborators so that they can best serve the task and each other.

The first conversations

The first set of Cultivate Collaboration conversations focus on the work shared by the total team (if there is any). That's the work at the center of the Radar Screen.

These initial discussions take place in two directions: top-down and bottom-up.

- Top-down: Team leader to the team
- Bottom-up: The team to the leader

Not every group has so clear a hierarchy. For some groups, like communities of practice, "top-down and bottom-up" won't work. They're more egalitarian. I'll discuss an approach for those teams a bit later. For those of us in groups where the hierarchy is clear, it makes sense to pay attention to the authority structure.

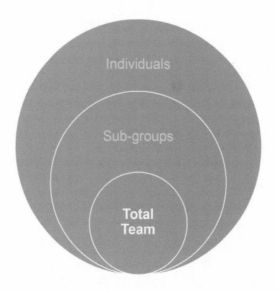

The first variety of conversations actually involves two conversations that are mirror images of each other: the leader talking to and making requests of the team, and the team talking to and making requests of the leader. They happen best when the two conversations are part of one process and both halves of the process are addressing the same question: "How do we need to work and be together as a total team when it comes the work we all share?"

The whole process is anchored in the Clarity that has been created in the preceding Practices, Inspire Purpose and Crystallize Intent. The first thing the total team does is to look back at their purpose and Radar Screen, and ask themselves: "What is expected of all of us if we're to live into our purpose and work effectively together on the work we all share?" This will end up as a single conversation between the leader and the group about mutually agreed expectations. It begins, though, with the leader and the team working separately, thinking about and writing down their ideas about what they expect of themselves and each other.

The leader will specify what they're looking for from the

group in terms of collaboration. Some typical expectations from managers might include:

- Bring issues related to center-of-the-Radar-Screen projects to the total team for consideration and problem solving
- Act and speak with an assumption of positive intent when it comes to your teammates
- Speak candidly about the mistakes and missteps you make so we can all learn
- Provide feedback to me and to our teammates within a day of a situation requiring it
- Celebrate your successes and those of your peers in small ways every day
- Make only collaborative commitments you can keep, and consistently keep the collaborative commitments you make.

These expectations are only useful if they employ behavioral language. Notice, for example, how "Bring issues" and "Provide feedback" describe observable behaviors. Throwing around teamy language isn't helpful. Expressions like "Show a positive attitude" and "There is no 'I' in team" are either vague or so hackneyed as to be useless. What does a "positive attitude" look like? That's a question with many possible answers.

To enable the other side of this conversation, the group members will specify what they will need from the team leader to be successful. Team members may come up with a list something like this:

- Timely updates on decisions and situations that you have visibility to and that may or will affect us
- Timely feedback based on what you're seeing going on in the team
- Regular check-ins with each of us as individuals

- Share leadership during our meetings; allow us to both design and facilitate our team meetings
- Input into and involvement in hiring new members to our team
- Ask before you tell; coach us to solutions rather than providing them

Notice again how each one of these describes observable behaviors.

These lists are often longer than the examples I've offered. It's generally better to start with a robust list, but the number of behaviors isn't what's critical at this point. Good conversations are what counts here. Once the two halves of this conversation have created their lists, the leader and the team work together to establish a mutually agreed set of expectations of each other. This isn't an exercise in command and control: "This is what I, your manager, need and I will settle for no less!" This is all done in the spirit of opening up conversations that will surface relevant differences that need to be sorted as well as areas of quick agreement. The final lists—one for the team leader and one for the team—are intended to act as guideposts and to ensure that everyone in the team knows what is expected of them. Remember, this is all about working together to fulfill the team's purpose and to deliver on the work the total team shares. These agreements get written down and become part of the evolving team charter. These conversations can be facilitated in several ways, one of which I cover in Appendix C.

As I mentioned, not all groups have a clear hierarchy. These groups are less bound by the "top-down, bottom-up" dynamic. Instead they work collectively to answer the same question: "What is expected of all of us if we're to live into our purpose and work effectively together on the work we all share?" The outcome of this conversation is a single set of shared behaviors that team members declare they're all equally accountable for.

The lists that come out of behavioral contracting conversations frequently include 12–15 behaviors. At this stage, numbers count and this is too many. The Ten Commandments are the cornerstone of several world cultures and most of us can't remember those. For all our good intentions, we can't keep lists longer than three to five in mind. I invite teams to find a way to get their lists down to five behaviors—sometimes with limited sub-bullets—and to make the list as specific and descriptive as possible. Here's an example from one of Mars's regional P&O teams. This was agreed to by the leader and all team members:

Mars Asia Pac P&O: Shared collaborative commitments

To have **CURIOSITY** around ideas—Don't leap too soon to solution mode.

To focus on **CLARITY** around communications—Keep things as succinct as possible.

To be **RESPONSIVE** to others' needs—Don't make them chase you & be proactive wherever possible.

To **KEEP PROMISES** with other team members—Follow through on your commitments first time every time.

To constructively **CHALLENGE** each other—With the intent to respectfully make things better for all.

I like this list because it's simple without being simplistic and it includes clear behavioral statements.

Not norms

Lots of groups create "team norms." You know the ones. They end up as posters on the wall, right next to the one of the rowers at sunset and the other one that declares, "There is no 'I' in team!" This ain't that. Your average team norm list comes out of conversations about how team members say they want to treat each other. That's not a bad conversation to have. It may be helpful, at least while the conversation is still fresh in people's minds. Team norms, even when posted on walls, don't have lasting effect. The conversations I have just described, and the agreements they lead to, create accountability for collaborative tasks and behavior. They're anchored to the team's inspiring purpose and connected directly to the work the team has declared they will share. Come performance management season, having these behaviors integrated into the team's expectations of one another makes a difference. We'll talk more about performance management in a bit. There is a second variety of conversations that we need to cover: group member to group member.

The second conversations

These conversations focus on the middle ring of the Radar Screen, all the work that is going to be done in pairs or small groups.

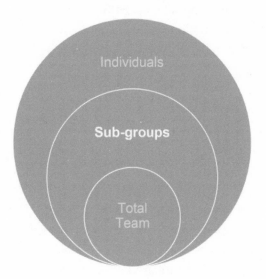

The few people involved in each piece of work start by ensuring that they all understand the work that is being done. They'll discuss questions such as, "What is the expected outcome of this project?" "What is the completion date?" "What resources are required?" and other project-specific details. Once the details of the project are clear, then they move to discussing their respective roles, who will be doing what, and how they would prefer to work together. These roles conversations are more personal and involve self-disclosure about style and work habits. They're beginning to bleed over into relationship topics, but not yet to a deep level. Things at this point remain in the "What do you know, what do you prefer, how do you like to operate?" domain. For instance, consider these "fill-in-the-blank" examples that small-group members might offer up:

- I prefer a lot of verbal communication, so...
- I'm already behind on this project, which has me worried, so what I could use from you is...
- I have seen how good you are with the details, so how about you...
- Based on my relationship with the VP in charge, what if I start a conversation with him, and you could...
- I'm totally new to this kind of content so I wonder if you would...

Get the idea? By the time they have worked through this contracting conversation, every member of each sub-group should be clear about what needs to get done, by when, and how the people involved like to work and collaborate. It's common sense really. This is the essence of intentional collaboration. By contrast, in the more typical reactive or "helpful" collaboration we discover responsibility overlaps and personal preferences after the fact. Instead, in Cultivate Collaboration we plan for how we can be most useful and helpful to each other and factor this knowledge into our everyday work. We're also awakening the achievement motive by being clear about what collaborative success looks like.

Performance Management and Collaboration

Organizations carry on ad nauseam about how important teamwork is. On the other hand, some pundits are now proclaiming that there's too much collaboration and teamwork thanks to how electronically connected we have all become. So long as organizations' primary rewards and recognition systems are focused on individuals, individual performance will reign supreme and teamwork will remain an overused buzzword. Unless, that is, we create meaningful accountability within our work-groups. The group is the only place in traditional organizations where we can make collaboration a specific, achievable thing that we hold each individual accountable for, that we provide feedback about, and celebrate as appropriate. All of the conversations I have described in this chapter are about creating interpersonal performance contracts. The next step is to wire the outcomes and agreements from these conversations into your performance management discussions and process.

As I write this, a number of firms have begun to do away with "old school" performance management systems. Good for them. This trend may continue to the point where the majority of Western-style companies have dispensed with annual performance ratings. That would be great. I'm not, however, holding my breath. Today's reality is that most of the big companies I'm aware of continue with what some say is a bankrupt notion. If your focus is collaboration and you're using our approach, having a performance management system can work to your advantage.

What's required is that the expectations that have been set in the conversations I've just described get recorded in your performance management system. To illustrate I'll use an example from my own team. My manager knows that I have committed to work on "The Big Project" with my teammate Claire. There was a sticky with both our names on it in the middle ring of our Radar Screen.

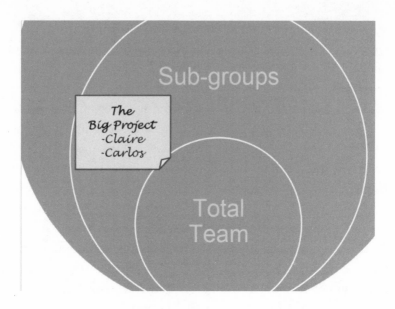

Though Claire is my peer, in this project she's the lead. I have agreed to certain accountabilities with her. Those go into my performance expectations for the year. Come time for my mid-year performance check-in, both my manager and Claire will provide feedback on this objective. My collaboration is now a part of the company's system that formerly seemed to work against it. What is more, taking this step makes the accountability for collaboration feel that much more "real" and achievable to individual team members.

The same holds true for the expectations at the center of the Radar Screen. Each of us has agreed to be held accountable for performing the work that we all share. We then participate with each other at performance review time, sharing our perspectives on the quality and impact of one another's collaboration.

Performance management isn't just a manager's job, anymore. It's the work of the entire collaborative entity/team/group. For managers, the big shift will be the one I mentioned earlier: from managing individuals and work to managing individuals, managing work, and managing collaborative effectiveness.

For team members, the toughest part in a hierarchical team will be developing a willingness and openness to talk about their effectiveness with their peers. There will be no genuine, intentional collaboration, though, without the willingness and ability to offer and receive feedback within a group.

Again, Clarity is paramount. This does not work without clear agreements and accurately described behaviors coming out of the conversations I've described. Whether you're talking about managing individual performance or collaborative commitments, it won't work where the expectations are ambiguous or vague.

Performance management and the trap of collusion

Collusion is toxic collaboration. As I use the word, it means a benign conspiracy to hide the truth about lousy collaboration. Imagine a team leader sitting down with a couple of folks who have been working on a project together. The truth is that these two, for whatever reason, just didn't connect all that much. They held their collaboration expectations discussion, but had never really bothered to do much about it or with it. They fell into their individual contributor habits and got a good bit of work done as a result. Neither one of them wants to look bad or cares to throw the other person under the bus. So, their conversation with the group leader might go like this:

Boss: So, how would you two rate the quality of your collaboration on this project?

A: Oh, I'd say we did pretty well, wouldn't you, B? I mean, we got the job done, didn't we?

B: Oh, yeah, totally. We did what we said we would. We didn't violate any of our agreements with each other. I mean, not intentionally. Hey, we're all human, right? Stuff happens. But like A said, we delivered.

Boss: I'd agree. You got the job done. It wasn't your best work, though. It wasn't awful. But things were falling through the cracks. It appeared to me that you weren't all that well connected.

A: Yeah. Well, you know how busy we get, right? So maybe we dropped the ball once or twice, but the proof is in the results, isn't it?

Everyone in this little scenario is a good soul just trying to do their best. Their unwillingness to own up to less-than-stellar collaboration is understandable. They might say they "have each other's back." In some places, their covering for each other would be called teamwork. Trust me: If the people in the rowing poster on the wall had been collaborating like A and B did, they'd be getting nowhere.

If I were their manager and I sensed the game these two were playing, I would want to ask, "So, tell me, how did your collaboration, the way you worked together, add value to the results you're so proud of?" Or, "Can you give me a few concrete examples of your collaborative behaviors and how they helped?" I'm not looking to beat up these two. Let's assume that the project got done adequately, based on how capable these two are as individuals. Remember, this is supposed to be about adding value via collaboration. A good result is OK. Our objective, however, is great results through collaboration. If these two missed the chance to go beyond good, then we ought to discuss that and get to the root of why. They will still each get an acceptable performance rating. They need to realize, though, that more was possible and be encouraged to make changes to the way they collaborate in pursuit of even better outcomes.

Behavioral Contracting Wrap-up

If this sounds like a lot of work, well, it can be. The outcome of this process, though, saves time, work, and aggravation. It cuts down on time wasted in the traditional "reactive" collaboration approach. In a typical environment, if we're lucky we stumble across the overlaps in our work before they get us in trouble, before we have to undo stuff and back-track to fix what we missed. If we're really fortunate, we find the overlaps and work the whole thing out without driving each other crazy or our manager finding out. I have just described the world of teamwork as most of us know it. Our Framework can liberate you and the groups you're a part of from the stress and inefficiency of too much reactive collaboration. I think the greatest thing about our approach, though, is the sense of ownership and involvement it generates in a team. I have heard from team after team about how, once they begin this process, they begin to feel their destiny really is in their own hands, and collaboration and teamwork come to have genuine meaning for them.

The Radar Screen is a wonderfully versatile tool that has applications in several of the Practices. We'll come back to it again in the next two chapters. Now, we need to go deeper on the topic of relationships.

Deepening Relationships

So far, what we have covered has been pretty technical—who is doing what with whom and what agreements can we reach with each other about all of that. It's been about creating even more clarity in order to fuel and focus intentional collaboration. As I suggested above, we cannot—absolutely cannot—ignore the underlying human dynamics, the interpersonal side of the relationships that are the foundations of all collaboration. These conversations begin with the work at hand, and go deeper. They directly address questions such as:

- What kind of person am I? What kind of person are you?
- What are the deeply held values that shape you at work?
- What are your greatest strengths?
- What drives you crazy? What are your pet peeves?
- What gives you energy? And what saps you?

These conversations may well begin as part of your work-focused contracting discussions. It just happens, especially where we like one another. They also benefit from a separate focus; time to talk about how who you are is likely to affect your work with your colleagues. These conversations need structure. We want to ensure they cover significant topics and answer consistent, meaningful questions. Many leaders and teams like to use personality instruments to assist in relationship building. Let's consider this common practice.

What letters did you get?

Carlos, what our team needs is to get to know each other better. We've been working together for six months or so and we're in that "storming stage" that I've heard teams go through. I think a light touch is in order here. I'd like you to take us through the Myers-Briggs Type Indicator®. When can we set that up?

Whether it's letters or colors or icons, people love their personality instruments. I get these requests less than I used to, but I still get them. There is a persistent story out there that if we get more familiar with each other it will breed collaboration. "If we get to know more about each other," the story goes, "we'll appreciate each other more, trust each other more, and therefore treat each other better and work better together." I'm a firm believer in building relationships at work. I'm a regular user of psychometric instruments to support teams in their collaboration. This approach of "let's get to know each other better so we'll work together better" is often flawed in application and execution. It's a little bit like the team spirit problem—it's a good thing, but we're going about it the wrong way.

We can administer and debrief a personality instrument with a group and create that nice little buzz of teaminess. Some might even get genuine insight into their own or others' behaviors. The instrument and the information it provides don't generally make a lasting difference in the effectiveness of people's collaboration, though. That's not to say they can't. It won't happen, though, when the instrument is administered as a solution in and of itself; that is, when it's administered and debriefed under the assumption that "familiarity breeds collaboration." Here's the provocative proposition:

There is no causal relationship between familiarity and the quality of collaboration.

I haven't seen studies on this. This is experience talking. There are plenty of people who I know pretty well, well enough to know that I'll never collaborate successfully with them. I hate to sound like Rodney Dangerfield here but, as well as I know my wife and she, me, we will never, ever try to wallpaper a room together again. Ever. Similarly, knowing that I'm mostly Blue and you're mostly Yellow isn't going to enable intentional collaboration between us.

In the worst case, teams use personality instruments as a way to avoid tackling the real and sometimes tough underlying issues that they don't have the courage or skills to raise and resolve. I've been there, and maybe you have, too. We go through all the amusing exercises, lining up along scales taped to the floor, making drawings of our dream homes, and sharing our colors. The entire time, there is an unspoken, almost unbearable tension knowing that the real problems within the group are being glossed over.

Making personality instruments work

What does it take to make surveys and psychometrics work for you and the team? Go back to the three dimensions of managing collaboration I talked about before we discussed the Radar Screen: the individuals, the task, and the relationship. You have to account for all three in your relationship-building work. Using the language of the Imperatives, what's needed is Clarity about why building the relationships matters and Intentionality in connecting the knowledge about one another to the task at the core of each relationship. Team members will know specifically what projects or initiatives require collaboration and therefore which relationships need quality attention. Which isn't to imply that we don't want all the relationships to be solid. What we're after is, once again, tapping into the desire of most team members to have clear, understandable, and achievable objectives. By pinning relationship building to the tasks the team has to do, we impart a sense of importance to what would otherwise be a general exercise in interpersonal affairs.

How might this look? Start just as you would with any psychometric instrument starts. Administer the instrument, whether it's MBTI®, FIRO-B®, or anything else. Debrief the findings with the entire team. This creates a shared "personality language" for the group. Then, break the group out into sub-groups based on who is collaborating with whom. Have them discuss how their particular style or preferences might show up in their collaboration. They should be asking themselves, "If this is who you are, and this is who I am, what are the implications for our work together on this specific project?"

When you anchor interpersonal work to the specific work of the team, you connect relationship with the achievement need that drives people. They will see clearly how the interpersonal links to the work, and how understanding others will help them to achieve both collaborative excellence and their personal goals.

A few years ago the team I'm part of used a less-well-known personality instrument. We were sitting in a coffee shop for the debrief. There were only three of us and a mutually respected colleague who was acting as our facilitator. It was late in the day and the coffee shop was largely empty except for us. This allowed us to be fairly animated and expressive without being disruptive. The instrument was complicated, and had 12 or 15 dimensions. No colors, just words. We focused on the dimensions where we saw strong similarities or striking differences among us. One insight from the survey confirmed what most of us suspected: my boss and I were polar opposites on one dimension of our personalities. He was an extremely rapid processor of information whereas I prefer to take my time integrating new ideas and concepts. We talked it through and offered examples of where in our work together this difference was showing up. We also talked about what it meant for us going forward. Our little coffee shop workshop lasted about 90 minutes and then we wrapped up for the evening.

A few months later, my manager and I got together to discuss a new piece of work, one that hadn't been a part of our coffee shop discussion. We had been asked by our VP to prepare a proposal for the global P&O leadership team on how to move a certain high-profile project forward. I began, "OK, this is a chance for me to work on developing my influencing skills. Can we talk about how we want to work together?" Immediately my boss jumped in, outlining an approach, offering next steps and a range of other ideas to make this proposal work. He was doing what he did — thinking fast (and aloud — he's highly extroverted) about getting the thing done. For a few moments I was silent, taking it all in, processing in my patient way. Then I realized what was happening. I stopped him and said, "OK. I appreciate your quick thinking and good ideas. But I think our style differences may get in the way here. If I'm going to use this as an opportunity to develop, I need you to play a different role, to slow down, to be more of a listener and a coach. Can you allow my more deliberate way of processing to work? Are you up for that?" Of course he was.

Back in the coffee shop we had drawn clear lines between the personality concepts we were learning and the work we were doing together. It made those concepts real and sticky for us. If we had just learned a personality model, played with the information in engaging but not directly work-related exercises, I wouldn't have retained what I did. By putting the two, the personality information and our work, in immediate proximity to each other, the connection between the two became lasting and useful. We still refer back to that coffee shop debrief to this day.

You can take this same approach with other team exercises and outdoor challenges. (You may even be able to make the Haka into a useful team development undertaking.) In most outdoor team challenges, your facilitator will work with you to draw out lessons learned. You'll talk about, not just how you worked together, but about how your individual tendencies affected the outcomes of the challenge. My experience has been that these exercises often stop there. Sometimes, I've had facilitators go on to ask something like, "What could these insights mean for the way you work together back at the office?" The right direction, but that question leads to vague, non-committal responses. You'd hear things such as, "We *could* do this," "Or we *might* need to look out for that." Don't settle for generalities, for "mights" or "coulds." Go deeper, get more specific. You can use the insights coming out of exercises like these more effectively by taking time out to apply them to a few real projects or initiatives you and your colleagues are working on back at the office, plant or job site.

Whatever you do in the name of relationship building you will find it more effective if you link it to the real work that is the focus of most high-achievers' attention.

What's Trust Got to Do with It?

The conversations and exercises I have just described are the key to unlocking collaboration in groups of achievement-focused individuals. If you have spent any time thinking about or working with teams and teamwork, the topic of trust is bound to have cropped up. "What role," you might ask, "does trust play in creating and sustaining productive relationships and teams?" It has a role to play, but it's not what most people think it is.

Plenty of smart people whose books I have on my shelves talk about the importance of trust in teams and how essential trust is to collaboration. I've taken and even led courses that focus on building trust in teams. Some team models even have the word "trust" built right into them. Yet, after more than 20 years of working with teams and their issues, I can't help but feel that we're getting it wrong when it comes to trust in teams.

If dissing the Four Stages wasn't enough, this doubting of the accepted wisdom on trust is flat-out heresy. Hear me out. I'm not saying trust isn't important. Trust is important. All of those contracting conversations I've described and the performance management conversations that have to take place have a trust element to them. All I'm suggesting is that we aren't thinking about trust in the context of teams and collaboration as productively as we could.

Before reaching this conclusion, there were a few questions that I needed to answer for myself about trust.

- What is trust, anyway? What do people mean by the word?
- Why does it so often appear as a problem in groups?
- What can we do, really do, about low trust in a group?

Many teams and their consultants jump into trust-building exercises with a certainty that suggests they know the answers to these questions. I don't know about you, but trust-building exercises have consistently disappointed me. I've been blindfolded and made to lie on my back for deep conversations, dropped backwards into the arms of strangers and teammates, crossed a rushing brook walking on a length of rope stretched between two trees, and more. These experiences have been fascinating, amusing, even nervous-making, but they never seemed to shift the needle on trust.

Having long pondered these questions and experimented with techniques in an attempt to understand the role of trust in teams, I want to make the following provocative proposition:

> When it comes to team effectiveness, trust is never really the problem and trust-building exercises are never the answer.

You may disagree, maybe strongly. I'd like you to hang with me so that you can understand how I reached this conclusion. I'm going to walk you through a reasoning process that I spent a few years on. It will make clear how I arrived at my contrarian views on trust. It involves several steps that we'll take one at a time. It begins with trust and it ends with courage.

What is trust?

Let's tackle my first question: What is trust, anyway? "Trust," like "team," is a word that gets tossed around pretty freely. Agreeing to what we mean by trust is therefore important. Back to those books on my shelves. There are a number of folks who have written well and convincingly on the subject of trust—Stephen Covey[1] (father *and* son) and Patrick Lencioni[3] to name just a few. Both Stephen M. R. Covey[2] (the younger) and Lencioni describe trust as a feeling of confidence, and I agree; it's about feeling a sense of certainty, security, and safety. For me, though, the key was being reminded that trust is a feeling, first and foremost. I think many of us forget this. I start there.

Like all feelings, trust is an internal condition, both mental and emotional, and ultimately under the control of the "feeler." Trust, because it's a feeling, is not and cannot be under the control of the object ("feel-ee" just doesn't work) of those feelings. That is to say, no matter what you do or say, my feelings of trust towards you are mine and mine alone. We don't act that way, though. Too often we pin our feelings on others. This phenomenon is addressed in couples' therapy. It is applicable here for obvious reasons. For instance, when I say something like, "John, you make me so angry," I'm placing responsibility for my anger on John—he "makes me" feel a certain way. Of course he doesn't. The truth is that I feel anger towards John based on how I interpret and react to John's words or actions. I call this an "error of ownership." It's this error that so complicates trust in relationships and teams. If I'm feeling angry at John and blaming him for my anger, I make ending my anger his responsibility. I'll keep waiting for John to do something differently to change my anger into something else. Not reasonable, but it happens.

The same holds true for how we deal with our feelings of trust. If I don't trust you, I'll tend to make my feelings your responsibility; I hold you to be the cause. When this happens, we end up at an impasse while I wait for you, the source of this trust problem, to make the first move. If trust is a feeling, within me and my psyche, why would I do this? It's nonsensical. What's more, I may tell others on my team that I don't trust you. At least some percentage of the time, they'll say to themselves, "Hmm, I wonder what it is about that guy that makes him untrustworthy?" It's as if when it comes to the feeling of trust, we readily surrender control of our mental and emotional processes to others. As I say, this happens with other feelings such as anger and frustration. Rarely, though, do teams ask for anger workshops. Those are for individuals. They ask for trust-building workshops. I think this happens because most of us don't think of trust as a feeling. Trust is this ethereal thing that either exists or doesn't exist between people. It can be conjured by good acts, honesty, and reliability. Or it can evaporate just like that when we do something thoughtless, and be hard to reinstate. Honestly, we're overcomplicating it. As soon as we embrace trust as a feeling, things get easier. Even with that, trust isn't the problem.

It's not a trust problem. It's a distrust problem

I was working with a client team, conducting data-gathering interviews prior to a team effectiveness session. During one of the interviews one of the team members said to me, "I think we have a trust problem. I can't be sure of anyone's true motives on this team so I have to watch what I say." I have heard these same words repeatedly from my clients: "We have a trust problem." Since when is trust a problem? The truth is that statements like this describe feelings or an atmosphere of *distrust*. This shift to talking about distrust (or mistrust) isn't pure semantics. When it comes to feelings, if we're going to do anything productive about or with them, we have to describe them accurately. What we're talking about when people say they're having a trust problem is, in fact, a problem with feelings of distrust. Now that we've cleared that up, let's take the next step.

From distrust to fear

The conversation about the "trust problems" was part of an ongoing engagement with the leadership team of one of Mars's developing businesses. It was a relatively small team—only six people—and they had been leading through a tough business turnaround. They had made progress during our time working together as both a business and as a team. In terms of their effectiveness with one another, though, they had hit a wall; trust was low, distrust was seething, conflict was going underground, and tensions among them were higher than I had hoped or expected. No one, including me, knew how to break this logjam.

During another pre-session interview, this time with the team leader, it suddenly occurred to me that distrust wasn't the problem, either. Distrust was only the symptom of deeper, more elemental feelings which were causing the problem. The team's distrust, it suddenly seemed obvious, was born out of fear.

I don't know many people where I work who would readily admit to feeling fear. Recall the trust-associated words I described earlier—certainty, security, and safety. What are their opposites? Uncertainty, insecurity, and danger. How do most people respond to these things? With some measure of fear, even if it's at a low level. Businesses are full of things that create uncertainty and insecurity. So, there is no shame in feeling fear. In fact, for me and the team I was working with, it was actually good news. We didn't have a trust problem or even a distrust problem. We were dealing with fear. I found this to be a useful place to begin our work.

From fear to courage

Knowing that fear is the issue can be good news because once we acknowledge this common emotion, a response becomes clear. It's a response that isn't easy, but it's more available than we may think it is. What's more, this response is valuable, praiseworthy and worth developing: It's courage. Courage is something all of us could do with more of, personally and in those around us. Each of us already has it even if we don't know it. Dealing with fear at work, which is a comparatively benign environment, gives us a chance to develop and express this simple, awesomely noble attribute.

My wife likes to say that "fear" is an acronym for "False Evidence Appearing Real." In my work with teams I have found that almost without exception team members are responsible, caring, ethical, and results-oriented people; people I would feel good about trusting. There may be some people I don't like, but they aren't people I ought to fear. I wonder when I encounter a team that self-diagnoses with trust/distrust/fear issues, "Why would you fear each other? The reality is you work at a great company full of great people."

On teams where we tackle mistrust head on, I find that the underlying fears are indeed based on false assumptions, stories team members have about each other that don't reflect reality. The next session with this leadership team was built around the idea of summoning the courage to have a couple of what had felt like scary conversations. I began by teeing up the idea of trust and distrust as feelings. I then asked them to look around the conference room table, to think about conversations that they had been avoiding with their colleagues. I invited them to think about what it was they feared, very specifically: What did you imagine was going to happen? When? What would be said? How would you feel then? There was some pushback. "I wouldn't say I was afraid. Worried, maybe." We agreed that worry and concern were low-level versions of fear, and moved on. The next question was, "What is the likelihood that your fear will become a reality?" I knew these people pretty well by this time. They were rational and kind. They'd give each other the benefit of the doubt when considering my questions. Often, just this series of questions gets team members to realize that much of their fear is, frankly, unrealistic. But not always. The next step was to ask them, either alone or working with a trusted partner, to think about ways to protect themselves against the risk of what they feared. This sort of planning can often bring team members around to feeling more capable than they might have thought they were at first. It begins to summon their innate courage—the necessary ingredient to break the logjam in a fear-laden group. To a person, this reframing helped team members to feel comfortable enough to be willing to at least try to have those very conversations. I set them off into a series of structured one-on-one dialogs with each other. Some of those conversations worked better than others. All of them generated some progress in their relationships. None did any damage.

When someone comes to you with concerns about trust issues, reframe the problem. Think of trust as the outcome of dealing with the fear or fears that are present in a team. Ask yourself what you can do to help people find, build, and sustain their courage.

Courage doesn't always roar. Sometimes courage is the little voice at the end of the day that says, "I'll try again tomorrow."
—Mary Anne Radmacher, author and artist

Who is it that you need to trust?

Courage, I had to remind this team and others, doesn't mean acting without fear. It means acting in spite of our fears. It means doing what, in your heart-of-hearts, you know needs to be done, saying what needs to be said. What I take out of all of this is that how much I trust others doesn't matter. What matters is how much I am ready to trust myself. This is the heart of courage.

What is it that I worry about when I ponder that awkward conversation I need to have with a teammate? I worry about how they will react and—most importantly—I worry about how I might deal with their reaction. That's the most relevant fear, the fear of not being able to handle the other person's reaction in sound and productive ways. If you trust in your personal sense of right and wrong, your experience, and even your innate if not-always-obvious courage, then how much you trust others becomes less of an issue. You can handle it.

If you don't trust yourself, find someone who does trust you. Have a conversation with them about why they have confidence and faith in you. Invite them to help you reveal your most courageous self. Either way, here's the truth: a significant proportion of the time, when you take the risk, when you muster the courage and extend trust—Patrick Lencioni calls this a "willingness to be vulnerable"—the other person returns a corresponding level of courage and trust. What could be more inspiring, more humanly beautiful, and more productive than two people stepping into their courage together?

Where it appears that distrust and fear are the problem, think again. What's needed is a call to the courage that each of us has but many have forgotten. Courage comes from the Latin word *cor* for "heart." You have one. Every member of your team has one. What can you do to en-courage yourself and those on your team?

Fear, distrust and dysfunction

In Chapters 3 and 4 I talked about my belief that true team dysfunction is rare. When I do encounter the real thing it always involves fear and distrust. The causes of the fear and distrust vary. The two primary sources of fear and distrust are organizational dysfunction and misguided individual team members, sometimes in combination.

As I suggested in the earlier chapters, in a dysfunctional organization where fear predominates, groups within the organization usually reflect that dysfunction. It's tough for a group to escape the influence of the organization it's a part of. With the right leader and willing team members, however, teams can create a climate of their own that shields them from the broader cultural problems of the organization. Our Framework can help in these cases. When a team digs deeply into its purpose and identifies compelling reasons to work together, it creates a sense of meaning and aspiration that may be absent in the enterprise around them. The work I have been describing on creating accountable collaborative relationships shores up team members' sense of belonging and mattering. I won't say that our Framework can change dysfunctional organizations. It can make working in one less toxic and more rewarding.

The other driver of fear and mistrust is individuals whose behavior others find unsettling, even frightening. We'd call these people untrustworthy or sometimes dangerous. The Finance team I used as an example in Chapter 4 was led by a gentleman whose management techniques were perceived as manipulative and political. They were. This man was creating a toxic work environment, leading by the explicit use of fear. He ended up being let go, thank goodness. Thanks, too, to the courageous and persistent team members who called out his behavior repeatedly.

Bad leaders aren't the only ones who can infuse a team with fear. In another troubled group I worked with, the leader was one of the kindest guys I've ever known. He was also in completely over his head. He had been promoted into a factory manager role as a developmental move. Either he wasn't ready, or he wasn't given the right kind of support and coaching, or both. In any case, the team around him interpreted his efforts at managing them as meant to demean and belittle them. For instance, he assigned the same piece of work to two people at two different times. He had been expecting them to work together. He hadn't made this clear, however. Each of them thought he was playing them off the other, making them compete for his approval. He had meant to create a collaborative opportunity. His ham-fisted approach had them believing he was operating from a place of negative intent. Based on my interviews with him, his team, and his peers, he was well intentioned but failing. His team couldn't make sense of his actions, became afraid, and out of fear assumed he was out to get them. Their distrust and the apparent dysfunction of the team was all coming, ironically, from a good heart. The road to fear, like the road to teaminess, is paved with good intentions.

By the time I arrived on the scene with this team, the fear and distrust were so intense that they remained silent. I found it necessary to break them into small groups, not including the manager, where they could muster the courage to speak. I asked the team leader to privately review the data I had compiled while I worked with each of the groups. Finally, I got to spend time one-on-one with the leader. I shared with him what I had discovered both prior to the workshop and in my conversations with the small groups that morning. He was shocked, embarrassed, and anxious about trying to make things right. We ended up scrapping the team workshop. We later explained this to the team, while thanking them for their bravery and patience. I explained that it was their honesty and willingness to risk speaking that made this course correction possible. I spent the rest of my time with the leader and his P&O partner figuring out how we could get him the developmental support he needed. Only then did we discuss possible next steps for his team.

Once again we come back to the need for courageous choices and actions to break the impasse. We come back to you, your trust in yourself, your beliefs or fears about yourself in difficult, potentially conflict-laden situations. Can you identify your limiting beliefs and set them aside? Even if you fear you can't, remember it's likely that the moment you extend yourself to another in courage and trust, he or she will reciprocate with equal levels of both.

Christopher Avery co-authored a terrific book about teams and teamwork titled *Teamwork Is an Individual Skill*.[4] He asserts that one key to successful collaborative relationships is acting as if, in all relationships, you're 100% responsible for the success and health of the relationship. Of course, you aren't. If you act as if you are, though, if you step into the difficult, possibly fear-laden conversations with a sense of personal accountability, things will happen. The relationship will move, become unstuck. More often than not, your colleagues will meet you halfway, matching your courage and sense of responsibility. It may seem counterintuitive, but developing your feelings of trust in others begins with you having the courage to trust yourself.

Let's ground this in the basics for a moment. Teams are full of achievement-driven individuals. They crave getting stuff done. Through your work on Cultivating Collaboration, after all the conversations, you will have woven an intricate web of committed collaborative relationships. Whether working with the total team on projects you all share, or working in sub-groups, your intentionality and productivity will depend on your willingness to be courageous with each other. Without the essential element of courage, relationships will stall and the work will suffer. With it, the sky's the limit. Nothing is more likely to delight and engage an achievement-driven team member.

In the next chapter, we'll move from Intentionality and the quality of working relationships within the team into the Discipline Imperative. Activate Ways-of-Working, the first of two Practices that address Discipline, is about how the entire team will operate, including meetings and making decisions.

Summary

- The Intentionality Imperative comes to life in the Practice Cultivate Collaboration.
- This practice builds on the Clarity created through the work on the preceding two Practices, Inspire Purpose and Crystallize Intent.
- Cultivate Collaboration involves contracting between the leader and the team, and among team members, to create accountability for collaborative behaviors.
- With collaborative agreements in place, team members explore how their personalities and preferences may affect their relationships and the work they will do together.
- When and if trust appears to be waning, team members find ways to encourage each other to have the necessary conversations to keep their collaboration vital and thriving.

Chapter 11

Discipline and Activate Ways-of-Working

One of the first jobs I was assigned when I joined Mars in late 2000 was to work with a Sales team. The leader told me, "We just need to work on our ways-of-working." For starters, what the heck was a "way-of-working"? In all my previous experience I'd never heard the term used. Ways-of-working, it turns out, was more than the norms or ground rules so common among teams. It was what I would have called back then "team processes." Ways-of-working consisted of things like meetings, decision making, and communications. Ways-of-working are the operational cogs that keep a team clicking along.

In my brief exchange with that leader I was also struck by her use of the word "just." She was saying, "This is simple. The only thing we need to do is to clarify our ways-of-working and most of our problems (whatever they might have been) will go away." The consultant in me felt the need for some diagnostics. At that time Mars wasn't committed to a specific team methodology and I didn't know which of the many approaches they might have been using. Unsure how to proceed, I asked a couple of my new colleagues. Their advice was to go ahead and help this leader with her request, as presented. No further diagnosis required. They felt that I needed to develop a few working relationships and this would be a good start. That was almost 16 years ago. I don't recall what happened in my work with that team. What stuck with me was that term, "ways-of-working," and how this culture viewed it as a primary solution for troubled teams. People all over Mars used the expression. That's how those words ended up in the name of this Practice. Including "ways-of-working" in the name of this Practice made it feel immediately familiar to Mars Associates. The way we apply this notion in the

Framework, though, is different from what most Mars Associates had been used to. The difference, which I'll discuss in a minute, is suggested in the word "activate" and it has to do with how this Practice is connected to the other Practices.

In this chapter I deal with two ways-of-working in teams: meetings and decision making. I could have chosen to include more. These two ways-of-working, however, are two that most clearly benefit from the Framework and the thinking that underlies it. I'll cover others in a future book.

Both meetings and decision making have been studied and written about at length. You can download terabytes—maybe even gigaflops (I love that word)—of information on these two disciplines. That's why I'm not going to give you any prescriptions on how to meet or ways to decide. As many teams at Mars have learned, nicely defined ways of working in and of themselves don't lead to higher performance collaboration. If a team doesn't know why their work matters and what they ought to be meeting about and deciding on, processes don't help. Instead, I'll focus this chapter on how to use the preceding Practices to make both meeting and deciding more effective. I'll also spend time on the behaviors that are required for both. To begin, it's worth reviewing the basics of this Practice: what it is, what it isn't, and how it's meant to function.

The Basics

How it compares to Cultivate Collaboration

The previous Practice, Cultivate Collaboration, addresses how team members will work together. So, what's the difference between that Practice and this one? It's a common question at Mars. The short answer is: One is more about tasks and relationships, the other about processes and team rhythm.

Cultivate Collaboration emphasizes accountability for collaboration. It's focused on the individuals within the team and the specific tasks that they have agreed to share with their colleagues. Remember our three interdependent dynamics? Cultivate Collaboration is about aligning

- the work
- the people
- their relationships.

Activate Ways-of-Working, on the other hand, focuses on processes and routines that the entire team develops and signs up for.

The Radar Screen offers another way to make a distinction between the two. Cultivate Collaboration, with its focus on relationships and collaborative behaviors, draws from and affects all three rings of the Radar Screen. Activate Ways-of-Working, by comparison, deals exclusively with the center of the Radar Screen.

Activate Ways-of-Working seeks to help teams establish a flow and a cadence for their collaborative work through agreed-

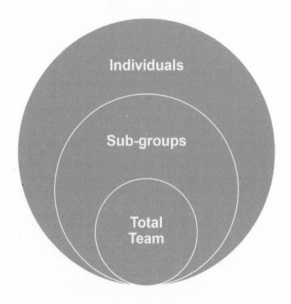

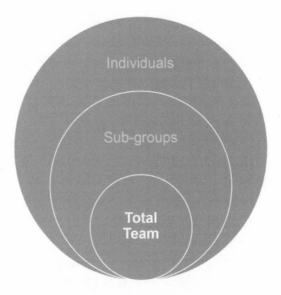

upon processes and protocols. The goal is to establish a set of routines and a healthy team operating cadence aligned with and supporting your inspiring purpose and shared work. In other words, your ways-of-working are created in ways that make them consistent with the rest of the Practices in the Framework. Outputs from this Practice include things like:

- Determining the frequency of team meetings
- Re-usable meeting templates
- An agreed set of decision-making approaches
- Templates to help frame and evaluate decisions.

Having consistent and aligned processes frees up the intellect and creativity within your team for the non-standard, often most exciting, challenges that always come along and that make teamwork so rewarding.

How it works

I noticed in the years that followed that early Sales team workshop, how often teams were self-diagnosing as having ways-of-working problems. Most of them were wrong. When I get this request—which I still do—I'm tempted to send the team a ready-made list of ground rules that they can choose from and leave it at that. Below is a selection from a much longer list of ground rules that was given to me by a facilitator friend. I used to offer this list to teams, back before I knew better:

- Treat the work seriously but don't take ourselves too seriously.
- Share the air(time).
- Challenge thinking, not people.
- Risk sharing your dreams.
- Be forthcoming about thoughts and ideas.
- Make the conversation as real as possible.
- Respect others' viewpoints.
- No finger pointing.
- Everything said here stays here.

Perhaps a bit hackneyed, but all good, right? As I said in the previous chapter, our Framework isn't about generic lists of potentially helpful, generic concepts or behaviors. If lists like this help at all, they don't help for long. When I get the ways-of-working request today, instead of sending my ready-made list, I pose a few questions. For instance, I might start with:

Me: Has your team agreed to its purpose, its reason for collaboration, beyond the sum of everyone's individual contributions?

This person might say:

Them: Do you mean do we have a vision or mission statement? Sure. We worked on that a few years ago.
Me: Not quite what I meant, but OK. Can you tell me what

your vision or mission is, off the top of your head? And how do you use it to generate effective collaboration?

By this time, I'm getting a blank stare. I then back things up and talk about our particular definition of team purpose, and why defining the shared work of the group is important. This is all to make the point that if you haven't clarified

- Why you're collaborating
- What work actually requires collaboration
- Who needs specifically to collaborate with whom

then all the norms or ground rules in the world won't do you a lick of good. Discipline that's not grounded in Clarity and Intentionality will crumble. Yes, your team may indeed need ways-of-working. Rarely, though, is the absence of them the root of a team's problems. Putting ways-of-working in place by layering new team processes over a flawed foundation for collaboration is akin to putting a shiny new coat of paint on an old car whose mechanical and electrical systems aren't sound. On the surface things may seem solid, but the thing will never run as well as it should. You want to begin with the most fundamental things if you really want to make a difference to your collaboration.

My first suggestion to teams that are struggling with meetings or how they decide or other ways-of-working is this: Begin with the first three Practices: Inspire Purpose, Crystallize Intent, and Cultivate Collaboration. Align your ways-of-working with the work done in the other Practices to "activate" and bring your ways-of-working to life. Connecting your team's processes to your collaborative purpose and your shared work is how you tap into that achievement drive I've talked so much about. Suddenly routines aren't just routines. They have a meaning and a valuable reason for being.

It's the same for individuals, by the way. If we have a purpose for what we're doing, and an intent, things become a lot easier. For instance, I've been meditating on and off for years. For a guy who likes to stay busy, nothing's harder than sitting still, seemingly doing nothing for 20 or 30 minutes. When I started, I experienced a lot of mental resistance to just being still and doing what I knew was good for me. I also suffer from a minor but annoying neurological disorder called benign fasciculation syndrome. Small muscles twitch at random intervals and at random places all over my body. It comes and it goes and it moves around. For months I'll experience very little. Other times it's almost unbearable. It turns out that meditation helps. It doesn't cure it, but it reduces the symptoms and, as importantly, my emotional reactions to them. So now that I have a clearer purpose and intent, the work of meditation is less problematic. Thanks to my disorder, meditation has become very easy for me. It has a clear and immediate payoff. I'm still not fully habituated to meditation. I'm way better than I was, though, because this routine now has a clear benefit for me.

I'm a typical Mars Associate in many ways, especially in my need to be active. Mars is full of individuals who cherish the company's action-oriented culture. Like me, they don't have much patience for routine and, dare I say it, Discipline. If you want a Mars Associate to accept a routine, to embrace a process, it had better be clearly relevant to them and their work. The "Why" and the "What" have to be crystal clear. That's what we aim to create in Activate Ways-of-Working.

Discipline—Forming new team habits

For collaboration to flourish, it has to feel relevant and important to the individuals involved. When it does, it will speak directly to the individual achievement need I've talked so much about. The same holds true for meetings and other team processes; if they don't feel germane and significant to team members, you'll have a hard time getting and keeping folks engaged.

By attending to the first two Imperatives, Clarity and Intentionality, and the Practices associated with them, you will have addressed the twin issues of relevance and importance. Now you want to apply the "Why," "What," and "Who" that were the outcomes of that work to your team's ways-of-working. As one member of a team I was working with said to me, "This team ways-of-working stuff is really about forming new habits, isn't it?" It's never been better said. As I discussed in Chapter 6 where I first talked about Intentionality, forming new habits is hard. Ask anyone who has ever tried to change their eating habits, started an exercise routine, or, say, made a New Year's resolution to meditate regularly. Success can be elusive. Taking new habits on board is challenging enough. It's even tougher because new habits don't occupy previously unused portions of your mind or time. They're always displacing or replacing some other way of being, of doing, of spending your hours. Take my developing habit of getting up every morning at 5:30 to perform some simple yoga and then meditate. My old habit of snuggling under the cozy covers and stroking the cat who's showed up to be petted has been getting in the way. I happen to enjoy that old habit. So does Carson, our little ginger cat. Letting go of that behavior/indulgence and replacing it with a few sun salutations and 30 minutes of meditation is no mean feat even when I'm feeling motivated by twitching foot muscles.

To further complicate things, breaking group habits is harder than breaking individual ones. We're dealing with the collective behaviors of several diverse individuals, each one with his or her own set of values, beliefs, interests and degree of personal discipline. Breaking habits involves unlearning and then relearning. For some of us, learning is easy, even fun. Unlearning's the drag. What's more, the more successful a group has been — especially if that success was based on individual effort and achievement — the harder it will be to break your group's habits. "If it ain't broke, don't fix it," is what you're likely to hear. It's not about fixing what's broken. This is all about taking collaboration to the next level, about not settling for "good enough" and instead going for greatness.

Fortunately, as with meetings and decision making, a lot's been written on this subject of changing habits. From magazines at the grocery store check-out line to business books, podcasts and PhD theses, you'll find a wide range of views on the subject. While most of what I've read deals with individuals, the same wisdom and techniques can apply to groups. Here is a short list of tips that I share with teams when it comes to the discipline of forming new, better team habits:

Know what you're about. Start with a clear and inspiring purpose as well as crystallized understanding of how your collaboration will bring your purpose to life. New habits infused with a sense of purpose and meaning stand a better chance of taking.

Start with what you have. Examine what your team is doing today. Does it support your purpose and shared intent? With your purpose clear and shared work mapped, turn a critical eye towards every routine and process the team has in place today and question them. Adjust as needed.

Start small. Once you've identified a list of the current ways-of-working that are serving you, and which aren't, start with just one habit to unlearn and replace. Keep your longer list handy so that as you progress you can move on to your next challenge.

Keep it simple. The new processes and habits you're introducing ought to be as simple as possible. We all have enough to think about without trying to implement complex new routines.

Plan for gradual progress. Don't expect to change your team's habits in a week or even a month. Have the discipline to be patient.

Be willing to experiment. Not everything that you try will work. Remember that even when your attempts fail, there is something to be learned, as a story I'll tell about my team will illustrate.

Reward yourselves for success. Don't just rush on to the next habit on your list. Take time to recognize that your efforts have paid off, even in small ways.

Turn developing new habits into a habit. Developing new habits is a skill that can be learned. Given the speed of change in the working world today, becoming agile at group change may be the ultimate team competence. We'll explore this more when we talk about team learning in the next chapter.

Putting the Practice to Work, Part 1: Meetings That Matter

Jon Petz wrote a great book with an even better title. *Boring Meetings Suck: Get More Out of Your Meetings and Get Out of More Meetings*[1] is a worthwhile read. Boring meetings do suck. When you bring a group together, you want to have everyone engaged and interested, getting as much as they give. The way to do that is to make your meetings about real work with tangible outcomes that align to your team's shared purpose and work.

Once more recall that team meeting I described in Chapter 2. There were about 13 people in a darkened room, only three of whom were engaged in the conversation. Everyone else was on their phones or computers. The meeting truly sucked because it was a waste of most people's time and the company's resources. Meetings, as I have already said, are costly. If you're going to invest time and energy in a meeting, make sure it does what good collaboration does and creates value at three levels: the individual attendees perceive value, the group and its dynamic get a boost, and the business sees benefits. First of all, 13 people is way too many for most meetings to be productive. Then, if 10 of 13 people are disengaged and otherwise occupied, I can guarantee that your meeting is eroding more value than it's creating. Your team meeting agendas are best and create the greatest benefit when they focus first on the work that you have all agreed you share. That comes from the center of your completed Radar Screen.

The internal consulting team I'm a part of at Mars only had a few things at the center of our Radar Screen. One was a project dealing with building change management and organization development capabilities for Mars, Incorporated. The other, less tangible one we called "hothousing." The idea of hothousing came from our team purpose where we declared we were "the hothouse for organizational health." Hothousing, as we define it, involves thinking together to tackle the tough problems that come up as part of our roles as internal corporate consultants. One of us raises a red flag, and we form into the "hothouse." We focus all our creative energies on the specific topic that one of us is wrestling with.

Focusing on these two, one a project, the other more of a team role, was intended to form the core of our team meetings. That,

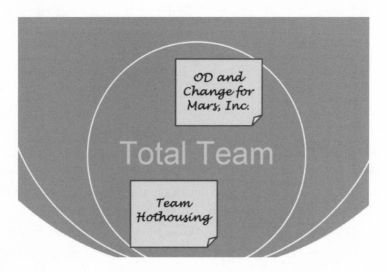

at least, was the new habit that we meant to form. One recent meeting illustrates why, even with the clarity we had, that's hard.

Our team is spread out on two sides of the Atlantic and in several locales. We've been using a desktop video app for our meetings. It's one of many so-called "collaboration technologies." It's a terrific tool and has made staying connected easier and richer than, say, teleconferencing. What it can't do is keep us from falling into the same old unproductive habits that we're used to in our face-to-face meetings. We'd done a nice job setting up this meeting, as we usually do. We only meet every couple of months, so one of our standing agenda items involves discussing what each of us has been up to. Prior to the meeting each of the six of us created summaries of what we'd been working on. These updates were posted to a shared document on our corporate network visible only to us. The idea was that before our meeting we'd review each other's updates. We'd use our precious time together in the video meeting to address questions our teammates had about our work. No reading out of the summaries, no repeating what everyone already knew based on our pre-meeting work. We had a total of three hours to meet. We allocated about a third of that for the Q&A on our projects. The rest of the time was to be dedicated to work the entire team shared, that is, the two pieces of work at the center of the Radar Screen. What did we do? We acted almost as if we'd never done the pre-meeting summaries, talking our colleagues through our summaries and embellishing what was written with anecdotes and additional detail. A mind-numbing exercise, unless you were the one doing the talking. Before we knew it, we were running out of time. We all regard each other highly. We like each other. So much so that no one was willing to speak up and call out what we all saw happening. The minutes just kept slipping away. Eventually someone called out the problem and we got back to our agenda, albeit with little time remaining for the rest of our agenda including our Radar Screen work.

Our meeting bombed because we'd lost sight of our team's purpose and shared intent. One big problem was that our Radar Screen didn't reflect reality. Only a few of us were actually working on the Organization Development and Change project at the center. It wasn't efficient or effective to include us all, despite our genuine desire to contribute. The only work we should share, we realized, was the practice of hothousing. Even that role, though, we had somehow failed to cover that day. Our behaviors and ways-of-working hadn't aligned with the commitments we'd made about our collaboration. Our collaborative purpose, we all agreed, felt right. We had to modify our Radar Screen by moving the OD and Change project to the middle ring of the Radar Screen, to be handled by a subset of us. Hothousing would be all that remained at the center. We then altered our meeting ways-of-working to align with those changes. We revised our standard agenda to ensure that every team gathering, virtual or otherwise, was built around what we had said mattered most to us as a whole. We'd still do a bit of catching up and reconnecting, but most of our time would be devoted to our shared work.

Meeting processes that are connected to a team's collaborative purpose and shared work are far easier to implement and sustain. They'll create more engagement in your team and make you far more productive. At the same time, a meeting is a complex set of human interactions.

To meet or not to meet

Here's a simple rule of thumb: Have a team meeting only if every member of your group or team has something at stake when attending. If your meeting doesn't feel to every person invited like it's creating value for them, like it's worth their limited time, skip it. Find another avenue for getting done what you need done.

Most of the collaborating in a team is done by sub-groups of two or three people. Much of the rest of the work is handled by individuals. These two classes of work, you'll remember, make up the outer two rings of the Radar Screen. Together they represent work that often does *not* require team meetings. Sub-groups meet whenever they need to, to advance the work they share. I don't think of these as meetings, though. I consider them working sessions. Even working sessions aren't always necessary. For small groups, a lot of collaboration can happen without them. They can do this by working asynchronously. The example I gave earlier of our team members adding to a shared document stored on our network was an example of asynchronous collaboration and co-creation. All of us had access to that document at any time of day or night. My colleague Damian might add his input at 9 in the morning UK time on Wednesday. That's 4 a.m. for me on the east coast of the USA. By the time I got around to adding my summary to the document, it was 4 p.m. EST two days later. That would have been 9 p.m. UK time on a Friday night. We each did our bit for the team, in a time and fashion that worked for us as individuals. Sure, we didn't use the outputs as intended. Nonetheless, this is a wonderful option for a team with members who are either in different time zones or who work different shifts.

Meet only when and if your meeting aligns with the team's shared purpose and the work at the center of your Radar Screen. This ensures that what happens at your meetings will feel important to every attendee. If the work doesn't meet these criteria, find other ways to get it done. This is how you'll ensure that when you do get together, team members will feel the meeting was worth it and you'll get the best from everyone. You will have provided them with an experience that feeds and satisfies their individual need to achieve and, therefore, achieves what you intend for the entire group.

Meeting beyond the Radar Screen

Lest we forget, what we're talking about here are team level ways-of-working. Sub-groups will have agreed their ways-of working in Cultivate Collaboration. In some teams all the project work happens in the outer two rings—there are no honest-to-goodness projects or initiatives in the center of our Radar Screen. These groups are still "real teams," by the way. My team has a "role" at the center of our Radar Screen, but no projects. We still meet every two months. Why? For one, we have our hothousing to do. Even if we didn't have that, I'd recommend that we meet. While the Radar Screen tells us what specific projects or initiatives may require full team meetings, it doesn't tell us what else may be important to keeping our little piece of the business running.

There are five things that are worth meeting, face-to-face or virtually, to do:

- Co-creating things like plans, recommendations and solutions
- Making decisions where the entire team is involved
- Celebration and recognition of team members and the work we do together
- Intentionally (as opposed to casually) deepening relationships across the entire team
- Group learning—more on this in the chapter on Sustain & Renew

The first two are related to the center of the Radar Screen. If there's work there, you'll end up co-creating and deciding as a team. Our team, for instance, has agreed that from now on, our regular meetings will be mostly about co-creating solutions with each other—hothousing. A few weeks before our scheduled meeting we will open up our shared document for ideas about what needs hothousing. We'll reach consensus, virtually, about which opportunity seems most valuable to address. We will then build that into our agenda.

The other three reasons to meet, if approached thoughtfully, will create benefits for everyone attending, to the team as a whole and by extension to the business. Celebrating success is vital to building and sustaining energy in a team. You don't need a meeting to do this, by the way. Group emails work; social media does, too. Adding an agenda item to all your meetings that is focused on affirming what's gone well will generate learning and energy—not teaminess but the right sort of team spirit. I talked in the last chapter about relationship building. When done with Clarity and Intentionality, and connected to the work of the team, it's something every team member will value. Golf outings and community volunteering are worthwhile but not nearly as effective when it comes to strengthening collaboration.

The fifth valid reason to meet is to learn together. In a team that is paying attention to itself, that stays mindful of how it's operating, team learning can and does happen as a total group. It even happens during meetings. Whether conducting a full-group After-Action Review of a project, or taking a few minutes after a meeting to check in on your team dynamics, you're engaging in group learning. Setting aside time to specifically tackle your group's learning and team development is essential. I'll say more about team learning in the next chapter. For now, make sure they become part of your team's ways-of-working. They ought to be on your calendar at least a few times a year. At Mars, our research demonstrated that teams' greatest deficit was in being aware of their own dynamic and consciously working on it. That's why we have a Practice—Sustain & Renew—that is focused on just this Discipline. Chapter 13 addresses Sustain & Renew.

There may be five valid reasons for teams to meet. There are all sorts of reasons for meeting that are less valid, less likely to create value for individuals, the team and your business. This is why the titles of books about meetings contain words like "Suck" and "Death." For instance, meeting just because you haven't met for a while is one lame reason to meet. Socializing is useful and fun. How about a rousing game of Cards Against Humanity? Then, have a few drinks together and catch up. Reconnect. That's all good. But don't convene a meeting primarily to socialize, not if what you're trying to do is to stoke collaboration. Remember, familiarity, while it can support collaborative relationships, doesn't usually make it better. If what you're getting together for doesn't involve the work at the center of your trusty Radar Screen and it doesn't align with your purpose, find another way.

There's another massively time-wasting reason for meeting that is a pet peeve of mine. It's mentioned in some of the fine books about meetings and it deserves restating here. Never, ever, ever in a million years use meetings for sharing information. Ever. Not in a zillion years, even. Not even if that information is related to your purpose and your shared work. Here's why: People truly are your company's most valuable assets, even if many of those who say it don't act that way. Each individual is precious. A room full of preciousness deserves to be treated accordingly. Talking at a room full of intelligent adults, dulling their minds with even the most inventive and seemingly relevant PowerPoint® decks, is an insult to their capabilities and a waste of everyone's time. Instead, send out content before meetings in emails, as booklets, as videos. At Mars we call this pre-work. Get folks reading it or watching it and thinking it over. Have them answer a few questions about it and submit their thinking before the meeting. Then use your valuable time together to discuss, debate, explore, examine, question, and query. When you're all together, do only those things that create value for everyone and for the entire group. Following the five reasons I cited above, meet to do things like planning the coming year, celebrating project milestones and working together to navigate difficult, near-term challenges (our hothousing role). Refer back to your purpose. Anchor your agenda in the center of your Radar Screen. Be sure it's linked to real business needs that your team feels immediately connected to, and your meetings will be worthwhile and engaging.

How often to meet

Meet as a full group only as often as your purpose and shared work require it. On complex, rapidly evolving projects that involve an entire team, you may want to meet every week and perhaps check in every day. I've seen several project teams working on urgent issues operate this way. Earlier in the book, I talked about a Finance team that realized the core of its purpose had to do with developing talent to ensure a healthy Finance function for the future. Based on this they stopped meeting every 28 days, a schedule that had been predicated on sharing information about company operations. Instead they agreed to meet only every two months. That was the right frequency for talking talent among themselves. In doing this they gave themselves back a full two days every other month to do the work in the rest of the Radar Screen. It may not sound like much, but they were thrilled. They could give themselves the gift of time because they understood their collaborative purpose and shared intent. In Appendix D I offer additional advice on how to think about meeting frequency and timing.

In short, if your purpose and shared work require meeting less frequently, do what you have to, to stay connected. As I suggested above, you don't need meetings. More and more, corporate social media platforms are helping teams to stay connected. Plan some social events that don't include work. Again, don't imagine that you're creating a more effective team by playing together. Sure, you'll enhance the climate of your group and that has an indirect, short-term impact on group effectiveness. Team outings, though, are no substitute for implementing and living by the Practices.

Meetings recap

- Meet based on what your purpose and Radar Screen tell you to meet about.
- Meet to do real work. Don't meet based on what's convenient for you, e.g. so that you can share some information more easily or because you don't get to see your team much.
- Meet only if you have decisions to make, need to co-create something, have something to celebrate together, seek to deepen relations across the group, and/or you want or need to learn together.
- Plan and set aside time to address team learning and development, whether you build it into your regular agendas or set time aside specifically for team dynamics work.

Putting the Practice to Work, Part 2: Deciding

Like meetings, decision making is a topic that scads of bright and accomplished people have studied and written about at length. My focus is limited to how the HPC Practices and theory shape decision making and the behaviors and attitudes that support it.

The key is—no surprise here—to align your decision making with your team's inspiring purpose and your Radar Screen. Where your work sits on your Radar Screen is a guide to where decision authority lies. The few projects that end up at the center of your Radar Screen—projects that the entire group has accountability for—will require team-level agreement about how decisions will be made. All other decisions, if you're following the lead of the Radar Screen, belong in the hands of either groups or individuals or small groups. Remember: Activate Ways-of-Working is exclusively concerned with processes that the entire team owns. It's making those decisions most effectively that I'll deal with in this section. Here's a hint—they won't always be consensus decisions.

Ways of deciding

I'm not a fan of consensus. More accurately, I'm not a fan of the way many people misunderstand and misapply consensus. I'm proud to say that the "Consensus Sucks" award was created just for me by the members of my OD Master's degree cohort group about 16 years ago. In the democratic ethos of that program, we were forever trying to reach consensus decisions. It drove me crazy. Despite my frustration with it, however, consensus has its place. Some decisions at the center of the Radar Screen may indeed end up as consensus decisions. There are other decision-making approaches that you're probably already aware of that we need to spend time considering, too.

When it comes to making decisions as a total team—again, the center of the Radar Screen—I've seen four approaches used. All of these are discussed at length, perhaps by different names, by decision-making gurus so I won't go into great detail here. My purpose is to make clear the differences among the ways of deciding so that you can make smart choices.

Consensus—The majority agree to an approach *and* the minority give consent; they agree to go along with the decision, to support it despite their reservations. Different from unanimity.

Pure voting—The approach that garners the most votes, wins. Similar to consensus but different in that those in the minority, the "losers," are typically less invested in the outcome.

Unanimity—A version of pure voting but where all team members must agree for the approach to move forward. Consensus is often confused with unanimity.

Authority-based—The group agrees that one member of the team—an expert or the team leader—will make the final decision based on hearing from everyone in the group in the process.

When it comes to business teams working as a total group, authority-based and consensus decision making work best, in that order. I'll talk about why in a moment. Pure voting can work, but only where the topic being considered is of minor consequence. For instance, a group may choose pure voting in order to decide whether to use their summer outing for paintball or a ropes course. Where the stakes are higher and the support of the minority is required for anything to move ahead, consensus is more effective. It's messier but more likely to ensure you have the support the decision requires. Unanimity is best saved for small groups where reaching it is a realistic possibility. As I mentioned, it's often confused with consensus. More on that in the next section. Authority-based decision making works and works well where any sort of hierarchy is recognized, namely, in most traditional companies. The hierarchy could be based on organizational structure with a boss holding the decision authority. It can also be applied using a hierarchy of knowledge and/or experience, allowing the person with the most information or background to make the decision. It's efficient and, if done right, involves the team in meaningful ways by seeking input, guidance and counsel.

What about my pet peeve, consensus? If you ask a Mars Associate to comment on decision making at Mars, you're likely to hear that Mars is a "consensus culture." I'd say it differently. We're a culture that is most comfortable involving lots of people in decisions. The great thing is that we get a lot of input to the decisions we make, often resulting in quality outcomes. The downside of this propensity for involvement is that decisions can move slowly. Owing to our egalitarian culture, many of us feel we have the right to slow down or even stop a decision-making process if we feel our view hasn't been adequately represented in the process. I've been guilty of this myself. Not long ago our team was hiring. My manager asked for the involvement of his team, including me, in creating the job descriptions. He then went about identifying and interviewing candidates. He involved his manager, P&O, and a few would-be internal clients in the interview process, but didn't include me. That ticked me off. Why wouldn't he include me? After all, I am a seasoned OD professional with a strong background in behavioral interviewing. Besides, these new hires would be my teammates. As it happened he found and hired two wonderful new teammates. When it came time to fill the last slot on our team, though, I voiced my dissatisfaction with his previous hiring process. I pressed hard to be involved the next time, and I was. I felt vindicated, but I must admit that the hiring took far longer and I can't say the outcome was better for it.

I've often seen decisions get made, then recalled and remade if not everyone who thought they should have been involved in the process was. When a Mars Associate derides our consensus culture, this is often what they are referring to. We call it "relitigation." I've seen it at other companies, too. In fact, I heard it said at IBM that "everyone can say 'no,' but no one can say 'yes.'" In a highly matrixed organization—and so many are these days—decision making is going to be complicated.

Let's deal with one other thing that makes consensus problematical. It's the "consensus-unanimity" problem. It's one of the biggest misunderstandings about consensus and it's the one that earned me that "Consensus Sucks" certificate.

"Consens-animity"

When a team claims, even believes, that it's seeking consensus but is, in fact, holding out for unanimity, watch out. They're on the road to "consens-animity," the make-believe land where everyone agrees with everything. It's a lovely, teamy, and misguided approach to deciding. It happens for a few reasons. Sometimes a leader or a vocal team member is overly concerned about disenfranchising the minority. "This project is at the center of our Radar Screen. Everybody has to be on board." If they were seeking consensus, they would acknowledge honest differences and invite the loyal opposition to live with the decision, while showing respect for their views. Instead, extra effort is put into cajoling and convincing resistant team members to go along. All this persuading eats up time. It could also cause the majority who *do* agree to feel that their authority isn't being respected. In the worst cases, any disagreement with an emerging consensus is seen as disloyalty or as a threat to the team's spirit. Think back to my earlier description of team dysfunction driven by an individual. It's the old "are-you-a-team-player-or-aren't-you" dodge. In these cases, certain team members try to "guilt" dissenters into joining the majority on a decision they don't support. Taking their opposition underground, the dissenters end up scuttling the decision in passive-aggressive ways. Regardless of what's behind it, striving for consens-animity over time silences the healthy differences and debate that a group of high-achieving individuals are prone to engage in.

True consensus and authority-based decision making, on the other hand, effectively preserve the diversity of voices in a team. At the same time, these two approaches rely on an expectation that every member will, at some point, need to "take one for the team." We might have to suspend a deeply held conviction or a perspective so that the team can move forward. This brings us back to the Discipline Imperative. There's an underlying set of small-D disciplines that team members need to cultivate to allow this sort of healthy deference to the team to take root.

The essence of team decision-making

If there is work at the center of your Radar Screen, you're bound to be involved in decisions that involve the entire team in some way. I've identified four sub-disciplines or behaviors that are essential for healthy decision making in working groups and teams:

- The discipline of letting others decide, a form of empowerment
- The discipline of deciding how to decide and who decides before it's time to decide
- The discipline of deep listening
- The discipline of letting go then moving on

Decision Making Behaviors

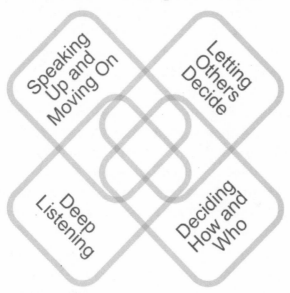

The discipline of letting others decide

Most of the decisions that will take place within your team won't involve the entire team. That's just common sense. Most of the work in the Radar Screen lies in the outer two rings. Therefore, everyone in the team has to be able to allow others to own decisions. Without this, collaboration bogs down and the Framework doesn't deliver full value.

In the earlier chapters I described some of my work with DDI. Empowerment was a major theme of that work at DDI and a big part of DDI's brand. Empowerment involves delegating work and decisions to the people who are closest to them. The term has fallen out of favor and part of me is glad. I never liked the word even when I was working at DDI. It suggested that someone higher up was conferring, out of the goodness of their hearts, power upon someone lower in the pecking order. I used to tell people, strictly off the record, that what was needed was for management to stop *dis*empowering people in the workplace. We all walk through the door with innate gifts and power. Too often we're expected to check our power at the door. What we need isn't empowerment but re-empowerment.

The HPC Framework requires (re-)empowerment. If your team is going to gain efficiencies through the Practices, it's essential. Projects that aren't at the center of your Radar Screen don't require full-group decision making. Where sub-groups are working on a project, the Framework suggests that the sub-groups have the authority to make decisions related to their project. Likewise, where no collaboration is required, where individuals own projects, they independently own decision authority. This isn't to suggest that sub-groups and individuals shouldn't be seeking advice and input from their colleagues or other stakeholders as a part of their decision-making process. Of course they should. The real challenge here, though, is faced by those NOT involved in all these delegated decisions. In the Mars culture where our default is historically set to consensus, it takes willpower to excuse yourself from a decision. We're not the only company that struggles with re-empowerment, though. Nor is this new news. The idea that decision making is most efficient when it's held at the appropriate level has been around since at least the 1950s and the beginnings of the Quality movement. By creating clarity of who owns which work, the Radar Screen helps place decisions where they make the most sense. Sometimes, though, depending on the company and its culture, decisions will still tend to flow up and sometimes out, to a broad audience of stakeholders. This creates enormous decision logjams. If higher-ups need to decide everything, nothing gets done. Even within a team, if every decision gets sent to the leader, or has to be made by the entire team, stagnation is certain. Team members using the Framework have to have the courage to allow decisions to be made as close to the work as possible.

The discipline of deciding how and who

Deciding how to decide and who decides before you decide is another habit that high-performing teams cultivate. It's actually more important to the smooth operation of your team than the final decisions themselves. It involves questions like:

- What decision process will we use? Authority-based? Consensus? Something else?
- If it's authority-based, who owns the decision?
- If it's a consensus decision, which group owns the final call?

The Radar Screen helps here, too. Full teams working on projects at the center of the Radar Screen will apply these questions to the work that they share.

Getting out in front of decisions like this requires thinking ahead and clarity, often more than achievement-driven folks are willing to take the time for. A group will assume that if they identify the work and a person to lead it during Crystallize Intent, then that's enough. The "how" and the "who" of deciding should take care of themselves. Too often they don't. Another mistake is assuming that consensus is the default. This is another one of those annoyingly common misunderstandings about consensus. Teams have to have the "how and who" conversation about every piece of work that will be shared. In fact, this discipline is at the heart of intentionality in decision making.

We're talking about the center of the Radar Screen, but the same guidance pertains to work that was placed in the middle ring of your Radar Screen. Effective sub-groups, during Cultivate Collaboration, impose on themselves the same discipline of deciding how a decision will best be made and by whom, even before the decisions present themselves.

The discipline of deep listening

Listening is a skill and an art. A few have a gift for it; most don't. It can be learned and it has to be practiced by any team fully committed to intentional collaboration. At every level, in the full team or in sub-groups, deep listening is a requirement. It's a complex topic, more complex than it seems.

Keep this in mind: Sound group decisions are based more on accurate and thorough understanding than they are on agreement. Deep listening is the path to genuine understanding on the way to effective decisions.

What do I mean by deep listening? Talk to your average manager and they're likely to tell you that they've learned about active listening. Many have been trained in it. I was. I also taught it. Active listening is a great start, but for most of us it's not enough. Active listening, as most understand it, is heavy on technique and focused largely on the person listening. We're taught a few behaviors like paraphrasing and affirming vocalizations—"I see," "So what you're saying is...," and my favorite, "Tell me more about that." We learn the right body language, too—lean in, remain physically open and relaxed. Then, with 3x5-inch job aids in hand to remind us of these techniques, we use them for a while. The techniques, first and foremost, give us a way to control our own urges to speak. They're a bit like the podium for a nervous public speaker that doesn't know what to do with his hands. We hold onto them for dear life until it's over. Often, though, we feel phony papering over our natural impulses with catchphrases and self-conscious body positions. Active listening works for some people who use it enough to make it natural. It is, nonetheless, based on prescriptions for what the listener should say and do. Deep listening, on the other hand, is grounded in what's happening within the other person. The ultimate question is one I first heard years ago: Are they feeling heard?

It's a simple question. Once again, though, the preference for action and achievement gets in our way. Remember the story of my boss and the project he and I were going to share? He heard me but only at the level of the problem, the work to be done. He wasn't listening for or hearing my deeper interest in professional development. He stopped listening and went right to explaining and action. I've done the same thing a thousand times. What he and most of us miss is the chance to awaken our curiosity, to use listening as an opportunity to explore and learn. I once heard an interview with a retiring CEO—this was years ago and his name escapes me. He was asked if he were given the chance to do it over, was there one thing he would do differently. He said, "I'd have been more curious." This was a guy who had made a ton of decisions. He had all the answers, or so he assumed. He'd done extremely well. Yet, he felt by the end of his career that he'd missed out by not being more curious, asking more questions. Like courage, curiosity turns out to be an indispensable attribute for high performing team members; it's central to deep listening and to others feeling heard. When it comes to group decision making, seek to understand, and then, with apologies to Stephen Covey the elder, seek to understand even more. Go deeper. Curiosity, again like courage, can be cultivated. A team full of curious people is a team that's likely to make sound decisions.

I said that decision making is more about understanding than it is about agreement. Still, there has to be some level of agreement, doesn't there? That persistent need to achieve gets in the way here, too. It's like an aggressive weed in our garden of collaboration. My deep need to achieve means I can't wait to get busy. When you describe to me your point of view, my instinct is to listen for where you and I agree and/or where we disagree. If we agree—hurray!—we can act together based on our agreement. If we disagree I want to resolve our disagreement so we can get to work. Either way, getting on with it is driving me. Deep listening be damned. Both the desire for agreement and attempts to "fix" our disagreement stymie curiosity and therefore undermine sound decisions and collaborative effectiveness.

Let's start with the disagreement problem. The urge to fix disagreement and turn it into agreement drives two behaviors: First, I'll try to talk the other person into my point of view with eloquent arguments. Or I'll demonstrate how the other's point of view is wrong so that they will change it to mine. In either case, I'll muster just enough curiosity to get the information I need to either figure out how to win you over, or convince you you're wrong. Either way, what I'm trying to get is agreement and, in doing so, invalidating the dissenter's point of view. I'm disempowering them. What I need isn't their agreement. Remember, we're working on either a consensus or an authority-based decision, neither of which requires everyone to agree. What I and the team need is for the dissenter to feel that their perspectives have been given a fair and thorough hearing. They have to feel they had some power in the conversation, indeed some power with you. You feed their sense of being heard, of personal power, by getting and staying curious. Once you've done that, a little old-school active listening goes a long way. It's been around for over 30 years, but the SOLER model never gets old:

S: Sit or stand *squarely* in relation to the person you're with
O: Maintain an *open* body position
L: *Lean* in a little
E: Make *eye* contact
R: Remain physically and emotionally *relaxed*

Affirm, genuinely, the validity of the person's points. Appreciate their perspectives. Invite them to provide feedback once the decision is implemented. They may never agree, but they're far more likely to support the team's decision if you have shown up as curious.

It's easy to see how hearing disagreement could complicate decision making. How could listening for agreement be a problem when we're making a decision? False consensus, another of my bugbears, is a real phenomenon that teams need to watch out for. It's what happens when full-team decision making meets teaminess. It results from, among other things, a failure of deep listening.

Speaking of old school, you may have heard of the Abilene Paradox. There's a book by the late Jerry B. Harvey that features this true story that was crafted into a parable about agreement gone wrong. It's a classic in organization development studies. It tells the story of a family, Dr Harvey's family, who all agree to travel to Abilene, Texas, from their home 53 miles away in Coleman, Texas. It's a hot, lazy afternoon and the family is sitting on their porch swatting flies and enjoying a game of dominoes. The father-in-law abruptly suggests a trip to Abilene. The mother, agrees, cheerily. The father (Dr Harvey) is very hesitant but doesn't want to rock the boat so he consents. He gives his consent, though, contingent on the mother-in-law's wishes, saying essentially, "Sure, I'll go if she wants to." Nice move, right? Foist it off on the in-laws. The mother-in-law, following the building consensus, agrees to go and they set off. The trip is hot and uncomfortable, going and coming. No one has a good time. When they get back home four hours later, it comes to light that no one really cared to go in the first place. The father-in-law had assumed everyone was bored so he made the suggestion. Once the mother agreed to go, they all joined in, none of them wanting to seem like the party-pooper of the family. They were all trying to do what they assumed the others thought was best, so none of them spoke up. They were, in the parlance of teaminess, trying to be good team players. No one expressed curiosity, though I feel sure someone felt some. Their good intentions, along with their failure to listen to their own instincts and the subtle messages being sent by others, ended up costing the whole family a pleasant and relaxing afternoon.

Agreement is so comfortable. It can make us feel all teamy and nice. We may even feel quietly proud of ourselves when we "take one for the team" by not voicing a niggling sense of unease with an evolving consensus. Social creatures that we are, we're prone to agreement even when it isn't real. In fact, I think our deep social urges often override the awesome power of the need to achieve. When consensus comes fast and easy, pause. Cultivate curiosity. Play the devil's advocate. Listen to your intuition and challenge the team to think again. Speak up, then listen deeply with curiosity.

By this time you and your team will have established a strong sense of collaborative purpose. You'll have made agreements about what needs collaboration. You will have agreed to how you'll work together to bring your shared purpose and commitments to life. Use this work and these agreements to frame and focus your disagreements. Connect back to the larger "why" and the expectations you've established with each other. The Practices will help turn differences into richer, deeper conversation and relationships. Then you can move on in whatever direction is best.

The discipline of letting go and moving on

In the end, team decisions require commitment. Ironically, sometimes we have to be willing to let go of an idea we may be individually committed to in order to help our team commit to a decision so that we can achieve a result. As my meditation practice might suggest, I'm a student, if not the most accomplished, of Zen. I have learned this: The practices of Zen Buddhism are grounded in discipline. A meditating monk seated for days on end in an unheated, unfurnished cave relies on discipline, not magic or New Age platitudes. Buddhism holds that the source of all our suffering is attachment: attachment to material things, to other people, to our own stories about who we are. Maybe that view works for you, maybe not. In any case, learning to let go is a decision-making discipline. It's learnable and necessary for team members and teams to thrive. I've spoken about the discipline a team has to have about deciding who decides. What if you think a decision ought to be yours and the team or your leader doesn't see it that way? How will you move things on if you can't let go?

Learning to let go and move on is similar to another time-honored practice: "agreeing-to-disagree," but it requires more mental and emotional energy. It's easy to agree-to-disagree with someone who you can turn and walk away from. It's tougher when the other person is someone you've signed up to collaborate with. You have to learn to be comfortable with discomfort. When we disagree with someone who we contracted to collaborate with, it's worrying. The fear that a disagreement and the emotions around it will affect our collaboration is understandable. You might adopt a well-intended but phony "agree-to-disagree" stance. You may try to act as if you never disagreed, as if you're moving along so you can get along. This is another error of teaminess. Great collaboration doesn't require that we all get along, that we operate in a state of continual niceness. Honest, frank differences make for a strong relationship but only when we learn to surrender the need to reconcile them all. Can you learn to be comfortable with this discomfort? It's a cliché, I know. Paired with patience, though, it works. Perhaps you'll return to your differences another day. Maybe you won't. Allow me to get all Zen again: Learning to let them go and patiently allowing things to unfold as they will is one of those life lessons that allow teamwork to work. Heaven only knows how many long-lasting marriages depend on this willingness to let go and move on. This isn't about love, I know. It is, however, about commitment.

When it becomes tough to let go, turn back to the Practices. If my team's sense of purpose is compelling to me and I feel I have been deeply listened to and honored, letting go and moving on is easier. If my teammates have spent quality time with me, sorting out who each of us will be in our collaboration, letting go will come more naturally. In the end, I can always fall back on my innate need to get busy and achieve something and let this carry me forward. Even if there is a powerful sense of shared purpose, if relationships are strong, and I've expressed my views and felt heard, I may still struggle. This is especially true if I'm emotionally attached to my opinions or if my ego depends on them. Sometimes there is just no getting around it. The sense of loss, of frustration at times like these, is essential to the experience of being part of a team. If things always went my way, then it couldn't be the sort of diverse and interesting team that I prefer to be a part of. When the team needs me to let go and move on, they're inviting me into the complete experience of being a part of a team but also of being fully human. It isn't and shouldn't always be about me—thank goodness.

Consensus, one more time

We've gone deeply into some of the behaviors that allow team decision making to work, including consensus. I've been hard on consensus but I'm not the only consensus crank out there. In our matrixed, ever more wired and wireless world, and in the land of the Open Office, some have said that consensus is one example of increasing "over-collaboration." Everywhere we turn, in the physical or virtual world, there's someone else we might want to include in our drive for consensus. Maybe, but if you ask me, consensus and collaboration are different and shouldn't be conflated. Consensus is about seeking consent whereas collaboration is about working productively together.

We need more, healthy, intentional collaboration. I'm not sure the same is true for consensus.

In cultures where consensus is overused, the felt need for consensus comes from different places. Sometimes, as I described with consens-animity, it arises out of respect for the views and feelings of others. It's seen as a kind of empowerment. "Hey, Stan, I respect you and your thoughts so I want to share power with you on this decision." Other times, consensus is ego driven, with people forcing their way into decisions—"I know things, so you have to listen to me." Other times it's fear driven—"If I don't provide guidance and wisdom, things will go wrong." Sometimes it's all three of these. No matter what the justification for overusing consensus, it's a curse for efficient collaboration. The Radar Screen is a useful first step in helping teams determine where consensus might make sense, and where it won't.

Use consensus sparingly. The most important step in avoiding your own trip to Abilene is to limit the number of decisions made by consensus. Authority-based decisions that use robust input from the team, paired with deep listening, are every bit as effective. Genuine consensus can be hard to come by, especially where the issues are complex. It takes time, even more time than thoroughly discussed authority-based decisions. The bigger the team or group, the more time consensus takes. Understanding is the soul of consensus. Understanding is developed via inquiry, balanced debate, dialog, and deep listening. The more team members, the more voices and perspectives to be heard and considered and inquired into, so the more time it takes. Then there are the risks of consensus decisions after the fact. What happens when we arrive or appear to arrive at consensus quickly, without everyone speaking up and sufficiently deep-listening? We end up traveling to Abilene. Worse still is consensus fatigue. Consensus fatigue results in people signing up to a decision because they're tired of all the talk and debate. "Can't we just get on with this—whatever 'this' is—and get to work?" This is what I experienced with my Master's degree cohort. The result is that assumptions aren't explored, potential risks are glossed over, and implications aren't fully considered. All these come back later to bite you. Again, use consensus advisedly. If you have a large group or don't have the time for quality consensus, find an alternative.

When does consensus make sense? Where broad and deep commitment to the final decision is essential. For example, remember the Finance team I worked with that decided to meet only once every two months? This was a group of detail-oriented people who needed to feel that they had a handle on their business, day in and day out. They believed that their internal customers expected this of them. Meeting every four weeks seemed like the right way to stay on top of what was going on. When they looked back to their team purpose and shared work, they realized that what they needed wasn't a meeting but information. As I suggested earlier, using meetings to share information is a bad idea. There are so many other more efficient ways to do it. Their purpose focused mainly on creating a robust talent pipeline for their function. Still, letting go of monthly meetings was hard for them. The conversations, the curiosity and the deep listening of a consensus decision process were necessary if they were to change and support a different way of working. Consensus also makes sense where authority isn't clear or well defined and everyone knows it. For example, in groups with a new leader who isn't the expert in something that's being decided, consensus works. The leader can empower the team to make a collective decision, knowing that they know the subject better than he or she does. Leaderless groups, such as small communities of practice, may also find consensus useful since authority in the group is diffuse and shared among them. The same disciplines apply, regardless.

Regardless of which type of decision making you choose in a given situation, you have to be clear about your decision process in advance. Know where in the Radar Screen each decision belongs. Be willing to let go of owning decisions when you aren't directly involved in the work. Get curious, listen deeply, and be willing to move on.

Decision-making recap

- Use your Radar Screen to sort out what decisions reside where. Many decisions can and should reside with individuals and with sub-groups.
- For those items at the center of your Radar Screen, work with the team to figure out the best, most efficient ways to decide. Not every project or initiative at the center of the Radar Screen requires a consensus decision.
- The skills of deep listening and letting go will be essential to a healthy decision-making discipline in your team.
- Listen for both disagreement and agreement and explore both carefully before finalizing any consensus decision.
- Use consensus sparingly and only where it makes the most sense. When it doesn't make sense, use authority-based decisions instead.

In Closing

"Discipline is remembering what you want." This quote appears on the wall of a yoga studio that I frequent. The Discipline of Activate Ways-of-Working is one of continually remembering what the team has declared is important to it. Teams evolve, of course. As they evolve, what matters to the team changes. The next chapter introduces the subject of team learning, and how teams learn and adapt to their changing circumstances.

Summary

- The Practice of Activate Ways-of-Working involves calling to mind what the team has said it wants and building these intentions into their standard operations or ways-of-working.

- The intent is to establish a rhythm and routines that support the team, its work and its aspirations.
- With the fundamental team operations accounted for, the team is freed up to attend to the non-standard occurrences and issues that make teamwork so interesting and so worthwhile.
- The team's inspiring sense of purpose, the work it has committed to share, and the agreements team members make about how they'll collaborate all inform how a team creates the positive habits and routines that are the heart of this Practice.
- Begin this Practice by looking back at your Radar Screen. Allow it to shape what you meet about and how often.
- Use the Radar Screen, as well, to guide choices about what decisions are owned by the team and which will be made by sub-groups or individuals.
- Beware of consensus and use it sparingly.
- Discipline and ways-of-working can seem unsexy at first, especially to hard-driving, achievement-oriented people. Keep your ways-of-working simple and clearly aligned with your other Practices.

Chapter 12

Team Learning

So far, I've presented a neat mapping of Imperatives to Practices. Clarity lines up nicely with the two Practices, Inspire Purpose and Crystallize Intent. Intentionality is paired directly with Cultivate Collaboration. Discipline aligns cleanly with the team processes that are part of Activate Ways-of-Working. This chapter and the two that follow it break that convenient pattern. All three are about learning; learning as a team Discipline but also learning in the service of the team's Clarity. In this chapter, I depart from the discussion of specific Practices and talk about the concept of team learning and its importance. Then, in the next two chapters I explain the remaining, learning-centric Practices, Sustain & Renew and Clarify Context.

You may wonder why Team Learning hasn't been called out as one of the Imperatives. It certainly is a need most Mars teams had. In fact, none of the teams in our research distinguished themselves when it came to learning. Most, in fact, were lousy at it. Learning is critical for Mars teams, any teams, to become more effective. So, why not a fourth Imperative? There are a couple of reasons. Remember that Intentionality is the heart of the HPC Framework. It's the one thing we found lacking that was most essential to stronger collaboration. The other two Imperatives, Clarity and Discipline, directly support Intentionality and were also found wanting. Clarity is the necessary precursor to Intentionality; if you aren't clear about what requires collaboration you can't collaborate, let alone be intentional about it. Discipline is the essential ingredient in supporting Intentionality. Once you've made your commitments and built relationships, you need Discipline to stick with them. Learning, while important, has a less central role than either of these Imperatives in making Mars teams more Intentional. Here's another reason: All three Imperatives were found lacking in teams *and the individuals* comprising those teams when it came to collaboration. Learning, on the other hand, is something that Mars team members, as individuals, do pretty well when they put their minds to it. For instance, a common strength among Mars Associates is problem solving. A fundamental part of problem solving is figuring things out and then figuring out what to do about them. "Figuring out" is learning. Our Associates have this skill in spades. They fail to apply it when it comes to teamwork, however. To my way of thinking, the application of one's learning capability to collaboration is a matter of Discipline and being Intentional. For these reasons, learning isn't one of our Imperatives. It supports the Imperatives and is still important enough to have two Practices that focus on it, however.

Learning and the HPC Framework

Both of the next two Practices I'll cover are about teams learning and then adapting. Sustain & Renew, the first of the two, is inward looking. It focuses on the team learning about itself and how it's functioning. This Practice is connected to Discipline in that it invites ongoing, habitual attention to all of what a team is doing. Because the outputs of Sustain & Renew potentially influence all the other Practices, it was placed at the center of our graphic.

Clarify Context looks outward. It's the crucial link between the team and the evolving world it works in. It's about what its name implies—creating clarity for the team, particularly during times of change. Clarify Context will address things like changes to organization strategy, structure, and leadership. Like Sustain & Renew, when practiced it can have implications for all the other Practices; when the world around a team changes, it has to respond to remain relevant. That's why Clarify Context is positioned at the outer edges of the graphic and wraps around

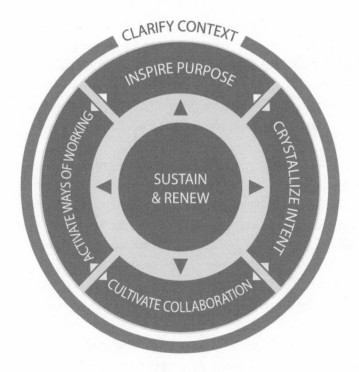

all the other Practices. Clarify Context is a less regular, less habitual Practice, that is, not a Discipline; it's used only when circumstances dictate a need for renewed Clarity. That's why we refer to it as "The Special Practice."

Learning without borders

Learning within a team, regardless of the Practice associated with it, is boundary spanning. Whether a team learns about itself or about the environment that it functions within, that learning has the potential to affect all the other Practices. If a team, upon reflection, realizes that its Inspiring Purpose isn't aligned with the work it has to do, either the purpose or the work has to change. For instance, if a team figures out that one of its key customer groups needs something vital from them that they hadn't accounted for, they'll have to revisit several of the Practices. This team would probably start with inquiring into their Inspiring Purpose; they might ask themselves, "Given this change, what is it that our collaboration is in service of?" Maybe it would stay the same, but it might have to change. Then, they'd rethink Crystallize Intent: "What work ought we to be collaborating on to bring our recently revised purpose to life?" From there, they would move on to Cultivate Collaboration and beyond.

The boundary-spanning impact of learning on a team is hard to depict with the circles and lines of our Framework graphic. We've used arrows to suggest the interconnections and influences. Even those are more static than I'd prefer. Learning makes things messy, the right kind of messy. Learning forces us out of our comfort zone and towards growth. Both of the learning-focused Practices insist that we break through all the lines in our lovely graphic in service of keeping collaboration within the team relevant.

Despite the disruptive nature of learning, learning as a behavior and a psychological phenomenon has consistent hallmarks, regardless of the Practice or Imperative it's associated with. Let's look at learning within a team, generically.

The Need for Team Learning: Back to Basics

When I began working with teams at Mars, I was a part of Mars University, our global learning and development function. My boss back then invited a consultant to come speak to our North American Mars U team about a diagnostic survey he had developed. I have no recollection of what the survey's specific focus was. Apparently, my manager thought the survey might be useful to our company. He also thought that learning about this survey as a group would be a good team-building exercise for us. The consultant agreed to administer his survey, gratis, to our team and then debrief it with us. He was a courtly gentleman, retired for the most part from corporate life and living in Hawaii. He traveled all the way to New Jersey to meet with us—I think he had a grown son or daughter in the area so it was doubly worth his while. I don't recall much about the debrief conversation with our Hawaiian friend. This I do remember as if it happened yesterday: At one point during our lively conversation, someone noticed him leaning back in his chair looking pensive and asked what he was thinking. He told us: "I've only spent a few hours with you, but I'd have to say that Mars may be the least reflective culture I have ever seen." We asked him to say more. He explained that based on what he had experienced of our team and a few others at Mars he'd had contact with, we didn't have much patience for stopping to consider ideas deeply.

We were inclined to get a piece of information, ask a bit about why it mattered, and quickly move on to acting upon that information. There wasn't much inquiry, little if any reflection, and minimal planning before going into action mode. What he was seeing was a combination of that Mars pragmatism I've talked about and our deep action orientation. In a few hours of phone calls and meetings, he'd landed on one of the essential messages that my far more involved research later uncovered.

What the research told us

This lack of reflectiveness was particularly evident in the data from the 20-item questionnaire that I had been using with teams and that fed my research. As a refresher, below is a list of the five lowest-ranked items from that survey, beginning with the lowest-rated one.

#20 The team regularly sets aside time to assess its performance as a team and to address team development needs.

#19 Team members are skilled at surfacing differences and disagreements, and dealing with them in a direct and timely fashion.

#18 The team has a well-understood process for identifying and making decisions.

#17 The team assesses its performance on important initiatives to capture lessons learned.

#16 The working environment within the team is open and generally free from unresolved tensions.

Every topic that showed up in this bottom five is addressed directly in the Framework and how we use it at Mars. Two of the items, #19 and #16, deal with conflict which the Framework covers in Cultivate Collaboration. One, #18, deals with decision making which we covered in the chapter on Activate Ways-of-Working. The remaining two have something to say about team learning and it's not positive. Teams' ways of addressing their team dynamics and development needs came in dead last at #20. Taking time to evaluate projects or initiatives came in at #17—not much better. The consultant from Hawaii had been on to something. When it came time to develop our Framework, our data made it clear that it would have to address team learning. The Practices of Sustain & Renew and Clarify Context are the result.

Learning as achievement

To get individually motivated team members collaborating, our Framework makes collaboration a thing to be achieved. The same thinking can apply to team learning. We move beyond the idea of learning as an occasionally useful by-product of our work, or learning-for-learning's sake, and view team learning as a thing to be achieved.

In Cultivate Collaboration, a team contracts for what their collaboration will look like so that they can hold one another accountable for it. They then build those commitments into their performance management plans, making them goals to be achieved. We aim to do the same with learning. The practice of contracting-for-learning includes making commitments to capture learning as a part of every project and every collaborative effort. After-action reviews and in-action reviews, which I'll discuss in more detail, become a habit. The commitment to learn is then included in every team member's annual performance objectives. "What did you learn this year about how you collaborate?" becomes as common a question as, "What did you achieve this year?" The achievement motive is a mighty force. Without this transformation of learning into a recognizable achievement, learning, like collaboration, remains either a nice to-do or an incidental outcome.

Learning-as-achievement, like collaboration-as-achievement, relies on accountability. I was speaking the other day to a senior Mars leader, one of our more successful General Managers, who is renowned for her team leadership. Her people love working for her and she consistently gets strong business results. She told me that for the teams she has led, learning is non-negotiable. Every meeting ends with a review of what worked and what could have gone better. Every one-on-one with a team member includes a discussion about what they're learning and where they might be stuck. Not everyone who reports to her gets it at first. Eventually, though, most do. Those who don't take to it eventually self-select out. She told me, "At the beginning, when it comes to making the discipline of ongoing learning stick, you have to act as an unenlightened leader." In other words, to get teams used to treating learning as another performance expectation, you have to dig in your heels and be tough for a while. We know they can do it. They're just not used to it and not accustomed to being held accountable for it.

Team Learning: What It Is, What It Takes

A significant part of my background involved adult learning. When I was in the training business at DDI, I spent a fair bit of time studying adult learning. As I learned, and you probably know, adults learn differently from the way kids learn. A big part of this is due to all the unlearning we adults have to do in order to learn something new. If unlearning is hard for individual adults, it's even harder for teams of adults.

Teams at work have to learn not only how to work together effectively, they have to learn how to learn collaboratively, even how to unlearn collaboratively. Teams operating in the typical Mars style have come to rely on lots of reactive collaboration, to see helpfulness as the primary expression of teamwork. They have to consciously work on learning about intentional collaboration and how to foster and cultivate more of it. What's more, they have to overcome the urge and habit of near-constant doing—read: achievement—to make room for learning.

Team learning involves a group seeking and gaining insight together and then planning to adapt or improve based on their insights. Team learning is both inwardly focused and outward looking. It involves examining team ways-of-working, collaborative effectiveness, as well as the environment the team is working in. It has three aspects:

Task-related learning—focuses on the work the team is doing together

Team dynamics learning—focuses on the way the team interacts and works together

Strategic learning—focuses on what is happening around the team that affects it

Sustain & Renew covers the first two, more inward-looking areas. Clarify Context is primarily concerned with looking out from the team. I'll discuss each as we cover the two Practices in their dedicated chapters.

Team learning, whether inwardly or outwardly focused, whether it is addressing team tasks or team dynamics, is comprised of five actions:

- Pause
- Inquire

- Reflect
- Plan
- Act

PIRPA is a lousy acronym. It's not surprising then that we call them The Five Actions of team learning. They're more a description than a prescription. They're based on what I've observed successful teams do. For instance, I spoke in Chapter 10 about a cross-functional, international Supply Chain team that had started to use the HPC Framework about eight months earlier. They weren't seeing the hoped-for results of their collaboration. Not only that, despite having a strong sense of purpose and great clarity about their shared work, they weren't feeling much like a team. In particular, their meetings didn't engage them. This team of Supply and Commercial professionals lacked a compelling need to be together. Each had a big job and lots to do within his or her own function or business. The pull of their various silos still trumped the perceived value of their being together. The team leader consulted me. We agreed that they would take a pause and carve out at least a day at her next fact-to-face team meeting for some team dynamics learning. We devised a simple survey that drew on the HPC work that the team had already done. The survey asked them to grade themselves on how well they were living their purpose and collaborating on the work at the center of their Radar Screen. To make the survey feel relevant, we used our Mars five-level performance management language for part of it: Outstanding, Exceeds Expectations, Meets Expectations, Below Expectations, Unsatisfactory. At this point, I left the leader and the team to their own devices. I agreed to check back in with them after they'd completed their survey and spent some time inquiring into and reflecting on the results at their next meeting.

As it turned out, they rated themselves "below expectations" on one aspect of living their purpose—creating simplicity—and between "below expectations" and "unsatisfactory" on two of their center-of-the-Radar-Screen projects. With the survey results in hand, the team self-facilitated a discussion about why they had rated themselves the way they did. Mind you, they had thoughtfully created their purpose statement and committed to it. They had selected the work at the center of their Radar Screen, work that they pledged to rally around. They weren't rallying, though. They were underperforming in areas that they had said mattered most and required their collaboration. "Why," they wondered, "are we not more engaged with each other?" Behind that were other questions like:

- Is our purpose the right one?
- Is the shared work the right shared work?
- If we're right about our purpose and shared work, why weren't these things tapping into our achievement drive and spurring collaboration?

After all, isn't that third question what this Framework is supposed to do?

They spent a morning conducting their inquiry into the survey results, and I joined them that afternoon via video conference to help them make sense of it all. It turned out to be a relatively simple problem.

A year earlier they had taken time to develop on their inspiring purpose and agree to their Radar Screen. When these were done, they agreed without much discussion to maintain the meeting timings and agendas they were then using. They were a geographically dispersed team; some sat in the northeastern USA and others in the UK. Their rhythm of meetings was a typical rhythm for a team of their type. It was anchored by two face-to-face meetings, six months apart, usually in June and December. One would be in the USA, the other across the Pond. In-between these two meetings, they alternated monthly between half-day video meetings and 90-minute conference calls. In retrospect, the cadence was probably fine. What they hadn't addressed were the purposes and agendas for these various meetings. They just went back to running their meetings as they always had. They'd talk about how the business was doing, how their respective factories were running, and where there might be hiccups in the supply chain.

We can apply the Five Actions of team learning to this scenario. In the name of "just getting on with it," this team had only used actions one, four and five as it related to their meetings. They had **paused** in order to create their purpose and Radar Screen. Then, when it came to their meetings, they **planned** and they **acted**. What they didn't do was take time to inquire and reflect as to whether the content and cadence of those meetings was clearly aligned with their purpose and their shared work. It's no wonder that they weren't making more progress on their purpose and the initiatives they meant to share. They hadn't intentionally set up their meetings so that they reflected these commitments.

They ended up modifying their meetings to bring them into line with their other collaborative commitments. It's more how they did this than where they landed that's the point. As they faced into this meetings problem, they did what they hadn't done previously and applied all five of the Five Actions.

- They set aside their "doing" and **paused** specifically to learn together about their team dynamic.
- They **inquired**, collectively, into a few questions they had posed for themselves.
- They **reflected** together and identified the insights gained from their inquiry.
- They used those insights and **planned** to make changes to the way they were collaborating.
- They took immediate **action** on their plans, made the

necessary changes, and scheduled a follow-up in a few months to check on their progress.

Using the Framework as a guide

After stumbling out of the gate, this team did the things more typical teams don't do. What's more, they benefited from having used the Practices of the HPC Framework. It provided a roadmap for their inquiry and brought focus and clarity to their learning process. For the sake of comparison, imagine the team had assessed itself using the Four Stages model instead of our action-oriented Framework. They'd have been left with little more than a description of the stage they were in. They'd understand their problems as being in Stage Two somewhere but have no path to solving them. Or what if their goal when they paused for team learning was to improve so-called team spirit, and they'd done this without having used our Framework? They might have done some orienteering or gone bowling as a team and had a lovely time. The odds are that their meetings would not have improved. They couldn't have built the action-oriented plan that they did without the Framework. The team I've been talking about completed their HPC Framework-based learning exercise and got back to work with a renewed sense of what they were all about and higher odds of getting things done well. There hadn't been any team psycho-babble or phony team spirit involved.

The Framework: What It Can and Can't Do

The most effective groups seek to understand their effectiveness and what's driving it so that they can address problem areas and optimize their collaboration. Our Framework addresses six Practices or elements that demonstrably influence collaborative effectiveness based on our research.

Obviously there are more than six things that affect collaborative effectiveness. What our Framework does, it does well. What it doesn't try to do is to directly address elements of team functioning that are better dealt with by other organizational systems and processes. Most notably, the Framework doesn't directly tackle team member and team leader capabilities. To be sure, the people on a team make a significant difference to how a team operates. As I've said, team leader and team member issues are the most common cause of team disruption, if not real dysfunction. Teams, while they can identify these sorts of performance problems, aren't the best source for fixing them, at least not in traditional organizations. At Mars we deal with these two influencers of team effectiveness primarily through our talent management and talent development processes. Hence, talent and team member capabilities aren't overt parts of the Framework. Remember the story I told of the dysfunctional leader whose peers were insisting that he run a team development workshop with his direct reports? They were hoping that his traumatized team would call him on his abysmal behavior, that he would learn and that this would fix things. They hired a team consultant and ran the workshop in spite of my guidance not to. It melted down, ending abruptly and badly. P&O, with their expertise in people performance and development, had to step in. In the end, the organization turned to the established process for dealing with poor performance, but only after it was too late.

I'm not suggesting you ignore the role of people in influencing team learning and effectiveness. There are certainly times when a team needs to pause and reflect on who it's comprised of, their skills and capabilities, and adapt appropriately. This happens pretty frequently when using our Framework, in fact. For example, when team members are contracting in Cultivate Collaboration they need to talk about who each of them is and what they can and can't do. When we get to Sustain & Renew you'll see that there are times when a team has to take stock of its members' capabilities. The suggestion I'm making is to assiduously avoid addressing what appear to be team issues when in fact they're individual performance problems. Your company, like ours, probably has policies and systems already in place to address these situations.

Business strategy is another powerful influencer of teams. The Practice of Clarify Context, which I explain in detail in Chapter 14, considers changes in business strategy as a thing to be learned about. The Framework, however, doesn't pretend to develop or fix business strategy. At Mars, we have processes and people to help our senior teams think about and develop strategy.

By no means should you leave people and the business out of your team learning conversations. The two learning-focused Practices we'll discuss are about diagnosis and sense-making leading to learning and action. Some of that learning and action may be directed within the team; it may touch on team members and their issues. Some of what's learned may be connected to business strategy. The point is that our Framework doesn't claim to fix underperforming people. Nor does it seek to steer the business or inform financial decisions. No team model or framework should. We leave those critical things to the people and processes already in place to do them, and I recommend that you do the same.

Team Learning as Team Spirit

Let's talk about team spirit one final time. I acknowledge that it's a real phenomenon. What I question are many of the common beliefs about team spirit and the things teams do in pursuit of it—bowling, orienteering, the Haka, and so on. What most people think of as building team spirit—creating a buzz, a positive sensation associated with team membership—produces nothing more than pleasant, short-lived feelings of connectivity. They're lovely feelings, but not lasting or change-producing.

There's another version of team spirit that's more valuable and more lasting. Groups that employ the HPC Framework begin by creating an almost tangible sense of team identity through their inspiring purpose and the clarity about the work they share. Then, guided by their shared purpose and work, they cultivate an environment of continuous learning and growth. Taken together, these things generate a sustainable field of collective energy, what I call "true team spirit." Teams working in this way foster an energy that is sparked whenever they're together, that nourishes them all, and that draws them together when they have been working apart. If you have ever experienced this buzz, you know what I'm talking about. I have felt it as a cast member in plays I've done where, every rehearsal, we learned something new. I experienced it when I coordinated our supposedly dysfunctional production team at the stock photo agency. We tussled and we sweated, but we did it together and made each other better. The fundamental element of true team spirit is that feeling you get around people who consistently bring out the best in you, whose energy and smarts you admire. You're drawn to these people because they spark energy, intellect, and even vitality in you. This is team spirit well worth cultivating. It doesn't require motivational posters, paintball or trust falls. It requires a focus on team learning.

Team spirit and team climate

David McClelland, he of the Three Motives, also studied what he called "organizational climate." In particular, he was interested in how climate within groups was affected by their leaders. McClelland's approach was well researched and can be measured using commercially available surveys. I prefer to keep it uncomplicated. Climate can be simply but accurately defined as, "what it feels like to work in a team."

Climate is often confused with culture so let's tease them apart. Culture describes norms, values, and attitudes that develop over time, that permeate the entire organization, and that subtly shape behavior. Culture tends to endure. Mars is justifiably proud of its unique corporate culture. I didn't want to challenge the Mars culture when I was developing the Framework. Since cultures persist, I wanted to dance with it, to work with its prevailing energy of drive and individual achievement. Climate, by contrast, is a shorter-term, local phenomenon that grows out of and reflects what's going on within a group. Many climates may exist in one culture. For instance, our Mars University team used to sit right across from the Americas Treasury and Benefits Center (ATBC) in Mt Olive, New Jersey. In the open office our two groups were fully visible to one another. As you walked through the door into our common area, the Mars U team was on your left and the ATBC team was on your right. We were all good Martians, all punching the clock every morning, all committed to living the Five Principles and the Associate Concept. We were all active participants in the Mars culture. Yet you couldn't have found two more contrasting team climates. It was evident when comparing our respective workspaces. On your right, where dedicated Mars Associates dealt with weighty things like our pensions and benefits, there was an appropriate sense of order, control, and composure. Desks were free of clutter in accordance with the Mars "clean desk" policy. Conversations were subdued, as they once were in the lobbies of stately old banks. Looking to the left, at the Mars U team area, you'd see and feel the air of creativity and kinetic energy. The clean desk policy was honored more in breach than practice. It seemed every horizontal surface was covered with cartons of training supplies, some being assembled, others waiting to be shipped. Alongside those boxes were scattered miscellaneous memorabilia and photos, some of Associates' families but many of Mars U class cohorts. Here and there were mementos from past courses: a rubber duck, a bizarrely decorated hat. In the midst of this essential clutter, Mars U Associates could be seen wandering around, cell phones in hand, in animated conversation. The energy of the two groups was dramatically different. Both worked in the same company and prevailing culture, but each had its own vibe, its own climate.

It's this more general sense of "the feel of the team" that I'm talking about when I discuss climate. As teams infuse themselves with the more powerful, learning-based team spirit, their climates reflect the energy created. What's even better news is that while culture is difficult to change, climate can be addressed relatively easily and quickly. Three to six months is all it takes for a group to alter its climate. A group that was, in January, struggling to work with each other and experiencing a heavy, energy-sapping climate could by June have turned things completely around. Learning as a group is the path to true team spirit and a healthier, more positive team climate.

Engagement

Lots of companies measure and report on employee (or in the case of Mars, Incorporated, Associate) engagement. Engagement is roughly defined as an employee's emotional connection and commitment to the company they work for. Engagement is an individual experience, but it's often measured within teams. Studies have demonstrated that more highly engaged groups produce stronger results across all sorts of metrics — higher sales, fewer lost time accidents, and so on — than less highly engaged groups. It's not clear, though, whether higher engagement tends to foster more collaboration. Nor is it clear how much of the improvement in group outcomes, if any, can be attributed to better collaboration versus those stronger feelings of engagement. At Mars, however, we're seeing a connection. We haven't formally studied it, but teams that work on their dynamics and effectiveness using HPC report increases in their engagement scores. So we're fostering a link between the two frameworks. We're connecting the two frameworks through the concept of climate.

Gallup's engagement methodology, which we use, focuses on engagement at the team level. Similarly, McClelland studied and reported on climate as a team-level phenomenon. What's more, both Gallup's engagement methodology and McClelland's climate model recognize the importance of the team leader in influencing and shaping the thing they're measuring. Sure, team members have an undeniable role in their own engagement and the climate they're part of. Managers, though, have a larger proportional influence on both engagement and climate, based on studies that have looked at both.

While climate and engagement parallel each other, the relationship between engagement and HPC is one of contrasts. The Gallup engagement survey, while it's administered to and reported at the team level, makes no overt reference to teamwork or collaboration. HPC, on the other hand, is about nothing but collaboration. The engagement survey asks individual team members for their views on its 12 items. The survey mentions the supervisor; it infers relationships, making specific reference to co-workers and friends; it also refers to the company and its vision. It mentions growth, progress, and development, but only at the individual level. The words "team" or "group" aren't used. HPC, by comparison concerns itself only with the team and how it works as a group. The two Frameworks are complementary in these respects.

They do have this in common, though: Teams with higher engagement scores report having more positive team climates, that is, the team feels good to be a part of. Likewise, teams that actively employ HPC, which is solely and overtly focused on the team, also report higher engagement and better team climates. We propose that one reason (there may be others) the two different approaches create better team climates is that they both rely on team learning.

Engagement data is fed into what's called the Impact Planning process. Gallup will tell you that teams that are rigorous about Impact Planning, that review their data together, create a plan, and then implement it are far more likely to raise their engagement scores. At Mars, teams that create and follow through on their Impact Plans are 18 times more likely to be engaged. HPC, through the Sustain & Renew and Clarify Context Practices, asks teams to follow a similar process focused on their collaborative efforts. What we're seeing is that teams have, of their own accord, brought the two learning processes together. They're using HPC as a central element of their engagement Impact plans and using engagement survey data in their HPC learning efforts. In fact, we now recommend that teams use the two frameworks together and conduct their Impact Planning as a team Sustain & Renew workshop. We have every reason to believe that the impact on team learning, on team climate, and on true team spirit will be positive.

The next chapter explains the HPC Practice of Sustain & Renew. It invites teams to implement the learning Discipline of regular self-examination, assessment and planning for improvement to ensure they remain relevant and keep growing.

Summary
- No matter how successfully a team has employed the HPC Framework, regardless of how clear their purpose or how intentional they are being about their work, if they aren't adapting they will falter.
- For learning to thrive in an achievement-oriented culture, it must be framed as something to be measured and achieved.
- There are three kinds of team learning: task learning, team dynamics learning, and strategic learning. Sustain & Renew covers the first two and Clarify Context the third.
- The same five learning steps apply to all three types of learning: Pause, Inquire, Reflect, Plan, and Act.
- The HPC Framework and Practices can act as a roadmap

to guide a team as it inquires and reflects on itself and its work.

- Team learning is the essential element of team adaptability, team member engagement and positive team climate.

Chapter 13

Discipline and Sustain & Renew

"Plus Ça Change" Ain't What It Used to Be

Plus ça change, plus c'est la même chose. The more things change, the more they stay the same. It's a truism that is less true for workplace teams. As things within and around a team change, the team has to respond, adapt, and change appropriately, or it risks losing its effectiveness and relevance. Team learning is what's required for team change.

Originally this Framework had only one Practice dedicated to team learning. Today it has two. This doubling has to do with who Mars Associates are. Mars Associates are generally quick students; they're natural learners, at least in some regards. We love a good discussion about the business, what's working, where our struggles are, and what we can do to respond to such things. We're less interested, though, in introspection, in digging into the "why" of things, especially our own processes. Teams, if they're going to thrive, have to be able to do both; they must critically consider both the external environment and their internal functioning. We realized that we needed Practices dedicated to each of these kinds of learning so that teams didn't lose focus on the more introspective variety. Sustain & Renew is the Practice focused on the team and its collaborative ways of being and working, and it's the focus of this chapter.

The Practice of Sustain & Renew

Sustain & Renew focuses on teams learning about themselves as collaborative entities. This Practice can be uncomfortable; it sometimes forces teams to face into their shortcomings. It doesn't have to be complicated. Engaging in Sustain & Renew can be as straightforward as this: Pause, inquire, and reflect. Look back at your work on the Framework just like the integrated Supply Chain team I described in the previous chapter. Review your purpose, your collaborative commitments, and ways-of-working, and ask yourselves:

- What's working?
- What would we have to change to make things even better?

Answer these two questions. Reflect together and figure out what you need to do differently. Create a plan, get busy, and then check back on yourselves in a few months. It is really that simple.

Simple is good and often just the thing. We could just stop there. My goal, though, is to enable you to apply every part of this Framework to your own teams and organization, which will be of various types and kinds. To do that, I'm going to share some of what sits behind this deceptively straightforward Practice.

Why Sustain *and* Renew?

Start using the HPC Framework and your collaboration will undergo a shift. You'll want that change to last. What's more, you'll want to be able to repeat not just your successes but to get even better at succeeding. You and your team will want to **sustain** the good stuff you're creating through using the Framework. You'll also want to figure out how to adapt and **renew** yourselves as required. Hence the name of this Practice.

The high-level question associated with this Practice is, "What now and what next?" It's intended to remind teams and team members to inquire into the state of their collaboration here and now and to think about what they would like to move on to or grow into.

Two kinds of learning

When a team using HPC takes a critical look at itself and how it's operating, it considers two sources of potential learning: the work it's been doing and its group dynamics. These two classes of inward-focused inquiry form the heart of Sustain & Renew. Let's go back to that questionnaire I used in my Mars research. It asked team members to rate, among other things, these two different aspects of learning. I asked how much they agreed with these statements:

- The team assesses its performance on important initiatives to capture lessons learned.
- The team regularly sets aside time to assess its performance as a team and to address team development needs.

The first statement dealt with task learning and the second with group or team dynamics learning. Task learning was rated seventeenth out of 20 items. Team dynamics ranked twentieth out of 20. Let's tackle task learning first.

Task learning

Task learning links neatly back to the Radar Screen and the specific work that the team agreed required collaboration. A common form of task learning is the "after-action review" or AAR that comes to us from the military. An AAR applies the Five Actions of learning from the previous chapter in an elegantly simple way. It involves pausing to look back at a recently completed project or program and inquiring about, "What worked and why?" and "What didn't work and why?" These two questions form the foundation for the team's reflection, planning, and subsequent improvement actions.

An AAR can be a straightforward team discussion or it can be a more elaborate facilitated experience. It can last an hour or involve a days-long investigation. One of the high points of my career with Mars involved learning with a team using the AAR approach augmented by what's called "graphic facilitation."

In 2005–6, two years before I was dedicated to working with teams, I was part of a team tasked with reorganizing our North American business into three strategic business units. The project was complex with several phases. It would affect every salaried Associate in what was then called "Masterfoods, USA" (this was before we used the Mars name widely across our businesses). Our project team was an appropriately diverse group, including project management specialists, Associate relations experts, talent assessment specialists, a member of our Finance organization, and two internal OD consultants. One of the OD folks was our leader. The other was me, in charge of human change management. One of the most involved phases of the project was the placement of hundreds of Mars Line Managers into roles in the newly designed organization. It wasn't about taking out costs and cutting heads. It was entirely about creating three smaller, more focused and nimble businesses from one large and unwieldy conglomeration of three different categories: chocolate confections, pet food and pet care, and human food.

Towards the end of the placement phase of the project, we conducted an organizational pulse survey along with a number of interviews to find out how it had gone. We heard the expected and understandable complaints from those who hadn't gotten exactly what they'd hoped for. By and large, however, the reviews were positive. Managers at all levels praised our rigor, efficiency, and compassion. We had done a lot right. We wanted to know what, specifically, so that we could apply the lessons to the rest of the project and share them with others in Mars, Inc. We arranged for a facilitated AAR. In order to make the process as engaging as possible, we hired an experienced graphic facilitator to help structure and record the discussions. We spent a full day answering a series of questions that were essentially all variations on, "What worked, what could have been better, and why." Our graphic facilitator led the program while at the same time capturing on large sheets of paper the key messages and themes. It was quite a feat on her part. Here's a sample of what she created.

That was over ten years ago, but the lessons we extracted from the process have stayed with me. For instance, we had set ourselves up for success by having functional experts as dedicated members of the team change instead of working with them on an as-needed basis. That helped tremendously with ongoing learning and course correction as well as building interpersonal relationships. We'd also requested and been given a dedicated, relatively secluded space within the office where we could conduct our work in relative privacy while remaining a part of the larger community. This choice enabled the high levels of confidentiality we required and it supported building a strong team dynamic among us. It was an engaging and effective way to set up and run a team.

As elaborate as our AAR process was with its graphic facilitation, all we did was employ the Five Actions, distill lessons learned, and then deploy those lessons. There's more information on the generic AAR process in Appendix E.

You don't have to wait until the end of a phase or the completion of a project to extract lessons learned. A group can also use "in-action reviews," IARs. As the name implies, IARs are similar to AARs except that they're applied to work that is still underway. You use the same questions to drive your inquiry: What's working, what isn't, and why? Lessons learned from in-action reviews get fed right back into the project they're addressing. The impact of the learning can be felt right away.

Team dynamics learning

Task learning is fairly straightforward. What did we do? How did it go? It's the sort of thing that good project managers can lead. Team dynamics learning, the second sort we'll consider, is where things can get tricky. It's typically the realm of psychologists, consultants, and woo-woo team building. It needn't be.

Over time, teams and groups develop patterns, habits of interaction and behavior that show up in everything they do together. That's what's meant by a team dynamic. Lots of things influence a team's dynamic: the clarity of their purpose, the mix of skills and abilities on the team, their understanding of the strategy they're following, the admixture of team member personalities, and levels of engagement, to name a few. Many of these influencers aren't part of the HPC Framework. Some, such as individual skills and abilities, can be dealt with through other channels, like HR. The question is, "From the extensive list of things that influence a team's dynamic, which are the ones that matter most and that we can do something about?" There isn't a single, right answer. The HPC Framework, however, covers a lot of what makes for successful collaboration. What's more, it empowers you and your group to do your own inquiry and learning. You don't need a consultant or an organizational psychologist to ask the right questions and to answer them. Use the HPC Framework as your guide. Think back to earlier in this section and those two questions: What's working? What would have to change to make us even better?

Broaden your inquiry by using the Imperatives

Reviewing how your team is doing against the commitments you made while working through the HPC Practices is simple. Many teams at Mars have taken this approach. In fact, in Appendix E you'll find a diagnostic questionnaire built around the Practices. An inquiry built around the Practices, though, has limitations. The Practices are interdependent. They overlap and interact with each other in sometimes subtle ways. Diagnosing them as if they were discrete from each other won't reflect the messy, organic reality of teamwork. To strengthen your team dynamics inquiry, you can use the Three Imperatives as your diagnostic guide.

The Imperatives, you'll recall, arose out of my research. They were the summary diagnosis of what was going on with teams at Mars. In short: There was a lack of intentional collaboration driven by low levels of clarity about what required collaboration. This was exacerbated by a general absence of discipline when it came to team operations, including learning. These issues were widespread among Mars teams. It makes sense, then, to begin the diagnosis of your team by inquiring into how a team is doing in terms of Clarity, Intentionality, and Discipline. The simple process I encourage you to follow looks like this:

Step 1: Overall assessment of collaboration
Step 2: Clarity assessment
Step 3: Discipline assessment
Step 4: Intentionality detailed assessment and conclusions

Within each of these steps, you employ some version of the Five Actions of team learning. Take the steps in the order I've shown. It's most productive to begin with a team-level assessment of collaboration. Once you have a read on how things are going, conduct inquiries into the Imperatives: Clarity, Discipline, and finally Intentionality. What you learn through your more detailed examination during steps two, three, and four will usually explain what you're seeing overall.

Let's go into more detail using the Five Actions from the previous chapter. We'll apply them to Step 1, above.

Pause. Create the space and time for your team's self-diagnosis. You can't squeeze this in at the end of a meeting. If you've worked your way through the entire Framework, you'll need a minimum of a half day to as much as a full day to do this work.

Inquire into how things are going generally, asking yourself how collaboration, as HPC defines it, is going in your team. Are you doing what all those teams from the research were claiming they wanted to do—collaborating more often and more effectively? Yes, no, or maybe. I often recommend that teams refer to the Levels of Collaboration graphic and ask themselves, using percentages, how much of each type of collaboration they're engaging in.

For instance, you might tell me, "We're at the Co-operation level 60% of the time, Reactive Collaboration 30% and Proactive 10%."

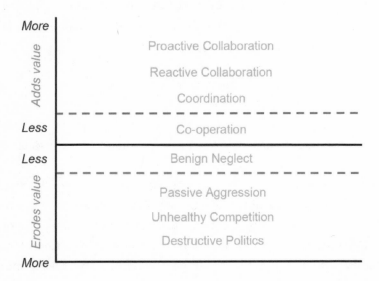

Reflect on the implications of your current level of collaboration for the work you're doing. The simple question to ask is, "Is this working for us?" It could be that spending 60% of your time in Co-operation is appropriate to your mission and business deliverables; most of your work may be in the outer ring of the Radar Screen. If that's the case, you can stop right there. If not, if you feel you aren't using collaboration as effectively as you could, it's worth conducting a deeper level of inquiry.

Plan for how you want to approach your deeper inquiry. You'll be looking for information about the reasons for your level of collaboration. You'll want to conduct further inquiries into levels of Clarity, of Intentionality and of Discipline. You can do this in the same session as the broad inquiry I've just described. Or you can plan to follow up later, and do some additional information gathering among yourselves in the meantime.

Act on your plan. Either conduct further exploratory conversations in the room or initiate the next steps in preparing for deeper inquiry later.

Mind the steps

The sequence for inquiring into the Imperatives matters. Following your overall assessment, Clarity comes first. The research told us that Clarity is what unlocks more intentional collaboration. Discipline comes next. Discipline as we define it is only relevant once a team has sorted out the "why" and the "what" of their collaboration. Once both of these Imperatives have been examined it makes sense to ask about Intentionality and to assess the impact of the other two Imperatives on the group's collaboration.

I think of the Imperatives as a series of lenses, like the ones used by an optometrist when figuring out how much vision correction you need. An eye exam, like an inquiry into collaborative effectiveness, begins with a general evaluation. They'll talk to you about your vision—is it getting worse, staying the same, are you having any symptoms of any kind? They may take a few images of your inner eyes. This will give your doctor a good idea of how things are going generally and let them know if they need to be on the lookout for anything. It's a great start, but not enough to prescribe the right glasses. So they'll dig deeper. One eye at a time, they'll have you look through a series of finely gradated corrective lenses. They'll flip through them one after the other, asking you to compare each to the one before it. "Is this one better, or this one?" "How about this one? Better, worse, or the same?" There's a specific sequence to all this lens shifting that gets you to the ideal prescription. There's also a lot of conversation between you and the optometrist. The same is true when working with a team through the Imperatives as a diagnostic. Use the suggested sequence of the Imperatives and keep inquiring and reflecting until you understand what's needed.

The Supply Chain team I've discussed in previous chapters used the lenses of the Imperatives, though they weren't aware of it. The manager had observed that her team's meetings weren't working out as intended. People were opting out even though they had accepted invitations. When they did show up, they hadn't completed what they said they would at their previous meetings. To get a clearer picture of why this might be happening, we created our survey. The survey, along with her observations about her team meetings, served as her step one high-level diagnostic. Next, the leader and team got together to inquire and reflect, to review their data, and apply the lenses of the Imperatives. They started with the Clarity lens, the foundational Imperative. Together, they discussed how clear they were about their shared purpose and shared work. They extended their discussion to consider Clarity in its broadest sense. They went beyond the "what and why" of Inspire Purpose and Crystallize Intent. They talked about whether team members were clear about who they should be collaborating with and how clear they were about the commitments they had made during Cultivate Collaboration. They even inquired into how clear team members were about their ways-of-working regarding meetings and staying connected. Their inquiry into Clarity spilled over into all of the Practices regardless of which Imperative each Practice might be primarily aligned with. That's why I like this approach; it facilitates a broader exploration.

Following their first round of inquiry the team concluded that the culprit wasn't Clarity. In fact, they reaffirmed their shared purpose and shared work. The issue was how they had applied — or failed to apply — their sense of Clarity to other Practices within the Framework. They next went to the Discipline lens. Since their meetings were where they were seeing the problems, they paid particular attention to them.

They quickly realized they'd made a faulty assumption a few months earlier. They had agreed that their existing process and timings for meetings was "about right." So their prescription for themselves had been to keep things as they were. That wasn't working. In particular, the agendas for their longer meetings didn't focus on the work at the center of their Radar Screen. As a result, their meetings weren't compelling to them, weren't built to arouse the collective achievement motive of the team. Said another way, their meeting Discipline hadn't taken into account the Clarity of purpose and shared work that they had spent time developing. This is why people were canceling out of their meetings or showing up without work done.

The problem they uncovered was anchored in the relationship among the Practices, with the way they had strung them together. By applying the lenses of the Imperatives to their self-diagnosis, they were able to inquire into the Practices as an interconnected whole. They could then tease out the particular Practices that needed more work. These were smart people. If they had looked at the individual Practices as discrete areas for inquiry, they probably would have made the links eventually.

I'm not sure every team would, though, which is why I prefer the Imperatives approach. Whether you begin your Sustain & Renew inquiry with the Practices or the Imperatives is a matter of style and personal preference. Do what works for you and your team, always keeping in mind the organic nature of teamwork and this Framework.

The Challenge of Sustain & Renew, or "How I Learned to Stop Worrying and Love Failure"

Stuff goes wrong in groups. It's why I have a job. Yet, most teams I work with get stuff done despite their issues. I don't see a lot of honest-to-God dysfunctional teams. What many people label as team dysfunction is instead individual dysfunction that has gone unaddressed and is thereby disrupting the team. Deal with the individual issue using existing company polices and processes, and what was presenting as a team problem evaporates. I've seen it many times.

There are dysfunctional teams, however. I've worked with a few. In my experience, the most common cause of dysfunction is low Clarity. If your vision is bad, eventually you'll end up walking into a tree. Dysfunctional teams can be unclear about many things: where they're going, why they exist as a team, what business needs they are serving, or why they're structured the way they are. There may be answers to these questions, but they don't have them or have forgotten. So, they muddle along unhappily, doing what they've been doing and eventually starting to run into barriers. They can't see, if you will, so they can't adapt.

One productive way to think about team dysfunction is as a persistent failure of the group to take in appropriate information and adapt. They aren't learning. It's the counterpoint to the idea that ongoing team learning leads to great team climate and true team spirit. A persistent failure to learn leads to lots of emotional bruises and a dreadful team climate.

Some teams get stuck. To get unstuck they have to learn. To learn, groups, especially stuck groups, have to face into difficult stuff. It will mean taking time out to confront mistakes and failures. The Supply Chain team I've been talking about at first resisted their manager's instinct to apply Sustain & Renew to themselves. "Hey, so we blew off a meeting. Or two. We're all busy trying to run our functions and earn a living. It'll be fine." They weren't initially prepared to admit any issues or risk. That's an attitude that, if sustained over time, leads to dysfunction.

My life has been one continuous mistake.

Deep guy that I am, I first encountered these words on a Zen thought-for-the-day calendar my wife gave me. They were uttered by Dogen, a Zen poet and philosopher of the thirteenth century. I love this quote. Imagine these words spoken with absolute equanimity, without judgement but stated as simple fact. They exude the sort of counterintuitive wisdom that captivates me. Wisdom can be seen as the knowledge accumulated from a life of mistakes put into context. In fact, a lot of folks make a living at doing just this. It's common for successful managers and leaders offering advice via blogs and articles to admit that they learned a great deal from their failures. They cash in on their failures, though, only after they have reached a pinnacle in their careers. I don't fault the pundits for this. Heck, it's my stock in trade. It's harder, though, for early- and mid-career managers and employees with high achievement drives to embrace failure. For them, failure is akin to losing. They don't like to lose, and where they are in their lives it feels like they have a lot to lose. Achievers keep score, based on their successes, and eschew failure no matter what the EXPERTS like me tell them. Eschewing failure is a habit teams and team members have to unlearn.

For the Framework to work, failure has to work, it has to

become generative. Failure has to become something we look for and mine for the valuable lessons it has to teach. General Stanley McChrystal is one of those leader-cum-pundit types who is in the business of offering wisdom to others. For a time, he led the allied forces in Afghanistan. General McChrystal has written a couple of books and given a TED talk or two. You might have seen the TED talk in which he talks about failure as a teacher. One of the commanders early in McChrystal's career gave him a piece of advice that stuck with him: learn to "fail without being a failure." While it makes a lot of sense, this one is tough for the achievement-oriented team member. For many of us, what we do is who we are. Completion, crossing the finish line, and moving forward are essential to our identity. What if, though, we framed failure as just another kind of achievement?

It's one thing to turn collaboration into a thing to be achieved. Collaboration can help us get work accomplished. Learning, too, can be construed as an accomplishment. Neither of these is too great a conceptual leap. Can you honestly make collaborative failure feel like an achievement? Recall what I just said about achievers liking to keep score. Tallying up one's failures doesn't make sense on the face of it: "Look, guys, I blew it seven times last year. Hurray!" However, keeping a record of the lessons one has learned can be effective. Tracking how a negative outcome was transformed into a positive insight that was valuable, not just to the person who experienced it but to others, is a real win. As Thomas J. Watson, founder of my former employer IBM, once said: "If you want to increase your success rate, double your failure rate."

We can learn from the world of design on this score. Design thinking, a widely used product development methodology, thrives on failure. Design thinking advocates product development by working from the consumer, back. Do your research, develop a few hypotheses, then rapidly create prototypes. Put your prototypes into the hands of users and watch what happens. Pay attention to what seems to work, and pay closer attention to what doesn't. "Fail fast, fail often" is the mantra. What doesn't work serves the invaluable function of telling you what you can stop working on or building so that you can focus on what seems to be working. Success matters, but getting there involves ample failure.

As useful as failure is, most organizations have an understandably limited appetite for it where their people are concerned. There are exceptions I've heard about, like the group within Google called "X." This is a group that works on what they call "moon shots," on wild ideas for doing amazing things. This is the group where the self-driving car originated, and where Google Glass started and was eventually killed. It failed. They fail all the time and celebrate failure as an act of learning. Most of us don't work at Google, though. In most big companies, fail to deliver on an expensive, highly visible project and you run the risk of being shown the door. What I'm talking about is a different kind of failure. Remember: The focus of this Framework is collaboration within work-groups. Our aim is to have Associates learn about themselves and their effectiveness as collaborative partners and members of a team. Collaboration isn't natural for most of us. It's a choice, a learned skill that we have to keep on practicing. What's more, it looks different every time our collaborative partners change; collaboration is a moving target. Failure, or lack of success, in how we're collaborating will be common and present lots of opportunity for learning on our journey together. We may as well make the most of it. In the end, failure-intolerant organizations probably won't know about most of our collaborative failures. These will happen within our immediate collaborative environment—our team. We'll pull ourselves up by the bootstraps and get the work done, regardless. What's more, the businesses we serve will be better for our having embraced and learned from the failures along the way.

It's not a problem, it's an opportunity!

I bristle when people insist that there are no problems, only *opportunities*! I get it, of course. Focus on our problems and we can end up dwelling on them and not noticing or learning from our successes. Focus on opportunities, on the other hand, and we'll be less likely to blame and more likely to keep things positive and teamy feeling. Yet, despite my belief in these things and my commitment to learning and creating team spirit based in learning, I won't adopt the slogan:

It's not a failure, it's a chance to learn!

These kinds of declarations infantilize us. They dismiss our genuine feelings when things don't go well. Falling short can suck. We're not kids in the town soccer league, though, who will feel hurt if we don't get a trophy (even though we finished last). Some things are failures. Others are partial successes, tinged with failure. Other things are unalloyed victories. Our feelings about all of them are valid and actually help us learn.

Learning from success is important. It, too, is hard for many of us. It's not because we don't like to talk about success. Most of us enjoy the recognition and satisfaction inherent in doing something that paid off. Some of us do shy away from overt recognition, and deflect positive feedback as a function of our personalities. More often the problem is the time and effort that learning, even learning from success, requires. We don't want to take the time to pause, inquire, and reflect, especially if we got it right. We achievement-driven types just want to get on to the next thing. It feels good and it moves us forward. While learning from success may not be easy, it's easier to convene a conversation of achievement-driven folks to talk about their accomplishments than it is to get them together to talk about their failures. Hence my focus on failure as a path to learning.

Team feedback and learning

Teams are made up of real, flesh-and-blood, fallible individuals, most of whom are trying, day in and day out, to do the right thing. They usually get it right but sometimes not. At some point, our fantastic successes as well as individual foibles and faux pas need to be looked at in terms of how they're affecting the team's effectiveness. This is where feedback comes in. At Mars we believe in the power of group feedback, of openly discussing all of what's working and what's not, even if what's not working is me. This is a scary prospect for many: "Wait, we're going to discuss my performance in front of the whole group? I only do that behind closed doors with my manager once a year." It's not as scary as it sounds. What's more, the benefits are so great that they easily outweigh the imagined risks.

Group feedback is an inevitable extension of the Practices of HPC. We've declared a common purpose, one we've all said we will pursue and support as individuals and as a team. We've identified the specific work that we'll do together and committed to each other, publicly, how we'll get that work done. It only follows that from time to time we'll have to talk together about how we're doing relative to our shared purpose and commitments. It's essential for each team member to understand how they're affecting the total team. Group feedback is how that gets done. It's how individual team members can most effectively learn about and build on their collaborative successes as well as understand and address those places where they may be letting the team down.

The process is simple but structured. It's based on the "hot seat" feedback process I described in Chapter 2, with one vital difference: it's bounded by the agreements and commitments that the team has made as part of working through the HPC Practices. In the process I described in Chapter 2, everything and anything that might possibly be construed as affecting the functioning of the team was fodder for feedback. I once witnessed a Finance director give feedback to his Marketing peer about his choice of wardrobe. That's an extreme example, but that lack of boundaries does lead to a sense that anyone can say anything to anyone else so long as they can find a justification for it. Within the context of the HPC Framework, the boundaries for feedback are clear, which helps the process to remain focused on what's important.

This was brought home to me the first time I facilitated a team feedback process with a team that had just worked through Inspire Purpose, Crystallize Intent, and Cultivate Collaboration. We were in China, not far outside Beijing, meeting in a village school-house that been converted to a corporate meeting venue. It was a lovely, rustic spot in sight of the Great Wall and well suited to a team retreat. I was working with a small leadership team of about six. We'd spent the previous day focused on their team purpose and working through the Radar Screen. The debates, especially about which work would be shared and which wouldn't, had been heated, bordering on angry. Eventually they proved productive. The next morning we conducted the behavioral contracting conversations that are part of Cultivate Collaboration. That afternoon was devoted to team feedback. I'd never conducted a team feedback session with HPC as the backdrop. Given the intensity of the conversations the day before, I was worried that things might get tense and more uncomfortable than usual. It occurred to me just then that it might help to remind the team what this feedback process was about. "You've declared your purpose and agreed exactly which work requires your collaboration. You then went on to commit to behaviors that would support both your purpose and your shared work. It's now time to talk about how each of you is doing relative to your purpose and the behaviors you committed to." This wasn't going to be a feedback free-for-all. It was going to be a chance for each person to gather data on themselves relative to what the team was committed to. It worked. It was the most productive round of team feedback I'd been a part of up until that time. I walked away from that two-day workshop excited about how HPC helps teams with its emphasis on Clarity and Intentionality, by keeping them focused on and committed to what matters most to them.

The process goes like this: The team sits in a circle of chairs, no tables. Each person takes a turn, first sharing their thoughts about what they're doing well, how they're living up to their commitments and the team's purpose. Then they offer a couple of thoughts about what they think they could be doing differently to be even better. Finally, they invite input, reactions, and feedback from their colleagues. There are ways to do this well and other ways to make a mess of it. In Appendix E I lay out some detailed steps that we use to increase the chances that the process is productive and positive. Here are a few pointers for making group feedback work:

- The focus of team feedback is on how each person is contributing to the group's effectiveness. It's *not* about how any one team member is doing on a single project, that is, work in the outer ring of the Radar Screen. Those conversations are better held between the manager and the individual.
- Don't wait for a group feedback discussion to give feedback. If you have feedback in the moment for a team member, share it as soon as possible.
- Hold group feedback discussions throughout the year to ensure that feedback is timely and so that the team has a chance to become efficient at the process.
- If a team member is known to be at risk, tread carefully. If a person is on an official performance improvement plan and subject to action by the company, it's important to let that process take its course. Group feedback isn't where you want to address such issues. Delay team feedback, if

necessary.

- Ensure the people are learning from both successes and shortcomings. The energy of the group will depend on everyone understanding and feeling that they're valued for what they do and growing to become even better. The easiest way to do this is to ensure that your feedback process elicits both sorts of feedback. The process in Appendix E does just this.

- Start slowly and gently. Your first team feedback session is likely to feel uncomfortable for some. Don't feel the need to have everyone deliver hard-hitting, soul-wrenching insights on your first time out. Allow a few sessions for people to get comfortable with the process. As time goes on, expect and encourage high levels of courage and straight talk.

The concern that is most often raised with me is ensuring psychological safety within the feedback process. My response? You can't ensure it or promise it, even if you start gently. There's a saying that I learned from a friend in Australia: There is no comfort in the learning zone and no learning in the comfort zone. Feedback is about learning. It's going to be uncomfortable, especially at first. I'm not suggesting that teams ignore common-sense rules of respect and decency. At the same time, if you wait for everyone to be "OK" with the process it won't happen. Giving and receiving feedback is just another skill, a muscle that if exercised gets stronger. The best way to start? Find a simple process that seems sound, like the one in this book, summon your courage and begin. Remember that it's a discipline, and stick with it until it becomes a habit.

Build a team development plan

Part of the pain of failure is that it's unpredictable. Things that we had counted on working end up going south. If we're thoughtful, we'll extract lessons from these failures and move on. We might even pull a Google X and celebrate our missteps and the information they yielded. High-performing individuals and teams, however, don't wait around for failure to learn. If we treat team learning as a thing to be achieved, it stands to reason that we would plan for that achievement, even set goals related to it. This won't be a foreign concept for most of us. A team's learning or development plan is similar to the individual development plan a person might create for themselves. It's all about what you, collectively, want to learn and how you intend to learn it. You use the same Five Actions talked about earlier as the roadmap for building a team development plan. Pause, inquire, reflect, plan and act. The sole difference between the Supply Chain team I described earlier and what I'm talking about here is scope. They were focused only on why their meetings weren't working. They paused, reflected, and inquired specifically into that problem. A team could just as easily pause to consider what it is that they need to learn more broadly. How are each of the Imperatives or Practices holding up and what are we going to do about them?

It begins with data

Every team needs a development plan. No two teams are identical, so no two plans will be alike. Essential for a good team development plan is data. "What can we learn about how we're operating today and how this is affecting us as a team and the results we produce?" For a team that's just been formed, the essential data on them is their newness. They'll first need clarity about why they were created and they can move on from there. Their team development plan may be as simple as:

Starting on 1 June, we will work through the HPC Framework beginning with Clarify Context. We will have worked through all the Practices by 31 December and begin to consistently operate based on the HPC principles as of 1 January next year.

If they're an established team that hasn't yet started using HPC, a simple approach to gathering data on themselves is fine. One of our other favorite tools is a simple diagnostic table with four categories. Ask the team to think about how things are going, and then have them populate the columns of this tool that builds on the old "Start/Stop/Continue" model.

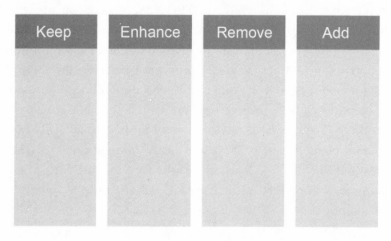

The team will populate each column with sticky notes. Each sticky note will contain a different thought about what the team might need to keep, enhance, and so on. For example, ideas you might see in the Keep column could be:

- Keep our once-monthly meeting
- Keep coaching us when we are stuck
- Keep our WhatsApp™ group—it really helps us stay connected

You'll find that team members will come up with a lot of similar or overlapping ideas. This kind of overlap is, itself, useful data; it tells you something about levels of agreement in the team. It gets interesting and tricky when a topic shows up in both the Keep column and the Remove column. In the same group that generated the Keep list above, someone else might suggest that the team remove WhatsApp™ from the tools they use.

Conflicting views like this will come up frequently in this exercise. Such differences within a team are common and healthy. They're one manifestation of diversity of thought and style. When your data reflects these kinds of differences, it's time to employ those Five Actions of Learning that I talked about earlier in this chapter. Take the time to explore the differences, find out what's behind them, what values, what assumptions, what feelings. Remember, this is just data. There's no need at this point to reconcile or resolve such differences. It's enough to know that they're there. If the data and the conversation suggest that collaboration isn't optimal, we find that for teams that haven't yet started it, embarking on the Practices, beginning with Inspire Purpose, works well.

Teams that have been working with HPC can generate their data using the Three Imperatives along with the Five Learning Actions. In addition, there's an HPC survey included in Appendix E—another good tool for those already using HPC. Finally, at Mars we use data from our Engagement surveys to help teams understand their climate and how well they're functioning together.

HPC isn't a panacea, as I've said. For teams whose dynamics may be more difficult, where there is a history of entrenched conflict and poor performance, you may want to consider getting help. Engage the services of an astute HR specialist or an external team consultant with a proven understanding of what drives and supports collaboration. In any case, don't create a team development plan based on your hunches and gut feel. Avoid team charlatans offering to transform your team's experience and productivity with exotic-sounding exercises and simulations. Insist on data, including any team-specific engagement data, and work from there.

A few examples

Team development plans can include a wide variety of different diagnoses and actions. It all depends on the team. I've used the Imperatives to organize a few examples of high-level diagnostics and related actions for a team that has been using the HPC Framework.

Diagnosis	Possible Actions
Clarity	
Our team's purpose doesn't seem relevant or appropriate.	Revisit, challenge and if necessary refine your team's purpose.
We aren't getting much done because we have too much that we're trying to collaborate on.	Review your team's Radar Screen, especially what's in the center. Challenge every piece of work at the center—does it benefit from total team collaboration? Could it be done better by a smaller group or an individual?
We've got some of the wrong people working on things.	Revisit and rework your collaborative Radar Screen. Review who is working with whom on what.
Intentionality	
Our behaviors in general aren't supporting our collaboration as	Go back to your agreed collaborative behaviors

much as they could.

(Cultivate Collaboration) and identify which behaviors are most in need of attention. Contract with all on what will be required to reinvigorate these behaviors.

People's varying styles and preferences seem to be causing problems in certain projects.

Identify which sub-groups are affected. Have them recontract with a focus on their individual styles and preferences. If appropriate, use a personality instrument and feed outputs into these sub-groups' collaboration discussions.

Discipline

Decision making is getting bogged down, especially on the work we're collaborating on as a team.

Check to see that each of the pieces of work at the center of your Radar Screen has a clear decision-making protocol associated with it. Will it be a consensus decision? An authority-based decision?

Decision-making authority isn't clear in our sub-groups.

Revisit the sub-group. contracting process (Cultivate Collaboration). Ensure all sub-groups agree to and implement a decision-making protocol for their respective tasks.

We're repeating mistakes across projects.

Agree to and implement an after-action or in-action review

	process for your team (Sustain & Renew).
We're getting negative feedback from internal customers largely through back-channels.	Develop and agree to a Sustain & Renew process focused on gathering and learning from feedback from internal customers.

Diagnosis isn't fancy or complicated. So much of what ails teams comes from simple problems that go unaddressed. Go back to the Five Actions. Slow down and get curious. Ask a few good questions and answer them together. Then, create a simple, achievable plan. The rest will come naturally.

Planning for continuous improvement is one way that teams remain healthy and productive. They also have to respond to changes in the world around them. Chapter 14 explains the HPC Practice of Clarify Context that addresses this need.

Summary

- Learning was the lowest-scoring item on the questionnaire used with the teams in our research.
- The goal of Sustain & Renew is to keep teams focused on productive learning about themselves and how they operate. Team learning makes the rest of your work on HPC stick.
- Sustain & Renew focuses on two types of learning: task learning and team dynamics learning.
- While the HPC Framework can act as a roadmap for your inquiry, the Imperatives do a better job of accounting for the relationships and connections among the Practices.
- Teams must learn to embrace failure and all that it can teach if they want to make the most of team learning.
- Team feedback is a natural extension of the HPC

Framework and it's one important discipline within Sustain & Renew. There is no better source of data on how the team is working than team members themselves.

- Use the data you collect on your team to create and follow a team development plan, an agreed set of actions for how you intend to keep learning together.
- Start small, keep it simple and data-based, and build your team learning discipline over time. When you do, you will find the energy and power that this Practice taps into to be the most powerful of all that we have discussed.

Chapter 14

The Special Practice—Clarify Context

What Makes This Practice "Special"?

Max DePree in his book *Leadership Is an Art*[1] says, "The first job of a leader is to define reality." Teams have the same responsibility, and Clarify Context is how they do it.

The other five Practices that we've talked about are inward looking; they concentrate on the team itself.

- Inspire Purpose asks the team to understand how its collaboration could add value over and above the total of everyone's individual efforts.
- Crystallize Intent focuses on identifying what work does and does not require collaboration.
- Cultivate Collaboration builds on the two preceding Practices and asks, "Who do we need to be for and with each other if our collaboration is to be as intentional as possible?"
- Activate Ways-of-Working invites the team to think about how its processes will enable their shared purpose and efforts.
- Sustain & Renew asks the team to reflect on how effective the team has been in its collaborative efforts.

Clarify Context, which is represented by a circle wrapping around the other five Practices, looks outside the team.

Every business team exists within a broader reality, an enterprise ecosystem that's like a Russian nesting doll. A team exists within a function like Sales or R&D, which itself exists within a larger organization, which itself may be nested within a holding company or conglomerate, which in turn exists within a

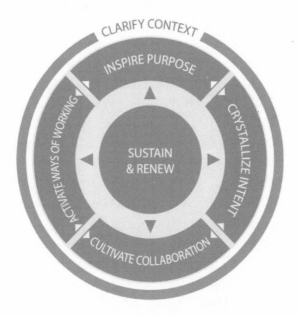

community, within a country, and so on. Not all of these layers matter to the team at the core. Still, every team has to ensure that it understands the various relevant contexts within which it works. This allows it to adapt appropriately to these contexts so that it can remain relevant and continue to add value for its stakeholders. In short, a team has to know and remain connected to its reality.

A context reality check is where thorough team effectiveness work begins. After all, if your team isn't relevant, all the team learning in the world won't matter. Crafting a team purpose and creating your Radar Screen will be wastes of time. If this sort of learning is so basic, why did I choose to talk about this Practice towards the end of the book? For two reasons: breadth of scope and frequency of application.

Most of our team Framework is practical and tactical. It's about the things a team can do right now and every day to optimize their collaboration. This one Practice, about learning and making sense of the team's operating context, is more strategic. It's meant to address a broader scope and time horizon and to connect the team to the bigger picture. Clarifying Context is existential. It can result in overarching choices and changes that can alter a team's reason for being and therefore its purpose, its shared work and ways-of-working. This is big stuff. It only needs to be addressed in response to fundamental or highly consequential shifts in a team's context. By contrast, I suggest that teams check themselves against their purpose at every team meeting. The team's Radar Screen ought to be refreshed every quarter. Collaborative agreements need to be revisited regularly as projects and tasks evolve. Clarify Context is invoked only when there's been significant change.

Learning about context

Clarify Context is potentially a big deal, but it isn't hard to figure out or execute. The Five Actions we used in "Sustain & Renew" are also applied to Clarify Context.

Pause: Clarify Context, because it takes in so much, can become involved. Teams may need to inquire both broadly and deeply. Be sure to allocate ample time for research, inquiry and reflection.

Inquire: While it may be an event or change that triggers work on Clarify Context, it's the inquiry into the meaning and impact of the event or change that is important. Take time to study the situation, and frame provocative questions that will get people thinking and debating.

Reflect: Dig deep into the questions you've posed. Look for connections and themes. Ask "why," then ask "why," again and again when considering any given topic. Don't settle for the easy answers, though in the end they may be what you return to.

Plan: Address the "so what" of it all. What will this team do about what it has discovered? How? When?

Act: Put your insights and plan to work.

Several years ago I conducted a Clarify Context workshop for a regional VP of P&O and his team of senior P&O leaders. There had been some organizational changes. The VP was going to take on a different role and someone else would be replacing him. Context was shifting. During this VP's tenure, the North American P&O function had broken out of a years-long funk and accomplished some important things. He wasn't the most popular leader I'd ever known but he was principled, tough-minded, fair, and his success was inarguable. He led the transformation of the P&O into a more credible, business-focused function. I was honored when he asked me to work with him and his team of P&O leaders to reflect on the two-and-a-half years since he had joined them. The goal was to assess the changes that had taken place and to distill important lessons as they prepared to enter a new phase. It was a bit like an AAR, but not limited to a single program or project.

By this time, I had come to believe in the power of graphic facilitation to enable deeper, more dynamic group dialog. I suggested to the VP that we use a graphic facilitator and he agreed. I contracted with the same facilitator who had worked with me on the organization redesign project. She knew our company and culture well by this time. One afternoon in the autumn of 2007 we gathered the VP's team. We invited their future leader to join us so that she could benefit from whatever was learned. Our graphic facilitator created a 12-foot-long, 4-foot-high timeline. We explained the process and they started telling stories. It was that simple. As the team told stories, our facilitator filled the timeline with characters, icons, words, and phrases that captured the major happenings and projects of that two-and-a-half-year stretch. Out of the recollections and drawings a coherent and surprising story emerged. Surprising to the team, anyway. Not to their leader. There was one roughly six-month stretch of time that stood out from the colorful clutter in the visual timeline. We had used human-shaped cut-outs to represent Associates who had left or joined the business. Red was for leavers, green for new arrivals. We'd written a name on each paper figure and placed it on the timeline at around the time each Associate had come or gone. The stretch of timeline representing this six-month period I just mentioned was a jumble of red paper figures. A number of long-serving P&O Associates had left Mars during that six months. Most had chosen to move on. Others had been offered the opportunity to leave. As it happens, most of the VP's major achievements came to fruition after this tumultuous time.

That difficult period of turnover had been the final phase of the VP's first 18 months on the job. It hadn't been a happy or productive time for the function as they got used to him and he figured out what he needed to do to succeed. After that span of time, though, there was a significant shift in what got done and how people felt about it. Things got better. They got better, it became evident, because certain Associates who hadn't been able to contribute, or who were somehow blocking progress, had left. What had been holding the function and its stronger Associates back were other, less well-suited Associates. The lesson was clear. People, or if you prefer, talent, matter. If you know what you want to get done and act courageously on people issues, it'll all come together. This wasn't news to the VP. For his team, who'd felt the sorrow of friends and long-time colleagues leaving, it was one of those honest-to-God "ah-ha" moments. There was no bitterness in their realization, just a kind of opening to wisdom. In some cases, practicing Clarify Context leads to clear and definable things that need to change, actions that need to be taken, in response to insight that has been gained. That wasn't the case in this example. It was, instead, a stellar example of how Clarify Context can provide broader lessons for teams and individuals making sense of transition.

Contexts to consider

Not every event or change requires a team to Clarify Context. For instance, when a single, new team member joins the team, the team needs to appropriately on-board and include the person. This may require redistribution of the work in the Radar Screen and recontracting of Cultivate Collaboration agreements, but that's about it. If, however, a team changes out multiple team members in a short time, that's an opportunity for Clarify Context; many relationships will have been affected. A significant percentage of the work captured on the Radar Screen will have new names listed as collaborators. More fundamentally, the personal nature of the team's inspiring purpose means that the team's purpose statement will need to be revisited. In all likelihood it will need to be rethought if it's going to work for a substantially new crew.

Similarly, if one of a team's multiple business targets changes, you'd need to adjust your Radar Screen and the agreements related to that target. You wouldn't, though, trigger Clarify Context. If, on the other hand, one critical leg of a three-legged strategy were altered or dropped, changing the essence of the strategy, that would be a different story. Such a change would alter much of the work the business expected from this team. Consequently, any team working against this revised strategy would want to Clarify Context.

When it comes to implementing Clarify Context it's all about scope. When Clarify Context is practiced, it often results in revisiting and reworking many of a team's HPC agreements. For that reason, it should be invoked carefully.

We've identified four kinds of change that generally call for this Practice: strategic change, organizational change, leadership changes, and broad changes within the team. We'll look at each of these categories.

Strategic—Every organization is, ideally, responding to the environment it operates or competes in. As the business environment evolves, organizations must adapt. As organizations adapt, the people and groups nested within them have to learn and adapt, too. A team's collaborative efforts are always meant to be in service of the intentions of the larger business. When organizational strategy changes, teams go back to their foundational HPC work. They reconsider all of the essential Practices, from Inspire Purpose all the way through to Sustain & Renew. As they inquire they might ask themselves questions like:

- What does this change mean for why we exist as a team?
- What about our purpose? Is it still relevant? What might need to change?
- How might the work we choose to collaborate on change?

In Chapter 8 I talked about my work with our ice cream business. They manufacture and sell iconic brands like Dove® Bars and Snickers® ice cream treats. For several years we called this business Ice Cream & Substantial Snacks or ICSS. They managed our ice cream brands along with a few other smaller but promising non ice cream products. They owned Combos®, a savory snacking product. They also owned Marathon®, a chocolate-based energy/nutritional bar. There were a number of reasons for what may seem to have been an organizational force-fit. These three non ice cream brands had at least one trait in common with our ice cream business: they were seen as strategically important in the overall portfolio but weren't yet major players in their respective product categories. This commonality suggested that all three groups of products would benefit from similar strategies and could therefore be managed as a portfolio.

The leadership team of ICSS operated on this assumption for about four years. It never seemed to work; growth was hard to come by. Then, last year, the ICSS General Manager proposed a strategic shift to the President and leadership team of the overall North American business of which ICSS was a part. Along with Dove® Ice Cream bars, many of our most prominent chocolate brands, like Snickers®, Twix® and M&Ms®, were represented in the ice cream portfolio. As the overall ice cream portfolio languished, so did the flagship brands within it. So, the ICSS business proposed returning to a stand-alone ice cream business. The change would allow the team and their business to focus on this highly specialized category. It would involve breaking out the ice cream business and transferring the other, non ice cream brands and assets to be managed elsewhere within the Mars Chocolate North America structure. The proposal was accepted. The implementation of the strategy triggered a cascade of work, not just for the ice cream business but for our entire North American chocolate enterprise. The organization design, reporting structures, budgeting assumptions, and more had to be rethought and reworked to accommodate it. As all this essential organization work was being done, the new Ice Cream Leadership Team (ICLT) had to Clarify Context, to reorient itself to a new, ice-cream-only strategy and the numerous changes it triggered.

In order to account for these changes the ICLT had to revisit their purpose and the entire HPC Framework. As you may recall, when they were the Ice Cream & Substantial Snacks Leadership Team they had seen their purpose as being "the stewards of the people and brands entrusted to them." This idea of stewardship had been entirely appropriate. They were shepherding a collection of diverse, small brands and nurturing a cohort of promising future leaders. Now, though, with a sole focus on frozen desserts and treats and a serious commitment to generate growth, stewardship, while still important, wasn't going to be enough. Working with an external consultant they agreed that their role as a collaborative unit was now "creating clarity, supercharging talent and enabling quality decision making." I discussed this purpose with them several months after they had devised it. I wanted to understand more. It felt too buzzwordy. Not surprisingly, it was more meaningful for them. In this new world of theirs, at least for the time being, clarity would be essential, especially for those who were used to how things had been before. What's more, people still mattered, but being stewards of talent wasn't sufficient. They meant to "supercharge" the capabilities and potential of the people they led so that this business could get to growth as quickly as possible. Finally, with their newly won freedom to act as a single-category business, decisiveness and quick action were indispensable. This small business, armed with strong brands and wonderful products, competes with the most powerful ice cream manufacturers on the planet—Unilever and General Mills. Freezer space in stores is costly and hard to come by. Gaining share was always hard for smaller competitors with fewer resources. Now, for our ice cream business, with its ability to be more focused and with a renewed will to win, decisiveness and speed could be a deciding factor in the battle for market share.

As a result of this shift in collaborative emphasis, not only the team's purpose but their entire Radar Screen had to be rethought. All the collaborative contracts that it drove needed updating. The changes that they had requested and made in the ice cream business strategy meant that they, as a team, needed to figure out, to devise, a new way of working together. Their organization also needed to change to reflect and take advantage of the shifts they'd made. That's covered in our second Clarify Context category.

Organizational—Somewhere, even if it's only in your boss's brain, your team exists as a bunch of boxes and lines within an organization chart. Think of the org chart as a graphical representation of the stakeholders with whom your team is in relationship. You and your team have internal customers and internal suppliers with whom you're in some sort of partnership.

When there's a change in the organization that affects this network of stakeholders and therefore your team's relationships, it's time to Clarify Context. Teams who are experiencing an organization change would want to revisit their purpose and shared work, as discussed in the previous section. In addition, they also consider questions like:

- How will we have to work differently together in order to reflect the changes taking place around us?
- Are there teams for whom we are customers who have been affected? What might they need from us now that is different from before?
- What changes might we need to make in our ways-of-working?

Where there had been two distinct sales forces in the ICSS organization, now there would be only one, ice cream-focused sales force. The VP marketing had been leading both the snack food and ice cream marketing teams in different sites. Now, there would be an ice cream-focused marketing organization under him. The same was true for almost every member of the leadership team. They were now leading a different business and each of them was leading a changed function.

The organizational changes that the ICLT initiated, while significant, were fairly simple in terms of their impact on their team. The group, at least at first, included all of the same individuals, minus one. The disruption to their dynamic was minimal. A better example of how a team confronts organization change comes from one of the P&O teams I have talked about. When one of our small petcare businesses merged with the larger Petcare segment in North America, the head of the smaller P&O team was chosen to lead the combined function. Her team added new members and shifted some responsibilities.

It was in some ways the same team and in other ways not. The collaborative contracts that had been established in the team's previous incarnation were no longer meaningful. For example, prior to the reorganization, the P&O team member who led talent recruitment had been working closely with her teammate, who supported the Finance function to fill some crucial roles in that division. The P&O Finance lead, however, had taken on a different role during reorganization. The P&O talent acquisition leader still had to help get those Finance roles filled. To do that effectively, she and a newly appointed colleague had to sit down and do a little Cultivate Collaboration contracting. The work they had to do was clear; the VP of Finance and his team were counting on getting people in those jobs. The newly paired P&O duo needed to develop clarity on how they would do it together in their newly constituted team.

Large-scale reorganization is complex and often painful. In the USA, at least, the implications of a corporate reorganization for outplaced individuals can be devastating. I'm proud of the lengths that Mars goes to, to respect the dignity and lives of those who end up without a job after a restructuring. Many companies I know of don't do half as much. Another big miss during and after reorganization is the failure to think about and account for disrupted relationships. For every individual who is let go or who chooses to leave, there is a web of working relationships that are affected. The impact that those disrupted working relationships can have on productivity and business results is considerable. A business may save millions by reducing headcount costs while hemorrhaging money as those who remain struggle to return to their former levels of individual and collaborative effectiveness. Here again, the team is the level at which a meaningful difference can be made. Clarify Context invites teams to consider the potential disruptions to their collaboration and to limit the collateral damage that results from organization change that is otherwise beyond their control.

Sometimes, though, turnover just happens. People move on, they get promoted, or they leave the workforce. Regardless of the reasons for turnover, changes in team membership in and of themselves will sometimes trigger the need to Clarify Context. Let's consider two instances when this makes sense.

Leadership—It's obvious. Leaders have more impact on the teams they lead than any other individual member of the team. Perhaps it's a weak leader whose individual problems lead to apparent team dysfunction. Maybe it's the strong leader whose efforts lead to an improved team climate. Whatever their impact, leaders deserve special consideration. Working on Cultivate Collaboration and contracting between the leader and the team is one example of how this Framework gives particular consideration to the role of the leader. We also do it in Clarify Context.

When a new leader joins a group, the group has to pause to reflect on themselves and their collaboration. No matter how robust their work on the HPC Practices, they'll benefit from this inquiry. New leaders frequently bring new priorities, even new strategies. They bring different preferences for how they like to work and how they prefer to have others work. Of course, the amount of change depends on the leader. Some leaders come in and, despite their different styles and personalities, pursue minimal change. Others arrive on the scene with an entirely new and contrasting approach. Still others will be somewhere in between. Regardless of the degree of change, both the leader and the team do well to pause and inquire as to what the change at the top will mean. Teams, working with their new leader, will address questions like:

- Who is this new leader? What makes them tick? What gets them excited and what keeps them up at night?
- What do we need to do to acquaint them with the work we

have already done on our dynamics? How should we best include them in that work?

- How much does our purpose resonate with what the new leader sees as our strategy and mission?
- How much of the work at the center of our Radar Screen aligns with our new leader's expectations and intentions?

About six months after the change to the Ice Cream strategy and structure, their leader was promoted into another, larger leadership role in Mars. When I met with them most recently, they were working under the interim leadership of their Marketing VP. The length of the interim period wasn't clear — it would be a couple of months up to as long as half a year. You might think, "You just moved the marketing guy into the big chair temporarily. No big deal. He knows the team and they know him." As I said, leadership matters. It changes things even when the leader comes from the ranks of those he must now lead and even when that change may not last. In fact, anyone who's ever been promoted to lead a team they were once part of knows that the shift from peer to boss is particularly difficult. This case was especially unusual in the way that he was asked to lead without fully leading. He'd been instructed in his interim boundaries by those who appointed him. He was to keep the ship on course but not totally take the helm. He'd be accountable to lead the business to a strong second half of the year, but he'd have no say in his team's year-end performance reviews. His context was contradictory.

While his team already knew him as a colleague, they didn't know him as interim leader operating under conflicting constraints. As I experienced them in our most recent work together, the team had little patience for the way the leader's role had been set up. The team spent a good deal of time recontracting the role their interim leader would play. They discussed the sorts of decisions that they felt he should be making, those that a full-time, dedicated general manager (GM) would make. They were clear that they expected him to hold them accountable for the performance of their functions and that he would be giving them their year-end performance management reviews. Finally, they expected him to take these expectations back to his boss and get her agreement to them. These conversations were vital to the team. No team can afford low levels of clarity about their leadership, interim or otherwise. Every minute spent clarifying leadership context is worth it. If, as Max DePree said, the leader's first job is to define reality, then clarifying leadership context is essential. It ensures that the entire team is living in the same reality as their leader, is connected and responding to the same sense of direction and priority as the person who coordinates their efforts and resources. This is true, even if, as would be the case with the Ice Cream team, they'd be going through a similar process again in a matter of months when a permanent leader was put in place.

This clarifying of context happens on both sides of the leadership equation. The team, as I've described, has to have their say. The leader's perspective is every bit as important. Even before stepping into their new job, the new leader will want to engage in related self-reflection. They may ask themselves questions like these:

- What specifically am I looking for in this job? What will I learn? What am I worried about? What am I excited about?
- What is the organization expecting of me? Is this team in turnaround mode? Are they already a highly functioning group? What are my bosses hoping I'll get out of and/or bring to this role?
- What do I have to offer this team? What skills, knowledge, abilities? What deficits do I have in terms of skills, knowledge and abilities that I need to address? How could this group help me address my deficits?

- How much change do I feel I need to lead? How much should stay the same?
- What does this team expect of me?

I wasn't part of the interim ice cream GM's process of self-reflection. Knowing the man as thoughtful and dedicated, I knew he wouldn't have accepted the appointment without carefully weighing the answers to a similar set of questions. It was an honor to have been asked, a chance to challenge himself and to be of further service to his teammates. In fact, his teammates benefited directly from the time he spent considering his choice. It enabled him to participate in the Clarify Context conversations I described above with cogency and commitment. His clarity and self-awareness became especially important when his team sent him back to his manager with a different set of expectations for the interim GM role. I know his boss. She's tough—smart, even-handed, but tough. His ability to stand his ground with her required that he know with certainty his mind, heart, team, and business. That's what this aspect of Clarify Context is meant to provide.

People and team—Our Ice Cream Leadership Team's new interim leader wasn't the only change in personnel they had to confront. After the interim leader's appointment, and unrelated to it, they also had three other changes to deal with. They on-boarded a relatively new P&O Director, their Finance Director was about to go out on maternity leave and be temporarily replaced by one of her team, and their Director of Sales was moving off the team shortly into a new role. Their business had stabilized as a dedicated ice cream business, but their membership was undergoing an upheaval.

Changes like this have a way of happening in clusters. In our day-to-day lives we'd just say, "All this stuff seems to happen at once." It does. In evolutionary science, this is called punctuated equilibrium. Mother Nature lopes along for a few eons without much changing, evolutionarily. The next thing you know, an asteroid the size of Manhattan hits the earth and the course of evolution shifts seismically. On a less dramatic scale these sorts of unexpected disturbances in a team's flow are common, if not always paid attention to. It's like that insight we had while creating the timeline graphic during the North American P&O workshop I described. Things had been stable on the team for a year or two and then, watch out! People were suddenly coming and going all at once. It wasn't clear until they looked back on it, though, until they clarified the context, how much impact that confluence of events had had.

When sudden widespread changes occur in the makeup of the team, regardless of the cause, it's time to Clarify Context. Apply the lenses of HPC with the newly constituted team. Inquire into and reflect on current levels of Clarity. Think together about how the changes will affect levels of intentionality and the quality of relationships in the team. It's particularly important to delve into the relationship aspects by asking questions like:

- Who is on this team now? Who are they as individuals and people?
- What are their skills and abilities? What deficits might they have and how can I help them address those deficits?
- What do my current teammates need most from me?
- How do my skills, abilities, and preferences fit in with theirs?
- What is needed to strengthen our relationships overall?

If, as was the case with both the Ice Cream Leadership Team and the Petcare P&O team, previous relationships were strong, there is likely to be some letting go that needs to happen. The former cohorts trusted and were courageous with one another as a matter of habit. Those members who remained following the change needed to develop new, similar habits of relationship with their new teammates. They'd have to unlearn one set of expectations to take a new set on board.

You'll want to think about the timing of these conversations. The comings and goings in the Ice Cream Leadership Team were in full effect the last time I worked with them. In fact, the interim GM and I talked about postponing the workshop until things settled a bit. They did the right thing by not waiting to do their Clarify Context work. You can wait for conditions to stabilize. They might, but they might not, at least not right away. We never know when one period of tumult will end and when a time of relative calm will take hold. It's a good idea to pause and learn even in the midst of change. Learning together, while it can energize a group, also serves to settle a group and bring it together. Reflection and inquiry induce a thoughtful calm and allow a team to focus and gain perspective. As with the rest of team learning, there is no single approach, no prescription, for adapting to the sudden turnover of team members. Here are a few things to keep in mind in the face of changes within your team:

- Remember that Clarity is organic and reality-shifting. You can't respond to every change in your team, so focus on the big ones first.
- Appreciate the disruptive impact of change on levels of the intentional collaboration and productivity in your team.
- Pause, take a time out to apply the Five Actions of team learning to the Imperatives or the HPC Practices as you have worked on them.

At this point, you've read everything that I have to tell you about the Mars Framework for High Performance Collaboration. The next and final chapter offers thoughts about how to make the

Framework work for you.

Summary

- What a team commits to and plans for through its work with HPC must be and remain relevant to the business they're a part of. Clarify Context is the Practice that addresses this need.

- Clarify Context is called the Special Practice because it is only invoked in response to significant changes.

- When a team's fundamental context changes—whether it's the business strategy, their leadership, the structure of the organization, or its own membership—a healthy group will pause to consider, or reconsider, their collaborative value, commitments, and plans.

- The same five learning actions—Pause, Inquire, Reflect, Plan, and Act—can be applied to any of the types of changes mentioned above.

- When clarifying context, the team's purpose, Radar Screen, collaborative contracts, ways-of-working and learning plans should all be revisited. They might not need to change. But they might, and that is the opportunity and the point.

Part III

Chapter 15

Putting the Framework to Work

You now have the HPC Framework in its entirety. You know everything about it that there is to know, at least so far. You know the background, the theory, and the history behind it. You've learned why it looks and works the way it does and how all its various elements function. You've been given its DNA, so to speak. Why would we do that, just put this out there for everyone to have and use? On one level, I've written this book because it's a cool story to be able to tell. It's something we're proud of, and we think that potential future Mars Associates and leaders, people we might one day hire, will find it attractive. It's bigger than that, though. We want this good work to last, grow and make the greatest difference possible. In the Introduction I told the story of how Mars led a consortium in discovering the cocoa plant's genome and then made the information public. Not every company would make that choice, especially when it concerned a raw material that's core to their business. Mars did and I'm enormously proud of that. The thinking that shaped the decision to share the cocoa genome was part of Mars agreeing to my writing this book. It's about our Mutuality Principle:

A mutual benefit is a shared benefit; a shared benefit will endure.

It's the reason this book exists. We want this work to endure and to serve us as broadly as possible. To ensure that, the work is best shared with those who share interests with us. HPC can make a difference to a lot of people and to businesses large and small all over the world. So, we're sharing it. Those are our intentions. Good intentions, though, only go so far. It's time to put it all to work.

Not surprisingly, we've learned a lot about what works when it comes to the Framework. We've also learned what doesn't work so well. Mars is a big company with one culture and several business units and divisions. Each of the major parts of Mars has a character of its own. Units and managers around the world have tried a variety of approaches to deploying and using HPC, approaches that were suited to them. As they've done this, they've learned and shared their lessons with me and our HPC community. This chapter is about our insights into the variety of ways that the HPC Framework can be adapted and applied.

The contents of this book could be used in a number of ways. Three strike me as most likely to make sense outside of the Mars environment:

- Adoption
- Adaptation
- Emulation

Here's a bit more detail on each:

Adoption: You take the contents from the middle chapters of this book and adopt the Framework, as it is.

Adaptation: You like the Framework but want to make changes, to adapt it to better suit your organization or your team.

Emulation: Instead of either adopting or adapting the Framework, you can emulate our research and development process. You use our development methodology to influence how you go about doing a similar thing for teams in your organization.

There is a fourth option that I call Mutation. I don't recommend it. Mutation would involve changing or removing parts of the

Framework or appending other unrelated frameworks to it. In other words, messing with its DNA. We've had experience with this approach and the results haven't been great. The Framework was designed as an integrated whole, all of the Practices connected in meaningful ways to the others. There's nothing stopping you using only one or two of the Practices, of course, or adding a seventh. While you may learn some things or generate some short-term energy in the team, you're not likely to see improvements in team performance or climate over the longer term. If you're going to take either the Adoption or Adaptation approaches, incorporate, in some fashion, all six of the Practices.

Before we go into the three implementation options, there are a few things it will be worth thinking about, regardless of the direction you take.

Is This Framework Right for Your Organization or Team?

Our Framework was developed inside of and tailored for one large, global company. The precepts it's built on, however, have the potential to work in almost any Western-style organization, large or small, for profit or otherwise. I make the distinction of Western-style because of the West's individualistic leanings and preferences. In companies that have arisen from cultures with a more collectivist orientation, HPC may not fly. I have used HPC with Mars teams in Asian countries that tend to be more collectivist—China, Vietnam and Thailand—with success. In these cases, however, the Mars culture had blended with the local and regional cultures enough that the Framework made sense. National and regional cultures do matter. Other factors, such as whether a company is global or local, whether it's profit driven or mission driven, are less critical. HPC, with its laser focus on unlocking and supporting collaborative behaviors, still applies, regardless of many of the things that differentiate one organization from another. The biggest variable may be the organizational culture you're working in. How you account for it can make all the difference.

Mind the corporate culture

If you choose to adopt or adapt this Framework or to develop your own, a lot will depend on your company's culture and how you understand it and factor it in. By the time I formally started to work on the HPC Framework, I had been with Mars for ten years. I was, not thoroughly but largely, acculturated. I had enough distance from our culture to be able to observe and comment on it, but was enough of an insider that I had a genuine feeling for it. The small group of us who collaborated on turning the insights from the research into what you see today spent months ensuring that what we produced felt culturally appropriate. We were flying into strong headwinds of individual achievement, so our Framework had to be sturdy and reliable. If you're considering using this Framework or the ideas within it in your organization, approach this question of culture as seriously as we did. In particular, know where to go with it, and where to push against it.

We were trying to work with and respect our culture. Simultaneously, we knew we had to nudge it in a productive direction that it wasn't aware it needed to move in. Our use of McClelland's motives theory to make sense of our achievement-oriented culture was just one part of it. One nod to our culture were the names and the sequence of the Practices. They were in flux for six months. We required labels that were descriptive and memorable without being too soft or poetic for our pragmatic culture. I have a spreadsheet with lists of words we considered as the name for the Practices. We started with a draft set of Practice names. We tried those out, working with Mars teams and managers, and in the end landed on what you see in this book. The same thinking went into the implied sequence of the Framework. We were aware that users would look at the graphic as they might look at a clock face, and move from the top, clockwise. The Practice at the twelve o'clock position would be significant as the presumed starting point. Originally, acknowledging our action orientation, I placed Crystallize Intent in the top spot, calculating that team members would want to know as soon as possible what the work was. A few of my colleagues challenged my calculus. They believed that if we caved in to this aspect of our culture, teams would start with this Practice and focus on just the shared work while potentially ignoring the rest of the Framework. In particular my colleagues were worried about achievement-oriented teams rushing past the valuable idea of collaborative purpose. So, we tried the graphic both ways. After our trial-and-error period, we knew what we had to do. The dissenters had been right. This was one place where we needed to challenge the culture. The teams I had worked with, once they had their tasks clearly in front of them didn't have the patience for Inspire Purpose or Cultivate Collaboration. If Inspire Purpose was going to work within the Framework, it had to take the top spot.

At every step of the way, we remained engaged with the Mars culture, feeling our way, deciding where to push against it and where to flow with it. In the end, the viral spread of the Framework throughout our business told us we had made smart choices. For the first four years of its life, the HPC Framework had no official sanction from the top of the organization. It was never announced as "the way" to do team effectiveness on our corporate intranet or elsewhere. It was embedded in one of our core management development programs and from there it took off. Today it's the standard for Mars teams. This couldn't have happened without our having engaged with the realities of our culture as we did. Our approach was time consuming and labor intensive. There may be more efficient ways to go about this sort of cultural harmonizing. Culture is an ethereal and difficult-to-pin-down thing, so I'm not sure. Whatever approach you take, take the time, put in the effort, and pay attention to your culture.

How to assess fit

Let's imagine that you've got a sense that HPC will work just fine for you the way it is. You have a strong hunch that you can put it right to work. You even have a team in mind that you want to start with. Pause before you do. Do a bit of inquiry. A major component of the HPC Framework's DNA is the idea that individual achievement tends to drive how people approach their work. Your firm may be different. Your culture may have a less pronounced level of achievement motive or it may be more pronounced. Maybe an overactive achievement drive isn't an issue at all. Since this single characteristic is so fundamental to HPC's functioning, be certain about the role it's playing or not playing in your organization.

If you're considering adopting our Framework largely "as is," or even in some adapted form, the first questions you'll want to consider are:

- Does your company's culture tend to favor individual effort and achievement over collaboration?
- Is this tendency suppressing or limiting levels of intentional collaboration?

If the answer to either of these is "No," then HPC "as is" probably isn't for you. If your organization isn't so swayed by the powerful forces of high individual achievement, consider a different approach. You may be able to adapt our Framework or to emulate our R&D approach. It probably won't work "off the shelf," though. What's more, there may be something else that's impeding collaboration in your organization. Perhaps it's a cultural norm. Maybe it's the nature of the work your organization does. Do some practical research to figure out what that might be. What could that practical research look like? In the section of this chapter on emulating our R&D process I offer a few ideas. Once you've done that, you can build or adapt an approach that will suit your needs.

The two-question test, above, may not be enough for you to work out whether HPC is for you or not. Another way to gauge just how attuned to your culture HPC is, is to use the "Levels of Collaboration" model.

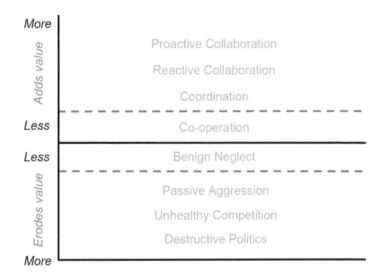

Go back to Chapter 3 and reread the definitions of the levels. Next, ask yourself how much of this collaborative dynamic you see playing out in your organization. If the co-operation-to-coordination-to-reactive collaboration cycle is common, you may be on to something. Check out your hunch with a few trusted colleagues. Explain the model to them and gauge their reaction. If, after this bit of inquiry, you sense a resonance, you may be able to adopt the HPC Framework as it is. If this test indicates that your company is different in some ways and similar in others, adaptation may be the way to go. If your company culture is substantially different from ours, you can either abandon HPC or emulate our research approach and see where that takes you.

Know other team stuff

HPC is different from many more overtly psychological team models and approaches that people are aware of. For instance, when I first started to introduce the Framework to people who hadn't been involved in its development, I got asked, "Is this for 'real teams' or just groups?" People who weren't all that team savvy were familiar with the fact that some team experts make this distinction. I was ready for them because I knew enough to know that this might come up. I still get questions like, "How is this approach similar to [insert team model of your choice here]?" I'm ready for almost any of these questions based on my research and experience. If you're beginning the journey of bringing a team effectiveness approach into your organization or to your team, know your stuff. At least a little. Be able to compare and contrast our Framework to the major models out there. At a minimum, bone up on Tuckman's Four Stages and read *The Wisdom of Teams*[1] cover to cover.

In your company there may be one or two oft-used team models that you'll want to get to know particularly well. In our company the Four Stages is well understood by teams around the world. I frequently find that I have to help others understand what I'm doing in relationship to it. For example, I've told teams that the initial work on HPC is focused largely on stages One and Two of Tuckman's Four Stages. I go on to explain that using HPC sets teams up to accelerate into Stage Three. Then, if practiced regularly, it paves the way for Stage Four and beyond, when the team needs to adapt to change. The links and comparisons you make will depend on what your organization is accustomed to. A little knowledge of the major team and group models will help you to navigate these challenges.

Forget the theory—mostly

I love the theory behind this Framework. I'm delighted by the way it hangs together theoretically, and how its intellectual underpinnings have held up over time. Almost no one I work with gives a damn about any of that. They don't want to hear about David McClelland or Maslow's Hierarchy of Needs. They just care that the Framework works. I'm guessing that most of the people where you work will feel the same way.

There will be instances, however, where having a bit of theory at your fingertips will be worth it. If all you want is to introduce the Framework to your team, as is, you won't need much theory. Familiarize yourself with the background that's in this book and with a few other team models for comparison purposes and you should be fine. On the other hand, if you intend to champion a broader deployment of HPC straight out of the box, get as comfortable with the theory as you can. You'll want to be prepared for the skeptics who challenge the quality of what you're doing. This applies just as much if you'll be adapting the Framework or emulating our development approach for broad usage. You'll need a good grounding in group and team theory. Without it, your product isn't likely to be credible. Save it, though, for those times when it's truly necessary.

Find a few partners

Maybe your organization will want to do something ours didn't: launch a formal campaign to introduce and deploy your team effectiveness approach. In this case, you'll probably get a lot of help from communications professionals and change management experts. Before you get to this point though, start small and in good company. Enlist a few colleagues who share your interest. Create a community that can practice and learn together. Get a few like-minded folks experimenting with the Framework. Then, share experiences and stories with each other. Create a minor movement. The lessons you learn will be useful input into the larger rollout campaign. What's more, you'll have developed your HPC chops just as teams throughout your organization may need a little guidance.

Ready, set...

With these thoughts in mind it's time to think about what you'll do with all of this information. I'll explore each of the three approaches—adopt, adapt, or emulate—below. In short:

Adopt—Use the HPC Framework just as it is explained in this book. No changes, no adaptations.

Adapt—Use the research and thinking but adapt how the main ideas are expressed to better suit your business or culture.

Emulate—Copy or use our research methodology to develop a collaboration framework that's more suited to your company and culture.

Option 1: Adopting HPC Off-the-Shelf

Let's assume that you've done the inquiry and testing as I've recommended and you're ready to put the HPC Framework to use. You may want it only for a one-time use. In this case, go for it. If it's a limited audience that you know well, what have you got to lose? You may be ambitious and want to create a movement inside your entire organization. If this is the case, as I've suggested, don't start with a broad campaign, even if you're excited about this Framework and its potential. Start small. You need a place to experiment, to learn about the Framework in action in your organization.

Every year hundreds of Mars managers complete the second-level leadership development program that includes several days of training on the HPC Framework. They come out of the four-and-a-half-day program tired but enthusiastic about putting what they've learned to work. The next section is adapted from the advice we give them.

Start with *your* team

Work with a team where you can make some mistakes and learn from them. The best place for that is with your team or with a team you know well that is willing to experiment with you. How you start is important. Let's talk about that now.

Introduce the thinking behind the Framework

You could just jump right in and start using the Framework. No preambles, no context. Just open your HPC book and get to work. Lots of folks at Mars have taken this route. It works, sort of. But it won't be as powerful as it could be and there are risks.

HPC benefits from participants understanding how it's meant to work by way of a bit of education. The difference between just jumping in and taking time to create understanding is a little like the difference between using a new smart phone and beginning to drive a car.

With a smart phone, you take it out of the box and, through trial and error and the internet, you figure the thing out, mostly. Any accidents or mistakes you make aren't likely to put anyone at risk. A pocket dial here, a name and address not stored there. Frustrating, but no big deal.

It's different when it comes to using a car for the first time. On the face of it, a typical modern automobile (not the self-driving sort, mind you) is pretty straightforward and fairly intuitive. Put it in gear, push one pedal to go, another to stop. Depress a lever to indicate you're turning. Lift another one to get the windshield wipers going; just likes apps on a smart phone. In fact, in some cases you can tell your car to do some of these things, just like you do with Siri or Google Now. What's more, if you're just learning to drive you've probably seen hundreds of others do it so you already have a good idea how it all works. Yet, we still spend hours in driver training. The reality is that we have to understand how all these automotive bits and pieces work together, to say nothing of mastering the rules of the road. By the time we get our licenses, we've invested time and probably some money making sure we know how it's all supposed to come together. This is for our safety and, more importantly, for the safety of all the other motorists and pedestrians out there. The HPC Framework can appear to be as simple and intuitive as a phone and its apps. Indeed, you can learn a lot by just using it. However, when you're working with a team you're involving others, who, if things aren't done reasonably well, might get hurt. No one's going to die, of course. The damage that can be done to individuals and relationships is nonetheless real. You'll want to be careful and responsible.

HPC makes sense on the face of it. It holds together nicely and it gives managers something to do for their teams, now. In their rush to build a better team, managers sometimes don't bother to figure out what "becoming a better team" might mean for them. HPC was designed to be an involving and immersive experience. You want others on this road with you. It helps for them to know what they're getting in to, what it is, and what it's all about. They don't need all the theory and background. But you do need to take the time to create context for your team. Help them see what's going on that's creating their present collaborative reality. Show them how this Framework can address that reality so that they can mindfully take part in creating a new one for themselves.

I've found that when introducing the Framework to a new audience, a combination of the Levels of Collaboration and the Imperatives is effective. This comes from an experience I had a few years ago with a skeptical team of senior P&O leaders in Europe. In fact, the Levels of Collaboration came out of my work with this group.

We had piloted HPC in the UK as part of a new manager development program. The Framework quickly became a viral phenomenon in Europe. This group of leaders had heard about HPC but they didn't get what all the fuss was about. They asked me to spend a day and a half with them so that they could get a deeper understanding of it and in turn support their managers who were using it.

I began by asking this group of savvy senior managers to think about the worst meeting they'd ever been a part of. I wanted them thinking about and feeling the pain of a specific unfocused, unproductive collaboration. I told them I wanted all the gory details: how it started, when you knew you were in trouble, what the worst moment was. It worked like a charm, generating a ton of energy, knowing groans, and laughter. We then got serious and talked about the potential costs of this sort of wasteful teamwork. We discussed how it kills group engagement and productivity. We also considered the costs if one takes into account the salaries and benefits of the individuals involved, how it inhibits their personal effectiveness. This all led, naturally, to talking about the need for more intentional, more thoughtful meetings and collaboration. It's at this point that I shared my Levels of Collaboration graphic. I'd sketched it out the night before while I worried over how to make a case for more intentional collaboration. I drew up a version on a chart and talked about how co-operation is the norm in our open offices. I described those moments of coordination around the coffee machine that lead to reactive collaboration. I applauded the helpfulness of Mars Associates. At the same time, I wondered if there was a way Mars Associates could more often think ahead about what required collaboration instead of turning to collaboration as a last resort. The recognition on their faces and their responses as I described this dynamic were unmistakable. They got it. To induce more intentional collaboration, I posited, would require two things: greater clarity and more consistent and appropriate discipline. In other words, I talked in terms of the Imperatives, even though at that time the Imperatives didn't have a name. From that point, I introduced them to the HPC Framework, talking about how the Practices addressed the need for clarity and discipline to unlock more intentional, proactive collaboration. By the time I'd finished, we were in high gear and cruising on all cylinders.

I developed the Imperatives and the Levels of Collaboration based on data and my observations at Mars, Incorporated. This fact notwithstanding, I've consulted to almost a hundred different companies in my professional life. I'd wager that these two simple sets of ideas, the Levels of Collaboration and the Imperatives, apply to many if not most of them. Use them. Ask your audience if they feel familiar to them. Get your team bought into why more typical, reactive collaboration has its limits. This will get them excited about the possibilities of intentional collaboration.

Now introduce the Practices

Now that you've got your listeners engaged, it's time to talk about the Practices of HPC and how they work within the context you've set. Now that you've laid the groundwork, this step is easy. Here's a brief on how to go about that.

Do it in the "implied order," beginning with **Inspire Purpose**. Make sure to draw contrasts between Inspire Purpose and concepts like mission and vision.

Next talk about **Crystallize Intent**, stressing the importance of clarifying the group's shared work using the Radar Screen. Contrast this to the idea of shared goals and targets. Talk about why shared work does more to drive intentional collaboration than either of these.

When you get to **Cultivate Collaboration**, which is next, be clear that the Practice is first and foremost about contracting for collaboration. This contracting is based on the Radar Screen that will be completed in Crystallize Intent. Talk about making collaboration something they'll be held accountable for. Talk, too, about the idea of deepening relationships and trust around the work that will be shared.

Activate Ways-of-Working is as much about applying the team's inspiring purpose and Radar Screen as it is about processes. Talk about meetings and decision making being most efficient and effective when they're clearly connected to and driven by the collaborative agreements the team makes in the earlier Practices.

Sustain & Renew will make a lot of sense in the context of what you've already spoken about. Stress that great teams are always learning from both their missteps and their successes, that they're disciplined about learning.

Clarify Context, too, will seem a natural part of the overall process by this point. Talk about how teams must be and remain relevant to the business they're a part of. Acknowledge that sometimes big things change and teams, smart teams, respond and adapt.

The Practices will make sense pretty quickly to people. At our website (www.collaborationparadox.com) you can find graphics and snippets of text that you can use to build a short White Paper or Presentation.

Use a common-sense diagnostic

You've got your audience on board and explained the approach. There's one more step I recommend and this one won't be a surprise: begin your HPC work with a diagnostic. There are any number of ways you can do this, a few of which I've talked about. For example, from Chapter 13:

- The Imperatives Assessment
- Keep/Enhance/Remove/Add table

I've even talked about using the Levels of Collaboration model and assigning percentages to each level of collaboration as a way to assess where a team is (also in Chapter 13). Diagnostics can be done anonymously by way of a survey. Another option is to conduct interviews, one-on-one, with each team member. A third option is to conduct a diagnostic conversation in the room in real time with the entire team. Each of the appendices offers questions you can use for these diagnostic conversations. Appendix E also provides the HPC survey that you can reproduce on paper or in an online setting. Every approach has its advantages and disadvantages. Find a diagnostic approach that makes sense to you and use it.

Start where it makes the most sense

Once you've done your diagnostic, do these two things: Get the team involved and meet them where they are. If you're doing an in-the-room diagnostic, involvement is inherent in the process so that takes care of itself. If not, if you used a survey or conducted one-on-one interviews, share the information or data you've collected and let them make sense of it.

Since you've exposed them to the Imperatives and the Practices already, you can create a few inquiry questions around them in order to get them thinking together about the data. For example:

What is this data telling us about:
- How clear we are as a team about the work that requires our collaboration?
- The clarity of our collaborative purpose and reason for being?
- How clear our business mission is?
- How effective our ways of working are?
- How well we adapt and learn as a team?

You can keep it more generic:

- What is this data telling us about our collaboration?
- What's working?
- What could be better?

No matter your approach, use your data and some structured debrief to find out what matters to them. Figure out where they are in relationship to the whole idea of working as a team on the Framework.

Next, you'll have to decide where you'll begin your work on the Framework based on the analysis of the data. Generally, if you're new to the Framework, you'll start with Inspire Purpose. I've seen variations on this, however. Some teams have a hard time understanding the concept of collaborative purpose and will push back against it. I don't recommend working too hard at explaining it or convincing them. If you have a team or functional mission, start with that. If you don't have one, take some time to create one. Work together to define a tangible thing or things the team needs to deliver. Once that's done, and it may take a few hours, you can back into Inspire Purpose by saying:

So, now that we're clear about our mission, I have a question: How do we as a full team need to collaborate to make achieving our mission most likely and most engaging for us?

Or I've had this work well:

How will you have to work together, who will you have to be as a team, to be in service of our mission?

Don't even tell them you're leading to a purpose conversation until you've got them talking.

You could start with Crystallize Intent. You may find, though, that it's difficult to define the Center-of-the-Radar-

Screen work—that which is shared by the whole team—without some sense of collaborative purpose to act as a guide. Don't let this stop you. Begin the Radar Screen exercise and when the team finds it hasn't any clear criteria for what goes at the center, you're back at Inspire Purpose. This same approach works for Activate Ways-of-Working. That is, how will the team know what its meetings should focus on if, as a team, they aren't clear what they're supposed to be focused on?

Cultivate Collaboration can work as a starting point, too. Again, because Cultivate Collaboration is largely about contracting based on the Radar Screen, it will lead you back to Crystallize Intent which, in turn, leads to Inspire Purpose.

A final thought on Inspire Purpose. Some teams won't have any work that they all share. There will be nothing at the center of the team's Radar Screen so there will be nothing that full-team collaborative purpose can address. Then you have a choice to make. You could just agree that HPC isn't for you. Or, as many teams do, ask yourselves, "What could we or should we be focused on together in order to optimize our business results?" Some teams choose to learn together, to use the team as a hothouse for individual growth as my team has. Others may see the team's role keeping people connected and engaged. Bear in mind that for purposes like the two I just mentioned, your ways-of-working should reflect their true nature. For instance, you'll make few business-related group decisions. Meetings won't need to be all that frequent or long. Let your inspiring purpose help you make sense of how you work, and if you don't have one, don't force it. Work through the rest of the Framework. Stumble and bumble a bit. If there's a purpose there, you'll discover it.

Teams who've set up their approach to HPC thoughtfully always find their way. If they've been equipped with enough understanding of the Framework to see how the pieces serve and support each other, they make sense of it. Give them the context, enough information to be informed participants and help them feel that they're in the driver's seat, and it will come together.

Going bigger

If you've had success with your team, and perhaps a few others, you may be ready to bring HPC to more people in your enterprise. By this point, you should be well prepared to do this. You've done the basic cultural assessment. You've had practice introducing the Framework and getting others to buy into it. You've even applied the Practices and got some lessons-learned under your belt. You know what you're talking about and what you're doing. From this point, it's all about lining up the right people inside your organization to design an approach and plan to take the Framework more broadly. How you do this is entirely a function of who you are and your particular organization. As you know, we never had to do this at Mars. There was no grand plan, no formal rollout. We were exceptional in this regard. I've rarely seen something go viral so effectively in a large organization. Who knows. Maybe you'll get lucky, too. It may happen; it may not. In the meantime do the work I've suggested and see what happens. Build your community. Find internal champions and communications specialists. Create a plan and put it to work.

Option 2: Adapting the Framework

The thinking and theory behind the Framework are sound. The way we've put it together, though, might not be appropriate or in tune with your organization. If this is the case, consider customizing the Framework while keeping its theoretical core intact. There are four aspects of the Framework that allow for tinkering:

- The visuals
- The language
- The implied sequence

- The division of the Practices

The first two provide the greatest room for creativity. The latter two give you less to work with but may prove useful.

The visuals

Our circle graphic actually began as the outline of a jet engine. It was meant to play on the flight and airplane metaphors I talked about in the early chapters. That imagery has faded but the circle still works. It's certainly not the only way to represent our Framework, though. Finding a way to illustrate the dynamic relationships among the Practices is important. Our arrows aren't perfect but they work. Don't lose this aspect. Beyond this one limitation, though, there are myriad ways of portraying the Framework and its various parts. You could even find a way to include the Imperatives, which our circular graphic doesn't do.

Below is one alternative I came up with early in the life of the Framework. It's based on some thinking my boss at the time did when he was trying to explain the Framework to a P&O group. It uses the Imperatives differently (you'll see only two of the three). Also, in this version, I nested "Clarify Context" into "Sustain & Renew" so you don't see the former as a distinct

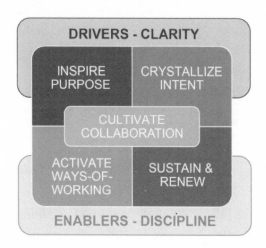

Practice. The main feature of this version is that it puts Cultivate Collaboration at the center to illustrate that it's meant to be influenced and supported by the rest of the Framework.

There's no reason you couldn't use this graphical idea in some form or fashion. It's by no means your only option. Another version I came up with (I sketched it out but never rendered it electronically) used natural imagery. Cultivate Collaboration was the trunk of a tree. Beneath, its roots were Inspire Purpose and Crystallize Intent. Activate Ways-of-Working was represented by branches. Sustain & Renew, if I recall, was represented by rainclouds. As a visual concept it never quite came together but you get the idea. Play with images and see what you can come up with. Better still, find a graphic artist, explain the concepts, and see where it takes them. Lastly, don't forget those cave paintings I talked about at the beginning of the book. The visual representation you choose has to tell a story that's meaningful and has staying power within your culture.

The language

The way we use language in the Framework is important. So important that we spent months looking for the right words and phrases. Our choice of words may not work for you and your organization. Fortunately, you have a thesaurus as close as the nearest computer. Start your own word list in a spreadsheet. Give the Imperatives and Practices different names and try them out with colleagues. Play a bit.

I've "genericized" the Practice names, below. Use them to think about words and phrases that could work for your organization.

- Inspire Purpose—Identify Collaborative Purpose
- Crystallize Intent—Define Shared Work
- Cultivate Collaboration—Contract Relationships and Deepen Trust

- Activate Ways-of-Working—Align Team Processes
- Sustain & Renew—Learn and Improve
- Clarify Context—Learn and Adapt

You may have noticed that I started each generic Practice with a verb. This way they retain the connection to our cultural preference for action. Since the entire Framework is built around achievement and action orientation, those action words are important. You could, however, strip those verbs out. You'd still have adequate, if somewhat less powerful, descriptors. In fact, while I was playing with the graphic above, I created a version that uses different words and no verbs.

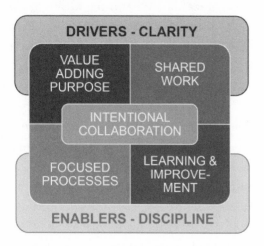

What doesn't work for me about this version is how generic it is and how many business buzzwords it relies on. It's trite and has no distinct personality. That may not be true for you, though. Either way, you'll want what you create to feel like it was made for your organization, not just copied out of a book. To help with this wordsmithing, go back to Chapter 7 where I summarize all of the Practices and isolate the essence of each one. As with the graphics, play, experiment, and feel your way to what works for your culture and people.

The implied sequence

We recommend that established teams begin with Inspire Purpose and work their way around the Framework, clockwise. Newly formed teams will find it helpful to begin with Clarify Context and then move to Inspire Purpose and follow the same path. That's what I mean by the implied sequence. I say "implied" because you can begin anywhere in the Framework. Granted, many of those starting points will lead you back to Inspire Purpose, given how the Framework is constructed. Nonetheless one can depart from our implied sequence and use the Framework successfully.

What if our implied sequence just doesn't make sense for you and your organization? What if the idea that a team should be grounded by inspiring purpose runs counter to prevailing company norms? For instance, I had one executive from outside Mars ask, when I explained our Framework to him, "Why would a team start with purpose if the strategy is clear and they know their role in it? Isn't strategy where everything begins?" What if another organization that's highly process driven feels that every team should absolutely begin with something like Activate Ways-of-Working? Is there a way to keep all the Practices while suggesting a flow that can accommodate other kinds of organizational preferences?

As of this writing, only a few other firms have been exposed to our Framework. I have, however, had ample experience with our own Line Managers and Associates questioning the sequence we recommend. I've frequently had to shuffle the parts of the Framework. To do that, I've created a few ground rules for myself in order to maintain consistency in my consulting. These can be applied to how you create a sequence, implied or otherwise, for your version of this Framework.

1) If you aren't beginning with the team's purpose, if at all possible begin with a team learning Practice: Sustain &

Renew or Clarify Context. Either is a great starting point. You'll often find that the insights or data point towards a need for a clearer team purpose.

2) If you prefer to start with identifying shared work, Crystallize Intent, create a solid link to Inspire Purpose (or whatever you call it). Make it clear that the "what" of your shared work has to be guided by some kind of "why" that clarifies the value of doing work collaboratively versus doing it individually.

3) You may choose, like many teams, to begin with relationship building, one aspect of Cultivate Collaboration. If so, circle back to do the rest of Cultivate Collaboration—the contracting part—later, once the team's purpose and shared work (Radar Screen) have been agreed to. You might even break Cultivate Collaboration into two distinct Practices, one dedicated to "getting to know you" exercises and the other to contracting around collaborative work.

4) If you prefer to begin with Ways-of-Working, ensure that everyone knows that once the team's purpose and shared work have been identified, Ways-of-Working will be revisited and checked against them to ensure there's the right fit.

5) If Sustain & Renew and/or Clarify Context make sense as starting points for your organization, refer back to #1, above.

One way or another, you and your team or organization will find that having a team purpose holds the whole Framework together. The Framework without some version of Inspire Purpose won't do for you what it's been doing for us. Get a read on where your organization, or team, is. Meet them there by adapting the Framework without losing the essential elements that make it work.

The division of the Practices

Despite my urging to use all six Practices, it may be that you don't feel that all of them are right for your organization. Perhaps your company is even more pragmatically minded than ours and the whole idea of team purpose seems a bridge too far. Or it could be that the contracting for collaborative work in Cultivate Collaboration appears to be at odds with your performance management system (I've heard of it). There are a few places where it makes sense to play with the Practices by, instead of removing any of the Practices, merging them. The Imperatives offer a handy way to do this.

I had one HPC user, who struggled with Inspire Purpose, suggest that we merge Inspire Purpose and Crystallize Intent into one uber-Practice called Clarity. So long as you address both the "why" and the "what," this merging could work.

You could also create an uber-Practice aligned with the Discipline Imperative. This would involve embedding the team-learning Practices within Ways-of-Working. They're all about discipline, about putting routines in place. They might be routines dealing with meetings or routines in the service of continuous improvement. They are, nonetheless, essential team habits that ought to be formed.

Finally, you could, based on your organization and culture, declare a fourth Imperative: Learning. Then, as I did in my alternative graphic, you could merge Sustain & Renew & Clarify Context. They're both about learning, after all. You'd lose the distinction between inward, team-focused reflection and outward connection to the business. That can be accounted for, however, in how you explain the Practice.

I've done some variations of each of these, but only in an effort to get teams started using the Framework. I needed to adapt to account for their concerns and predilections. In every case, I reverted to the form of the Framework I've described in this book. If you have reason to believe that any of these variants might work for your organization and culture, have a go. Remember, though: whatever your reservations about the way we've built our Practices and however you choose to put them together, I encourage you not to abandon any of the six. The Five Essential Practices and the sixth Special Practice are a fabric of interwoven concepts and actions. Pull out one of the conceptual threads and the Framework will be weaker and less likely to perform as described.

Option 3: Emulating the R&D Process

OK, so the off-the-shelf approach isn't for you. The adaptation option isn't right either because the underlying theory and thinking don't apply. You like the way we did this though, how we created a team effectiveness Framework based on our people and culture.

I have one piece of advice here: work from the inside, out. Don't begin with articles, academics, and consultants; they're likely to bring biases based on tools they prefer or studies they've done. Use them later to challenge your data and assumptions, to enrich your thinking, and refine your product. I got lucky. Even though it wasn't originally intended for this purpose, I happened to have had two years' worth of Mars team data to refer to. If I were starting from scratch, I'd want to begin with the same rich trove of information.

That's what a group of millennials at one large pharmaceuticals and consumer goods company did. They were all part of a cohort within a management development program. They were assigned to work together to develop and then share with senior managers a perspective on the future of the workplace. Collaboration emerged from their research as an important aspect of this future. I was invited to speak to them about what Mars had learned about collaboration. I spent an hour or so with them, via Skype™, explaining our research, our findings, and what it led to. They then went off to conduct their own research on collaboration within their global company.

How you conduct your research is important. If you're thinking about building a team effectiveness framework for your firm, figure out how to gain experience with teams in your organization. You can either do the work yourself or find someone, like me, who is willing to do it, and gather the data you can. Regardless of who does the work, remember: size— sample size, that is—matters.

I don't remember much from my Master's-level statistics course but the number 30 sticks with me. I recall our professor telling us that you want at least 30 samples to use in your analyses. I've since read that while 30 is a nice guideline, reality is more complicated. Speaking as a confirmed non-statistician, I found that having 30 teams in my research was just right. It was manageable and it ended up yielding a generally accurate picture of teams at Mars. Maybe 20 would have been enough. Forty wouldn't have served us any better. Five or ten teams I'm certain wouldn't have been adequate. The size of your organization, of course, matters when it comes to sample size. You'll need a large enough sample to appropriately represent the diversity of your enterprise. Ensure that your subject teams come from:

- A variety of functions
- Different organizational levels, and
- If your organization is global, from as many different places as possible.

One note about levels before I continue: Early in the development process, you may recall that I shared our Framework with the Harvard professor and author of a well-known book on teams. He was intrigued with my findings, but he was stunned that they were consistent across organizational levels. In fact, he was skeptical. "You're telling me that a General Manager and his team are subject to the same barriers and issues as a team at a factory?" When I showed him what I was developing, his skepticism softened. You may encounter similar skepticism where you work, so be prepared for it.

The idea that senior teams are different makes intuitive sense. At one level, they are. They deal with questions of global strategy and weighty decisions that involve tens and hundreds of millions—sometimes billions—of dollars. Their choices can affect thousands of lives of people in countries around the world. A factory leadership team, by contrast, deals with one physical site, and makes decisions that affect only that location and a few hundred people. The kind of scale that senior teams deal with—and less senior teams don't—makes a difference to team makeup and the team dynamic. Some people will be qualified for those bigger, global sorts of jobs and others are better suited for lower-level positions. Our Framework, however, is blind to scale and reach. All it seeks to do is to clarify where collaboration will create value and then to get group members more focused on collaborating productively. Senior teams benefit from this focus as much as factory teams, marketing teams, HR teams and not-for-profit teams. If you're developing your own team effectiveness model, keep level differences in mind. You may encounter questions about who your framework is for and where it's likely to work. You'll need to be prepared to answer in a credible way. This is where academic research may help.

I began my work on a team effectiveness framework with academic research: journal articles, books, interviews with scholars. It got me nowhere. It was all good stuff, but translating it for use inside Mars wasn't working out. In the end, I used external research only as an adjunct, as a source of information, inspiration, and to justify the reasoning behind our Framework. The reason was, once again, the culture. No matter how smart the professors and consultants writing the myriad books, articles, and blog posts, they don't live in your company. They aren't steeped in what collaboration looks like in your company today, and where your culture needs nudging and where it doesn't.

Closing Thoughts

The Mars Framework for High Performance Collaboration has become how Mars leaders and Associates think about, pursue, and achieve collaborative excellence. Since work on the HPC Framework began six years ago, most of the teams from the original research have either had complete turnover or been reorganized and live on in another form. The same is true for the other teams whose stories of applying HPC I've told. Change is really the only constant. The feedback on the Framework, though, has been consistent. It works, and it works better than other approaches to team building. Teams find it easy to understand and apply. It's creating more effective and more productive collaboration. We're not done yet, though. We continue to explore what's possible with HPC and the thinking behind it. It's being applied to help us get better at specific disciplines within the general realm of collaboration. For example, we know we can be better at decision making. HPC already addresses decision making; it's helped teams to focus on the most appropriate decisions and ways to make them. We're now looking deeper at how our cultural tendencies, our drive to achieve, and our egalitarianism may be keeping us from being as agile as we can be, even with HPC. It's early days, but it's becoming clear that the Three Imperatives will have a role to play in how we improve decision making. We're also thinking specifically about how to lead using the HPC approach. We know that the Framework works. We know that leaders have a particular role to play within it. We're now asking the question, "What are the competencies and capabilities required for a leader to make the most of this already successful Framework?" We haven't stopped challenging ourselves to make the most of HPC and the work that went into it. Just as with the cocoa genome work, we're inviting broader participation in the exploration.

That's where you come in.

It's now in your hands. My colleagues at Mars and I decided that writing this book was a good idea. More than that, we felt it was the right thing to do. We had learned a great deal about a subject that organizations large and small have been wrestling with for years. We found an approach to enhancing team effectiveness and to sustaining those improvements that teams themselves can understand and apply—no consultants needed. In doing this we found a way to make work a better place to be. Teams—healthy, productive teams and the relationships that they're made up of—can be among the most rewarding and fulfilling aspects of working for a living. If we must work for a living, and most of us have no choice, it ought to be as positive and life-affirming as possible while still delivering the results our businesses require. The HPC Framework is one way to make our work something we can honestly say we enjoy. In that spirit we wish you all the best.

Summary
- The Framework can be used as is, adapted for your culture, or you can research and develop a model that works for your organization.
- Before you choose to adopt or adapt HPC, assess the potential fit of the Framework with your organization and culture.
- If you're considering using the HPC Framework (or the thinking it's built on), first study the broader subject of team development to enable you to credibly compare HPC to other approaches.
- When it comes time to promote and explain HPC to others, focus mostly on practical applications, using your knowledge of the theory only when it's needed.
- If you decide to use HPC as is, begin with your team or a team you know well. Take your time introducing the

concepts behind it and only then get into the details of the Framework itself.

- When implementing HPC with a specific team, choose a place to start, a Practice, that makes sense for that team based on data you have collected about them.
- When you decide to take HPC more broadly, identify a few partners within your organization to support and champion the effort.
- If you prefer to adapt the Framework, the four areas that lend themselves to adaptation are the visuals, the language, the implied sequence of the Practices, and the ways that the Practices are grouped.
- If you choose to emulate the R&D approach we took, work inside-out, starting with research on teams within your organization, and then move on to the literature and theory to make sense of what you find.

Using the Appendices

Except for Crystallize Intent and the Radar Screen exercise, there is no indispensable tool or approach for any of the Practices. There are probably 20 ways to develop a team's purpose, a hundred ways to deepen relationships within a team, more than either of those for assessing a team's health. Each appendix provides at least a few tools or techniques that we use at Mars. Many of them are in the public domain and have been adapted for our use. There are doubtless many more potentially useful ways to go about any of the Practices. The appendices are only meant as a place to start. While I've striven to provide detailed instructions and templates, I'd suggest you not be limited by what I share here. Once you understand the principles of our Framework, feel free to find or develop your own tools and techniques.

The Conversation Questions

At Mars, Incorporated, we believe in the power of questions to unlock thoughtful, generative conversations. When we were originally testing and refining the HPC Framework, the Conversation Questions were the first tools we offered to teams interested in using the Framework. Since we had only recently begun testing it and using it ourselves, we didn't have a lot to offer to those who were anxious to use it. The group of us responsible for building the HPC Framework into the manager development program for which it was originally intended made a decision. We would create sets of Practice-specific questions as a simple but useful place to start. I could use the questions with teams during the testing phase and we could then build those same questions into the finished training program.

The Conversation Questions are the only thing that is consistent in the six appendices. Since their creation we've gone on to develop other techniques and tools that we offer both through our manager development program and during consulting engagements. The Conversation Questions, though, are still valuable. They can be used in a variety of ways. First and foremost, I find them helpful as part of other, structured exercises within the Practices. For instance, when I facilitate a purpose development process with a team, I use a few of the Inspire Purpose Conversation Questions. Below are two examples:

- What is the boldest thing you can imagine our team accomplishing?
- What is the legacy we want to leave as a team?

When I'm getting ready to work on the Radar Screen exercise with a team, I like to get them thinking about the current state of their shared work. To do that, I use two or three of the Crystallize Intent Conversation Questions. For example:

- Where are we under-utilizing the collaborative capabilities of our team today?
- What's the greatest collaborative opportunity our team could capitalize on?

The Conversation Questions are also a great place to start when a team doesn't know where to start, as an informal diagnostic. You can draw from the Sustain & Renew questions if you want to have the team discuss their effectiveness in a broad, open-ended way:

- In what areas can our team improve?
- What are the strengths our team has to build on?

If you prefer to do a deeper dive into a specific Practice, you can use a few Conversation Questions from that Practice. For instance, you may want to get a sense of how well sub-groups are operating based on the agreements they made. Pull a couple of the Cultivate Collaboration Conversation Questions and tee up the discussion:

- How can we best hold each other accountable?
- What consequences exist for lack of collaboration on our team?

Use the Conversation Questions as you and the team you're working with see fit. Add to them. Modify them. Play with them. No matter which tools or approaches you decide to work with, smart questions will serve you and the team.

Appendix A: Team Purpose

Introduction

Developing a team's inspiring purpose statement is more art than science. Below are three conversation-based approaches for developing or discovering your team's purpose.

A Simple Question-Driven Team Purpose Conversation

1. Copy the list of questions that appear at the end of this appendix. Provide a copy of the list for each member of your team.

2. Hand out the questions to the team. Ask each team member to select a question that they find compelling. To ensure the broadest, most diverse discussion, make sure each team member selects a different question.

3. Ask each team member to read their question and share their response with the group. As they read the question, record it on a flip chart. Ask that all team members listen carefully to the answer. Then have each team member contribute their own ideas and thoughts in response to this question. Get some conversation going and capture big ideas on a flip chart next to the question. Challenge team members to go deeper, think bigger.

4. Continue until every team member has had a chance to share their question and answer. Allow time for ample conversation.

5. Refer to your flip chart and ask: "What does this tell us about the most powerful reasons that we exist as a team, beyond the results that we create?" Facilitate a discussion and summarize the ideas in bullet point form on another flip chart.

6. Put the team into two or three sub-groups. Ask each sub-

group to craft one or two possible purpose statements based on the bullet points from step 5. Have the sub-groups share their statements with the larger group. Work together using input from all the sub-groups until you have created a rough draft of your team's purpose statement.

7. Use the BeCAUSE tool from later in this appendix to test the quality of your purpose draft. Refine it as needed.

8. Now that you have a team purpose statement, set it aside for a few weeks. Come back to it with fresh eyes to see if you all still agree that it works for the team

The "What-Who-How" Approach for Purpose Statement Development

Background

This approach to purpose statement development was created by beginning with what I considered to be a strong purpose statement, the one from the Global Petcare Management Team. I wasn't able to determine what process had been used to arrive at their purpose statement. I just knew that the statement worked. Its simplicity, its clarity, and its balance of aspiration and practicality were unmatched. Just as importantly, it worked for the team that developed it. I decided to work backwards from their finished product. I deciphered its structure and used that structure as a guide for this process. The process I describe below was developed working with the P&O team as mentioned in Chapter 8.

The structure has three elements that correspond to these three questions:

- What will our collaboration be in service of?
- Who will we be together?
- How we will play that role?

The process for distilling the elements of the team's inspiring purpose follows this "what, who, how" sequence. The final statement, however, is put together in the reverse order: "how, who, what." Since the Global Petcare Leadership Team's purpose statement served as the model for this approach, we'll use that statement as the example here.

- Their collaboration was in service of **what** larger ambition? Creating the future of the pet care industry.
- To support this ambition, they agreed they would act, collectively, as **who**? As architects.
- They further agreed on **how** they would have to play this role: courageously.

Their final statement read:

Together we are courageous (how) architects (who) of the future of Petcare (what).

Resources required
- A vision and/or corporate or functional mission statement; any documents describing the ambitions and intentions of the larger organization
- Fine-point markers
- Three pads of sticky notes of different colors
- Ample wall space or several flip-chart stands with paper
- Someone to facilitate the process, even if that person is from within the group
- Between two to four hours

This is an iterative process that requires a willingness to explore ideas, to listen deeply, and to play with ideas and words. Give yourselves a couple of hours for the first three parts, but don't rush if it runs longer. Take the time you need for quality conversations. The fourth part will begin on the same day that you complete parts one through three. It will continue, though, beyond the initial session. Some teams allow this process to play out over weeks to ensure they've given their purpose the reflection and attention it requires.

Part 1: What will our collaboration be in service of?

1. Pass out three different-colored pads of sticky notes to each person. For purposes of these instructions we'll use yellow, blue and pink pads.
2. Begin by asking each person to think about what their collaboration will be in service of.
    *   Refer them to the team vision, mission or other relevant strategic documents.
    *   Ask them to think beyond the obvious such as making products or more money. For instance, together they may be in service of a better future, more engaged Associates, a healthier world, a more mutual business, etc.
    *   Encourage them to think about their collaboration at its best and how it will support the business's or function's strategic intent.
3. Team members work individually without speaking, capturing each idea on a single yellow sticky note. Give them about 7 minutes for this step.
4. Next have them work silently to place their yellow stickies near each other on the wall or a large piece of paper.
5. Ask them to stay at the wall/paper and review these stickies and to add any others that occur to them.
6. Next have the group look for similarities among the various sticky notes. Place identical or similar ideas in clusters on the wall/paper. Note any outliers and be sure to retain them. Pay attention to ideas and words that seem to be most engaging for the group.
7. Have them return to their seats.

Part 2: Who will we be together? What role will we play?

8. Invite team members to think about a role that this team could play in service of their ambition.

    -   Are they going to be entrepreneurs, architects, stewards, curators, ambassadors—it could be anything.
    -   Have them write their ideas on blue sticky notes—one idea per sticky note.

9. Have them post all their blue stickies near, but not adjacent to, the yellow sticky notes from the previous discussion. Discourage conversation at this stage.

10. Ask them to silently review the collection of blue sticky notes and to add any other role ideas that occur to them.

11. Again, ask them to cluster identical or similar ideas. Note which ideas seem to generate the most conversation.

12. Ask them to return to their seats.

Part 3: How will we play our role? What will describe us at our best?

13. Using the pink sticky notes, ask them to write down adjectives that they think would describe their collaboration at its best: courageous, inspiring, persistent, innovative, driven, etc.

14. Have them place these stickies on the wall or flip chart near but separate from the first two sets of sticky notes.

15. Again, have them silently consider this collection of ideas, adding any new ideas that might occur to them.

16. Ask the team to create clusters of similar words and ideas.

17. Keep them on their feet for the next steps.

Part 4: Putting the pieces together

Clustering

18. Divide the group into three smaller groups, even if the sub-

groups contain only two individuals.

19. Assign each group one color of sticky notes to work with. One group will focus on Part 1, "What we are in service of?" Another group will focus on Part 2, the "Who" and a third group on Part 3, the "How."

20. The goal is to further explore and refine the clusters of ideas that were generated in the previous steps. Each group will title the clusters based on the themes they see. They will also discuss and think about the outlying ideas and how they may—or may not—be related to one or more of the clusters of ideas.

21. Give them 10–15 minutes to complete the preceding few steps.

22. Next ask each sub-group to choose two or three of the big ideas represented by the clusters to discuss and propose to the rest of the team. They will focus on the ideas they find most compelling and appropriate within their assigned category.

Finding consensus

23. Reassemble the three groups into a single group gathered around the yellow sticky notes that answer the question, "What are we in service of?"

24. Have the group that worked on this question present its thoughts about what it saw in the sticky notes. As the group shares its ideas, have them place the idea(s) they're discussing in a fourth location; call this the Purpose area. Encourage discussion and debate with the broader group. It's OK to move ideas back from the purpose area into their original grouping if, through discussion, these ideas lose their appeal or meaning.

25. Allow the discussion and movement of sticky notes to be dynamic as the larger group explores and advocates for the ideas that are most meaningful for them.

26. Allow the process to continue until a consensus begins to emerge. Ideally, by the end of this discussion, there will be no more than one or two yellow sticky notes in the Purpose area. The fewer the better, but nothing is final at this point.

27. Do the same thing with the other two groups of sticky notes. As the discussions unfold, continue to populate the Purpose area with the most compelling ideas from each of the three categories.

28. Once all three categories have been adequately discussed, move the entire group over to the Purpose area to consider the ideas that have made their way there.

29. Invite general discussion of what they see emerging from this collection of words and ideas. Ensure that everyone understands, as much as possible, what each and every sticky note is meant to convey or capture. Once everyone is clear about everything in the purpose area…

30. **Stop the process for at least four hours,** and preferably overnight. This "soak time" is extremely important in letting the subconscious make sense of the collected ideas. Capture the ideas in the Purpose area in whatever way makes sense, so that you have them for the next steps in the process.

31. Encourage them to think about this process during the hiatus, even as they go about other tasks or duties.
    • Stress the importance of this break for this process.
    • Individuals can, after at least four hours away from the process, work alone on a few draft statements that they might want to propose when they reconvene. But this isn't essential.

Crafting and finalizing your purpose statement

32. When a suitable amount of time has passed, reconvene the group.

33. Ask them to attempt to draft a provisional purpose statement based on the sticky notes that ended up in the Purpose area

during the earlier stages of the exercise. They will structure these statements in the "How–Who–What" format. Another way to explain this format is as adjective(s)–role description–aspiration.

Note: For large groups, consider breaking them into two or three sub-groups for this step, each of which will bring forward a draft statement. Then bring the small groups back together to share their draft statements. As each group presents their thinking, look for common elements across the drafts to help you create a single draft that represents the most widely held views.

34. Don't try to make this draft word-perfect. It only needs to represent the most compelling and widely agreed-upon ideas.

35. Once you have one or two "How–Who–What" drafts, request that two or three team members take away the draft(s) to craft a final, proposed purpose statement. Give them anywhere from one to four weeks to do this.

    Note: You don't need to wait to have a fully final purpose statement to begin your work on Crystallize Intent and the Radar Screen. At this point, your draft purpose statement(s) is probably clear enough to guide that work.

36. Once the drafting group has a proposal (remember, allow one to four weeks for this), convene the larger team. Have the drafting group share their proposal and lead a discussion about it.

    • Use the BeCAUSE rubric to assess the final version, tweaking it as needed.

37. When the group has agreed to its purpose statement, set a date about 30–60 days out, to sense-check the purpose statement one final time. Use the passage of time to test whether or not this purpose statement will stand the test of time.

38. Once the team is satisfied that the purpose statement is truly

final, make it the foundation of your team's charter.

The Iceberg Approach for Team Purpose Development

Introduction

A team's purpose at its best makes clear to all team members, and even those outside the team, how the team, through its collaboration, creates value.

This approach is predicated on the notion that all teams have the potential to create value at two levels: above-the-water-line and below-the-water-line. The water line imagery is drawn from icebergs. What's visible above the water line is always a small fraction of the totality of an iceberg. What's below the water line is always bigger, harder to see, but more powerful.

When talking about purpose statements, above-the-water-line refers to team reasons-for-being that resemble a team's mission. They answer the question, "What is the work that the team must undertake *as a team*, the things that if the team didn't do them, no individual or other group could reasonably be expected to do them?" These may include developing strategy, developing and managing a budget, managing talent, or simply completing the tasks assigned to the group.

Below-the-water-line are the things that the team agrees they must spend their collective time on but that are less tangible, less easy to see, but that will make the purpose inspiring or aspirational. This class of things includes anything that connects with team members at a more intuitive and emotional level than those things above the water line. This aspect might focus on things like Associate well-being, the environment, and sustainability.

This approach relies on the use of pictures, of images and imagery. The intent is to get participants out of their heads and into a more intuitive and instinctive way of thinking. If we begin with words and phrases, our expressive vocabulary is limited to the words we're most comfortable with. By using pictures as a starting point, we expand the possibilities of what our participants can imagine and express.

Materials needed:
- Flip-chart stand and paper
- Markers
- Center for Creative Leadership's "Visual Explorer™" cards, or equivalent source of images
- Room set up for conversation (a "U," for example) with other space for small-group discussion

Step 1: Define your approach

- Share the definition of purpose that includes the notion of how the team creates and/or adds value.
- Draw the outlines of an iceberg on a flip chart and explain the idea of above- and below-the-water-line.
- Explain that this is how you will approach the process of developing the team's inspiring purpose.

Step 2: Identify the above-the-water-line (AWL) responsibilities

Do this next step with the entire group.
- Explain that you want to brainstorm a list of those responsibilities that this team must own together.
- Sometimes, using the analogy of a job description helps them understand what you mean. "If we were hiring this team to do a certain job that included specific responsibilities and deliverables, what would those be?"
- Another option is to talk about this as developing the team's functional mission statement.
- Be prepared to share a few examples of what might be included in such a statement: creating budgets, completing projects, quality assurance, etc.

- Remind them, as needed, that this list should represent those tasks that support the achievement of their goals and that, if this team didn't do them, they wouldn't get done.
- Expect a list of five to seven things, only one or two of which will be unique.

Step 3: Identify the below-the-water-line (BWL) purpose

This work is done first at an individual level, then in small groups, and finally brought to the total group. It relies on using graphics (Visual Explorer™ cards or pictures from magazines or other sources) to transcend the limitations of words and lists.

Spread out your pictures on a large table.

- Invite team members, working in absolute silence, to go to the pictures and to choose three that represent their highest hopes/aspirations for the team.
- Ask them, "What would have to be true of how we work together if we were to not only complete the work we have to do, but also make our collaboration meaningful and enjoyable for all of us?"
- Next, put them into groups of three or four and have them explain to each other why they chose the cards they did.
- Then, have each group choose three cards, total, that they all agree can represent their shared aspirations.
- Have each group present to the total group their three cards and the big ideas that they represent. Capture all the big ideas on a flip chart. Allow for as much discussion as you feel is needed.
- Finally, remix the groups and have your new sub-groups of three or four create flip charts with three to five bullet points each that capture both the AWL and the BWL concepts. This step is *not* about creating a final statement; it is merely your first pass at pulling together the big ideas

that should be in a final statement.

- Have each group present their three to five bullets and discuss as needed. Be sure everyone understands all the big ideas that have been presented.

Stop here and either:

- Leave the exercise for the day and come back to it the next day, where you will have sub-groups propose actual purpose statements

Or...

- Identify two or three volunteers to take the bullet points away to create and then propose a draft purpose statement at a subsequent meeting.

  Note: Providing a time gap is important. It allows the discussion and concepts to soak in to a deeper intuitive level, allowing for a greater likelihood of discovering unexpected things.

Common Issues with Purpose Statements

Too tactical: Many team members are pragmatic. They get uncomfortable talking about their hopes and aspirations. Helping them to move past this pragmatism is one of the great gifts a facilitator can give them. How you do that is up to you.

Functional, not collaborative: Many first-pass purpose statements describe the functional purpose of the team, their AWL reason for being, and not the value-adding collaborative role of the team. For example, here's a first pass from a Mars Petcare R&D team:

Together we imagine and create amazing products that consistently delight pets and pet lovers.

There's no doubt that this is what they want do together. The question I would have for this leadership team is, "How will you have to BE together *a team*, that will create the environment and conditions to enable you to do what your current statement describes?"

The BeCAUSE Checklist

Once the team has a solid draft, you can assess its quality using the BeCAUSE tool. Compare your statement to each of the BeCAUSE elements to see how strong it's likely to be.

Be: What and how will our team "be"?

It's about how you want to *be* with each other, and what you want the team to be to your people and to the business. It's *not* about your functional goals, tasks, or outcomes.

C: CATCHY—sticky, clever, memorable

The purpose statement should catch your attention, and the elements should stick with you because they are memorable.

A: ASPIRATIONAL—hopeful, appreciative, future-focused

The purpose statement inspires the team to move forward with hope. It does not describe the current state but the future ways of being that the team wants to attain.

U: UNIQUE—original, differentiating, distinctive

The purpose statement communicates the unique contribution of this team. The statement is an original creation unlike any other team's. It is not a replica from the level above but differentiates the team from others.

S: SHORT—concise, brief, crisp, simple

The purpose statement should be easy to remember and share because it is brief and concise. Refine the statement to the simplest form while retaining all the attributes listed above. Team members should be able to remember and repeat it easily.

E: EVERYDAY—useful, practical, consistent

A purpose statement must be easy to understand and have

practical **everyday** application. It provides direction for meeting agendas, directs decisions, and guides thinking about how the team works.

Team Purpose Conversation Questions

- What makes you proud to work in our team?
- What is the boldest thing you can imagine our team accomplishing?
- What is holding us back?
- Vocation has been described as "the place where your greatest passion meets the world's greatest need." What would our team's vocation be?
- What is unique about our team (beyond functional activities) that if we did not exist would not get done?
- Why do we get out of bed every day?
- What if… [we were… we could… etc.]
- What's possible for us?
- Beyond pay and benefits, what inspires you to come to work every day?
- What unique possibilities exist for this team because of the individual talents, values, and passions each person contributes?
- How does our team, when we are working most effectively together, add value to the business?
- What is your greatest ambition for the team?
- What is the legacy we want to leave as a team?
- What will be required of us if we are to act as a wise team?
- How will we as leaders / team members show up courageously?
- This team inspires me because…
- What three words do you least associate with our team?
- What synergies does our team create?
- Why are we uniquely positioned to provide value to the business?

- What three words do you most associate with our team?
- What is the legacy that we want to create/leave as a team?
- What does our team offer others?
- What is the journey that we are on? From where, to where?
- If this team were a person, what attributes would best describe him/her?
- How much impact can we have as a team?

Appendix B: Crystallize Intent

The Radar Screen is the central tool for aligning the collaborative work of the team with most of the other Practices. I've found no more useful way to do this, hence it's the only tool explained in this appendix. Conducting a Radar Screen conversation can be done either face-to-face or virtually using desktop video. We'll start with the in-the-room version and then I'll offer a process for conducting the exercise virtually.

Face-to-Face Radar Screen Discussion

Time required: 2–3 hours. Timing will depend on team size, number of tasks and the complexity of the team's working environment.

Materials:
- Large white paper or flip charts
- One medium-sized pad of sticky notes for each team member
- Sharpie pens or markers—one per team member
- Artist's tape for hanging flip charts
  Note: A large whiteboard can also be used. Or you can create your Radar Screen electronically as described in the section on conducting the session remotely.
- Participants will need a list of their personal tasks/objectives to refer to.

Space:
- Large meeting room with plenty of wall space to hang flip charts

Set up
1. Provide each team member with a dark-colored, fine-point

marker and a pad of sticky notes.

2. Create a large version of the Radar Screen (see diagram) on either a couple of pages of flip-chart paper or another large piece of blank white paper. Hang it on a wall with plenty of room around it.

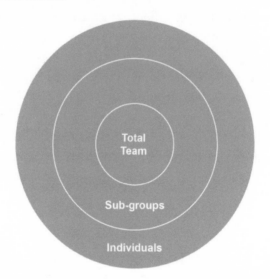

3. Explain how the Radar Screen works, how the levels of collaboration are represented by the three concentric rings.
4. Instruct team members to write each project or initiative that they own or lead on a single sticky note. One sticky note for each project or initiative that each person owns. Have them put their names or initials on all sticky notes along with the names/initials of any other team member with whom they may share the project/task.
5. Have all team members post all their sticky notes on a smooth, blank wall or large piece of paper—near, but *not* on your Radar Screen.
6. Have team members go to the wall and silently review all the sticky notes. When complete, have them all sit down.

The center of the Radar Screen

7. Explain that you will start at the center of the Radar Screen, limiting, as much as possible, the number of tasks placed there to three. This helps to focus the discussion.

8. Ask one team member to stand up and pick from among *all* the sticky notes the three that they feel require ongoing, full team collaboration. Have them place these three at the center of the Radar Screen. Have the team member explain their thinking briefly as they do this. Don't allow much debate at this point; that will come later in the process.

9. Ask a second team member to do the same. This person can either a) pick three new sticky notes and replace the first three (moving the first three to another position on the Radar Screen), or b) keep one or two of the first person's choices and replace only one or two, or c) simply leave the first three as they were. Ensure there is discussion about why this person is making the choices they are making.

10. Continue with this process until the entire team has had a chance to place their choice of sticky notes at the center, *or* until the entire team is comfortable with what has been placed there.

11. If there are still sticky notes left on the wall after the center of the Radar Screen has been completed, facilitate moving these remaining sticky notes to appropriate rings on the Radar Screen. Don't aim for perfection. Close is good enough.

12. There should now be three or at most four sticky notes at the center of the Radar Screen. Once about half the team has posted its choices, you can allow the center to expand beyond three if there is consensus that more than three is appropriate.

The rest of the Radar Screen

13. Review the sticky notes in the second ring and validate

who should be collaborating with whom on these projects/ initiatives. Modify the initials on the sticky notes as required.

14. Validate the outer ring as truly individually-owned-and-managed projects or initiatives.

15. Invite one final review of the entire completed Radar Screen. Challenge the team to consider if any of the projects should be removed entirely from the Radar Screen based on the amount of work that the team has committed to. These would be placed in a "not now/not us" category for later discussion.

16. Discuss with the team how they want to capture this output. Ensure ownership for the capture is assigned and a timeframe established for publishing the finished version to the team. Plan to review your work on the Radar Screen in three to six months.

Conducting the Radar Screen Exercise with Remote Team Members

When some or all team members are working remotely, use Skype™ or a similar desktop video application to conduct the process. Some pre-meeting work will be required.

Time required: 2–3 hours. Timing will depend on team size, amount of work, and the complexity of the team's working environment.

Before the session

1. Well in advance of your Crystallize Intent workshop, describe the Crystallize Intent process to your team. You want them to understand what the process is and why it's important.

2. Each team member will provide, via email before the session, a list of the projects and initiatives that they're responsible for. Each item they submit will include the names or initials of all Associates who will be working on it. Their lists should

not include general job responsibilities but only discrete projects or initiatives.

3. Prepare your draft Radar Screen ahead of time in PowerPoint® or a similar presentation software package. Populate it with the projects and initiatives that the team submitted.

   - Place each of the items submitted by the team into an individual text box; one project or initiative per text box.

   - Place each of the text boxes into the appropriate ring of the Radar Screen based on the number of people collaborating on each. Screen for duplicates as needed. Plan on sharing this draft Radar Screen during your virtual team discussion.

During the session

4. Begin by reminding the team how the process will work.

5. Share your draft Radar Screen via screen sharing if possible, so that it can be seen by all and modified in real time.

6. Start the discussion by having the team review the projects and initiatives at the center of the draft Radar Screen. Remind them that you only want projects in the center if they require the ongoing collaboration of the entire team. The goal is to end up with no more than three, maybe four, projects in the center by the end of your discussion. Those projects and initiatives that are moved out of the center of the Radar Screen will be placed in either of the other two rings based on the discussion.

   - If, by the end of this discussion, there are more than three projects at the center of your draft Radar Screen, ask for suggestions on which ones should be moved to other rings of the Radar Screen.

   - Challenge the team to think critically about what requires full team collaboration as opposed to work that could be done just as effectively and more efficiently by either small groups or individuals.

7. Once you have gotten the Center of the Radar Screen to the smallest appropriate number of collaborative projects/initiatives, conduct a similar discussion about the second ring of the Radar Screen.

   • Remind the team that if a piece of work can be handled more efficiently and effectively by an individual, then it will be better placed in the outer ring.

8. Review the outer ring with the team to ensure that the projects there are indeed individual tasks.

9. After working through each of the three rings of the Radar Screen, ask one last time if there are any final concerns about placement of projects. Address any concerns through discussion.

10. Once the final version is agreed, take a moment to recognize yourselves for a job well done. Save a copy of the Radar Screen and plan on reviewing it again in three to six months.

Conversation Questions

• What are the few things that you're sure require collaboration within our team?

• What projects or initiatives within our team require minimal or no collaboration?

• What do we need to let go of?

• What are we collaborating on today that doesn't require it?

• What do we need to minimize, subtract, condense, make smaller, omit, or streamline?

• Where are we under-utilizing the collaborative capabilities of our team today?

• What are the things you can't say "no" to?

• What are we doing today that we need to say "no" to?

• How does our team collaboration bring to life the Five Principles?

- What is the most important thing our team could do this month?
- The greatest collaborative opportunity our team could capitalize on is...
- What will it take for this team to be able to say "no" to what may be asked of us?
- Who would benefit by collaborating on a project with other team members?
- What center circle project could be moved to a smaller group within our team?
- What is important to you, and what are you doing about it?
- Select one of your personal objectives. How does this objective link to the objectives of the total team?
- How well does our Radar Screen align with our team's business objectives?

Appendix C: Cultivate Collaboration

An Approach for Leader–Team Contracting for Behaviors

Cultivate Collaboration begins with a two-way contracting process that involves the team leader and team members. It's essential that this conversation be approached with care and a spirit of collegiality. It's not a matter of one person—the manager—foisting his or her will on a group, or a group trying to get its way. The process assumes that the manager and the team can act as partners in crafting a set of agreements about what will be required to make collaboration flourish. Mutual regard is essential.

Note: This process can be conducted virtually. It involves negotiation, give-and-take, and the potential for disagreement. Therefore, conducting these conversations face-to-face is preferable.

The process flows as follows:

1. The team leader asks the team to prepare a list of their expectations of him/her. These expectations will be stated as behaviors that the team feels they need to support their collaborative purpose and shared work. This list can be created prior to the session or in the room in real time.

2. At the same time the team leader prepares a list of his or her expectations of the team. These expectations are stated as behaviors that the leader feels he or she needs from team members for collaboration to flourish in the team.

3. The conversations start with the team stating their expectations of the manager.
    *   The list of behaviors is captured on a flip chart or whiteboard.
    *   At this point allow only questions for clarity and

understanding. Limit discussion and debate. That comes later.

4. Once the team has shared its list, the manager shares his/her list of expectations/behaviors of the team. Again, limit conversation and focus on clarity of understanding what has been shared.

    • The list is captured on a flip chart or whiteboard next to or near the list generated in the previous step.

    • Typically, the lists will agree in some ways and contrast in others. These similarities and differences form the basis of the subsequent conversations.

5. Begin the deeper conversation with the manager working through the list of expected behaviors that was shared with him or her.

    • Have the manager talk about what he/she agrees with and why.

    • Next the manager will talk about the requests that have been made that he/she isn't comfortable signing up for. This conversation continues until the team and manager either become comfortable with the requests or the team understands why their request may not be included in the final behavioral contract.

    • Review the final list of behaviors for the manager. It's best if it's limited to five to seven easily remembered behavioral commitments. If necessary, pare the list down by merging similar or related requests.

6. Next the team responds to the manager's requests of them. Note: The team may need time away from the manager to prepare their responses, so build this time into your plan for this session.

    • As with the manager, have the team begin by talking about where they agree with their manager's requests and why.

    • Next they will discuss the areas of disagreement. The goal here is to find common ground with the manager, not to make the manager wrong and the team right, or the other way around.

- Discussion continues until the team and the manager agree to the list of behaviors that will be expected of the team members.
- As with the manager's list, this list is best when it's limited to five to seven behaviors.

7. Debrief and discuss the final two lists, side-by-side. Check to be sure that both the manager and team are comfortable with what they have committed to.
    - Validate the lists by checking them against the team's purpose statement and against the work at the center of the team's Radar Screen. Will they support the collaborative intent of the team?

8. Print the final contracts and ask the entire team to sign them.

Examples of Behavioral Contracts

Team leader
- Assign tasks equitably.
- Support the team publicly.
- Hold us accountable for managing our own conflict directly with each other.
- Deflect non-priority requests.
- Be available for decisions and to resolve issues as required.

Team members
- Honor collaborative commitments or be clear when you can't.
- Keep the promises you make.
- Go direct with conflict.
- Listen deeply for what's not being said.
- Challenge one another to exceed expectations.
- Communicate in advance of the need.

- Leverage strength in the team by acting and speaking as one.

Template for sub-group contracting

The second ring of the Radar Screen identified areas of collaboration for sub-groups within the team. The contracting among those sub-groups takes place as part of Cultivate Collaboration. Sub-groups can use the template below for each project/initiative to be contracted. One template per one shared project/initiative.

What I will provide to you: What I need to receive from you:

- •

- •

- •

Mutual adjustments to the contract:

Deepening relationships

These conversations are an opportunity to build trust and deepen relationships where it really matters—between and among team members team who share work. Below is one simple approach that Mars teams use.

These conversations are about seeking to understand how our styles, personalities and preferences might affect how we work together.

1. Ask each team member to prepare a flip chart (or slide if you will be working remotely) with responses to these four

points:
- Three deeply held values that make me who I am
- Three things that energize me at work
- One thing that brings out the worst in me
- The legacy I dream of leaving

2. Each team member then shares his or her responses with the entire team.

3. Following each person's disclosure, allow for conversation to explore how their responses might affect how they collaborate on team projects/initiatives that are shared by the entire team (those from the center of the Radar Screen). Note: Keep this part of the session brief, 5–10 minutes per person at most. Save the bulk of the time for the next step.

4. After all team members have presented, ask them to meet with their sub-groups to discuss how who they are might affect their shared work. Use the answers to the questions from the previous step to inform these discussions. Given the overlap of members across sub-groups this may require a few rounds for all sub-groups to complete the conversations.

5. While working in sub-groups be sure to refer to the sub-group contracts described above. This ensures that people's personalities and preferences are appropriately accounted for in your agreements.

Conversation Questions

- What motivates you to connect, personally, with other members of this team?
- How clear are you about your commitments with your teammates when working together on business priorities?
- Who on the team has the biggest network within the team?
- When you need to get something done, who do you go to?
- I need to make more time for connecting with...
- When I'm not feeling courageous, what I need is...
- I define trust as...

- Someone I especially trust is... because...
- My work has critical intersections with...
- I lack a strong relationship with...
- I have great relationships with...
- My key stakeholders are...
- What does healthy conflict look like on our team?
- How do you define healthy conflict?
- A teammate that inspires me is...
- To me, commitment means...
- One thing I can commit to my teammates is...
- My teammates are committed to...
- An expectation our line manager has for the team around collaboration is...
- One thing I think my peers expect of me when collaborating is...
- One thing I expect when collaborating with my peers is...
- One person I want to work more with is...
- Who do you feel most accountable to?
- How can we best hold each other accountable?
- What incentives exist for collaboration on our team?
- When and why would a team member come to your rescue?
- What consequences exist for lack of collaboration on our team?

Appendix D: Activate Ways-of-Working

Meetings

Chapter 11 covered many of the basics of applying HPC to your meetings to ensure that they're more engaging and aligned with your collaborative intentions. Let's take a deeper look at how to think about meeting frequency and length. This is based on work we've been doing recently within Mars on an initiative called Meeting Smarter.

The Three Levers

A smart meeting schedule creates a balance among three factors:

- Meeting frequency
- Meeting length
- Agenda topics

The team's Radar Screen, as we've said, helps to make decisions about all three. Let's consider how the three factors interact to help create smarter meetings.

It's about time

Meeting frequency, meeting length, and how one sets up their agendas are all about wisely allocating meeting time. Finding the balance among these levers involves:

1. Figuring out how much time the team needs to spend together based on the work that was placed at the center of the Radar Screen.
2. How they prefer to divide that time up. That is, how often they need to meet to get their collaborative work done.
3. How long those meetings need to be.

How much meeting time?

Meeting time is precious and costly, so budget it wisely. The higher the need for full team collaboration, the more shared work there is, the more time you're likely to devote to meetings. Remember though, not all collaborative work requires meetings. Sometimes sub-groups can handle parts of a project and bring them back to the larger group. A lot of collaborative working, even among the total team, can be done by sharing information and co-creating documents using file sharing and social networking applications like SharePoint®, OneNote® and Yammer®. Follow this rule of thumb:

> Allocate a full team meeting only for those complex tasks and issues that will demonstrably benefit from it.

Everything else can be done most smartly by using collaborative technologies appropriately.

How often?

Frequency will be a matter of the urgency and complexity of the work. If a project is on a short or urgent deadline, the team may need to meet frequently at least in the short term. Complexity can be a part of both short- and long-term projects. Complex projects, projects with multiple work streams and hand-offs within the team, benefit from high levels of connectivity among team members; meet more frequently in these cases. When urgency and complexity are combined in one project there is no substitute for using team meeting time to get the work done. Collaborative technologies can also be helpful in complex and urgent work, especially for remote teams working in different time zones. Between meetings, work can continue via file sharing, keeping momentum going until there's time to bring the team together again.

On the other hand, if the need isn't urgent or particularly

complex, meeting less frequently is fine. If a group is working together to create a long-range plan, and isn't bound by an immediate deadline, they can and should meet less frequently. There are likely other matters that are more pressing that will demand their time. Here again, collaborative technologies can be used to advance the work in-between actual meetings.

How long?

Short meetings are generally more engaging and effective. Neuroscience suggests that you can expect to hold the average adult's attention for no more than 50 minutes at a time. Short meetings—an hour or less—are fine for straightforward topics and deliverables. Again, how long a meeting or meetings should be is a matter of complexity and urgency. More complex topics will often require longer periods of active collaboration than simple topics. Breaking up longer meetings on complex topics into a series of shorter ones can work, but it can also backfire. Interrupting productive debate or critical Q&A simply in the name of keeping a meeting short can compromise the quality of your meeting deliverables. Give the work and the meeting the time they deserve.

Though I separated them in the preceding explanations, meeting frequency and meeting length are two sides of the same coin. When it comes to setting meetings, you can think about frequency and length together with the help of the diagram provided opposite.

There will be exceptions to this simple approach. Establishing a team's meeting rhythm is as much an art as a science. Take the time to consider the team's purpose, the nature of the work they share, and the overall environment they're working in. Apply this logic where it makes sense, but be ready to flex.

High	Longer, less frequent meetings	Longer, more frequent meetings
Complexity		
Low	Shorter, less frequent meetings	Shorter, more frequent meetings
	Low Urgency High	

Meeting agendas

Recurring team meetings

For regularly occurring team meetings, the work at the center Radar Screen forms the basis of your high-level agendas. If, for instance, your team has declared that it's working together on Projects Alpha and Beta, you'll put placeholders in your agendas for these projects. Of course, other items will make it onto your team's agendas. From time to time you will need to on-board new team members. There may be engagement activities you have planned. Occasionally, urgent matters will arise that require the team's attention. Any of these might need to be accommodated in a meeting agenda. But, when it comes to the regularly occurring work of team meetings, you turn to the Radar Screen first.

Your Radar Screen is a good start. When you begin to plan specific meetings, though, you have to get more detailed.

The O^2 deliverable

Smart meetings have clearly stated deliverables and each deliverable is the result of active co-creation. We use the O^2 format for stating deliverables in the clearest way. Each O^2 deliverable is made up of two parts: the Objective and the Opportunity. The Objective identifies in a general way what is being created or achieved. For example, we might be co-creating a plan, making a decision or co-creating a solution. The second O, Opportunity, refers to the specific benefit we'll get from the deliverable. We set this up as a "from–to" statement.

For example, maybe we need to make a decision (the objective) about moving FROM having three vendors TO having a single vendor (the opportunity). Another agenda topic might require an agreement (the objective) for moving FROM a variety of formats for submitting proposals TO one standard format for proposals (the opportunity.) The O^2 deliverable format forces greater clarity about what it is the team must accomplish. This focuses the team, helps them stay on track during the process, and helps you know when you have done what you set out to do.

Ad hoc meetings

Just because a piece of work isn't on your Radar Screen doesn't mean it might not require the attention of the team. Think about those urgent surprises that come up: an angry customer or a safety incident in a factory. Every so often teams have to call ad hoc meetings. These meetings benefit from the same thinking. Take time to frame a clear O^2 deliverable for even last-minute meetings.

Decision Making

Below is a simple tool that I first learned about when I worked at IBM and that we use at Mars. It's a way of gauging the levels of agreement within a group in a quick and non-threatening way. It's particularly useful when a group is trying to reach consensus. You can use it when beginning a decision process to create clarity about where the group is starting. It can also be employed later in a process if the group becomes stuck. It's called "Fist-to-Five."

It begins by stating the proposed answer or pending decision to the group. The clearer your proposition, the better for this process. Write it in a place where all can see it. Once everyone is clear about what is being proposed, you'll ask for a show of hands and fingers following the guidance (see table):

Fist-to-Five

Fist—complete disagreement with the proposed decision	**Three fingers raised**—I agree
One finger raised—I strongly disagree	**Four fingers raised**—I agree strongly
Two fingers raised—I disagree	**Five fingers raised**—I completely agree and support the proposed decision

It's essential that everyone raise their hands at the same time. This prevents those who might be inclined to follow the majority from being able to do what they see others doing. Sometimes, I ask team members to close their eyes or to turn their backs to each other when they raise their hands to ensure I'm getting an accurate read of everyone's views.

While all hands are in the air, tally the results and then state them aloud. For example: "I see that two of you have five fingers raised, two have four fingers raised, one has three fingers, and two of you have two fingers raised."

Next, confirm that your count is accurate by asking if this is what the group is seeing. If they've had their eyes closed or turned away from each other they'll need to adjust themselves to see what you're seeing.

When it's clear that everyone has the same tally, it's time for hands to go down and to begin the conversation. This can go many ways depending on the matter being discussed and how close or far apart your team members are, based on the "fist-to-five" tally. It's helpful to begin by asking the group a few questions such as:

- What do you make of this response?
- What does this mean for how we should proceed?
- What's the best next step for us to take?

Fist-to-five isn't always helpful. In fact, it can backfire. For example:

- When it's clear there's strong disagreement and the dissenters have made their positions known, fist-to-five can come across as putting dissenters in the hot seat.
- When it's clear that the group is ready to move forward with the proposed decision, fist-to-five will feel like postponing the inevitable.

Because it's non-verbal Fist-to-five can help the more reserved in the room feel better about revealing their positions. It's also sometimes just the break a team needs when they're feeling mired in too much talk and debate. The physicality of it has a way of easing the tensions in a room. Try it the next time the team is trying to close in on true consensus.

Using the Conversation Questions in a Ways-of-Working Discussion

The HPC Conversation Questions for this Practice are most useful for teams that are already using HPC, who want to understand how they're doing. They're ideal for taking a Sustain & Renew approach to your ways-of-working. Below I describe a simple exercise that can surface good data for teams that want to take their ways-of-working up a notch or two.

I've found it most useful not to limit the inquiry to just one way-of-working, like meetings. To do so ignores how connected, how interwoven a team's processes and interactions tend to be. For example, decision making often happens within meetings. Decisions are informed by the many connections people have had outside of meetings. So, keep your inquiry broad at first and then zero in on the ways-of-working that seem to be the biggest opportunities.

The steps

Prior to your meeting about ways-of-working, select two to three questions from the Activate Ways-of-Working Team Conversation Questions located below. Provide them to team members in advance of your conversation. Then:

- Ask them to send their responses to you a few days before your meeting.
- Collect and sort the responses to the questions based on any themes you see.
- Provide the consolidated responses to each team member for review just before the meeting or as you're getting started. Be sure they have time to digest the information prior to the next step.
- Begin your conversation based on the themed responses you have distributed.

There's no telling where a given conversation will go. As I said, this is a Sustain & Renew exercise. Apply the Five Actions of team learning and see where it takes you:

- Pause
- Inquire

- Reflect
- Plan
- Act

Activate Ways-of-Working Conversation Questions

- A way-of-working for our team that is not effective is...
- A way-of-working for our team that works well is...
- What decisions are truly team decisions?
- What process do we have for making decisions?
- What decisions are we trying to make as a team, but should be delegated to individuals on the team?
- What does a crucial confrontation on our team look like?
- Our team could be made more efficient by...
- An example of high efficiency on our team is...
- I define efficiency as...
- A role model for efficiency is...
- A best practice from our team I would share with others is...
- A best practice way-of-working I've heard of is...
- How can you play a stronger role in supporting team ways-of-working?
- What are we spending time on in our meetings that could better be spent on something else?
- Our team's fundamental processes are...
- What systems are fundamental to the team's ways-of-working?
- What communication mediums are best for connecting with the team?
- How does the content/agenda of our meetings serve our team purpose? What can be improved?
- What is the best thing about our team meetings? What is the worst?
- What stops the flow of communication on our team?
- Our team needs to make more time for connecting with...

- What is the best way of communicating with you? ... among the team?
- A new way of working I would propose for our team is...

Appendix E: Sustain & Renew

We've talked about two kinds of team learning: task learning and team dynamics learning. I'll address both in this appendix, as well as provide a questionnaire for use that covers both by looking at the whole HPC Framework.

Task Learning

The after-action review

An after-action review (AAR) is conducted at the end of an initiative or project. It encourages productive discussion about what happened, and what can be learned. After-action reviews aren't about success or failure, right or wrong. They're professional discussions of specific events designed to distill important lessons learned—positive or otherwise. Use the graphic below to structure an AAR with your team on a specific initiative or project.

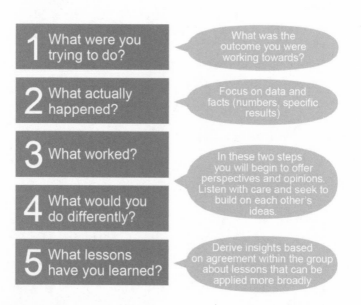

1 What were you trying to do?

What was the outcome you were working towards?

2 What actually happened?

Focus on data and facts (numbers, specific results)

3 What worked?

4 What would you do differently?

In these two steps you will begin to offer perspectives and opinions. Listen with care and seek to build on each other's ideas.

5 What lessons have you learned?

Derive insights based on agreement within the group about lessons that can be applied more broadly

Team Dynamics Learning

Assessing a team using the HPC Practices

There are two approaches for using the Framework and the thinking behind for assessments. The first approach involves inquiring into each of the Practices discretely. The second involves using the Three Imperatives to drive the inquiry, an approach that can better account for the relationships among the various Practices.

HPC PRACTICES ASSESSMENT

This questionnaire is designed for use by teams that have begun working with the High Performance Collaboration Framework. It will provide a sense of how effectively the team has taken on board the Practices of HPC.

This questionnaire can be used in a number of ways.

- You send the questionnaire to every team member and have them send the completed version back to you. You then gather their scores and use a spreadsheet to total the scores yourself. You bring this compiled data back to the team for discussion.
- You use one of the many fine online survey companies and create a version of this questionnaire there. These services will compile the results and provide a report for use with the team.
- You ask individual team members to complete and score the survey themselves. Then have them bring their results to a team meeting where the team can compare and discuss their findings.

The Questionnaire

1. Score each statement in each Practice based on the 1–5 scale below.

1	2	3	4	5
Strongly disagree	Disagree	Neither agree nor disagree	Agree	Strongly agree

2. To determine the score for each Practice:

A. Total the Score column and place the sum in the cell marked "A".

B. Divide the total by the number indicated in (B) SCORE. This is the score for this Practice.

For example, for Clarify Context, your scoring might look like this:

CLARIFY CONTEXT

#	Item	Score 1–5
26	When there are significant shifts in the organization (new strategy or structure) our team takes time to reassess our team purpose, commitments and ways-of-working.	3
27	When there are significant changes in our team (new leader or several new members) our team takes time to reassess our team purpose, commitments and ways-of-working.	2
	(A) Column total	5
	(B) SCORE (column total ÷ 2)	2.5

INSPIRE PURPOSE

#	Item	Score 1–5
1	We have developed a team purpose statement.	
2	Our purpose statement is focused on the value	

created by our collaboration and not on our functional reason for being a team.

3   We actively apply our purpose statement in the operation of our team.

4   Our team's purpose statement is both aspirational and pragmatic; it inspires us and it helps guide our day-to-day collaboration.

Column total   **A**

SCORE (total ÷ 4)   **B**

CRYSTALLIZE INTENT

#	Item	Score 1–5
5	Our team has agreed about which work requires full team collaboration.	
6	We have agreed about which work requires sub-groups within our team to collaborate.	
7	We have agreed about which work in our team will be owned and performed by individuals.	
8	Team members' efforts are guided by the agreements we have made about which work requires collaboration and which doesn't.	
	Column total	**A**
	SCORE (total ÷ 4)	**B**

CULTIVATE COLLABORATION

#	Item	Score 1–5
9	Our team leader holds us accountable *both* for our individual performance objectives *and* for specific expectations of how we will collaborate with each other.	
10	Members of our team expect their teammates to work with them based on specific	

collaborative agreements they have with each other.

11   We regularly set aside time for building and maintaining effective relationships with each other.

12   Members of our team consistently handle conflict effectively.

Column total   **A**

SCORE (total ÷ 4)   **B**

ACTIVATE WAYS-OF-WORKING

#	Item	Score 1–5
13	Our team meetings are consistently effective.	
14	All of our meetings are built around clear deliverables.	
15	We have a clear process for how we make decisions within our team.	
16	We use our decision process consistently.	
17	As a team, we are consistently effective at making decisions.	
18	We have agreed to a set of team communications protocols.	
19	We apply our communications protocols consistently.	
20	Communications within our team are consistently effective.	
21	Our team uses collaborative technologies to their fullest potential.	
	Column total	**A**
	SCORE (total ÷ 9)	**B**

SUSTAIN & RENEW

#	Item	Score 1–5
22	We regularly assess how effective we are as a team, that is to say, how well we are living our HPC commitments.	
23	Our team consistently conducts after-action reviews on significant projects.	
24	Our team has a plan for how we will assess and improve our collaborative performance over the next six months.	
25	Our team follows our team improvement plan consistently.	
	Column total	**A**
	SCORE (total ÷ 4)	**B**

CLARIFY CONTEXT

#	Item	Score 1–5
26	When there are significant shifts in the organization (new strategy or structure) our team takes time to reassess our team purpose, commitments and ways-of-working.	
27	When there are significant changes in our team (new leader or several new members) our team takes time to reassess our team purpose, commitments and ways-of-working.	
	Column total	**A**
	SCORE (total ÷ 2)	**B**

Summarize the scores below. Use the summary to lead a discussion with your team.

Scoring Summary

PRACTICE	SCORE	NOTES
Inspire Purpose		
Crystallize Intent		
Cultivate Collaboration		
Activate Ways-of-Working		
Sustain & Renew		
Clarify Context		

Imperatives-based Diagnostic Questions

To get a thorough picture of how effectively the team is collaborating, conduct an inquiry using the Three Imperatives as your guide. Below, grouped by the Imperatives, are questions you can use to conduct your inquiry. You don't need to use all of them. Select a few from each Imperative to initiate your diagnostic conversations. Then dig deeper using follow-up questions based on the ideas and issues that arise. You can conduct these conversations one-on-one or with the entire team.

Clarity

- How clear is the team about their reason for being and acting as a team (versus working as a collection of individuals)?
- How clear is the team about how their collaboration is intended to add value over and above the sum of their individual efforts?
- How clear is the team about why their collaboration matters beyond the specific business deliverables expected of them?
- How clear is the team about what work, specifically, is shared by the total team?
- How clear is every team member about who they should be collaborating with?
- How clear is the team about where decisions for key

matters reside, and with whom?

Intentionality

- How thoroughly have team members contracted with each other for how they will collaborate?
- If you're the team leader, how intentional have you been in contracting with team members about what you expect from them in terms of collaboration?
- If you're the team leader, how intentional have you been in finding out what team members expect from you in supporting their collaboration?
- Have team members included expectations for collaboration in their annual performance plans and objectives?
- How much work has been done with the team in strengthening important collaborative relationships?
- How intentional has the team been in using their agreed-upon ways-of-working? Do team members actively remind one another of their ways-of-working agreements?
- How intentional and engaged has the team been about assessing their performance as a team?

Discipline

- What ways-of-working has the team developed?
- How well documented are the team's ways-of-working?
- How well-aligned are your team's ways-of-working to your team's purpose and shared work?
- How consistently does your team use your agreed-upon ways-of-working?
- How disciplined is your team when it comes to conducting after-action reviews on specific projects?
- How disciplined is your team when it comes to assessing how well you are working together as a team?
- How disciplined is your team about implementing improvements to your ways-of-working?

Team Feedback

A crucial element of continuous learning and high performance collaboration is the giving and receiving of feedback within the team. In high performing groups, feedback isn't a once-a-year event, but rather part of how the team operates. It's sought out and offered freely, one-to-one as well as in the group, real time.

Delivering and receiving feedback are skills that can be learned and practiced. A powerful tool for thinking about and then delivering feedback is represented by the acronym SBI. The letters SBI stand for situation, behavior, and impact. The intent is to ensure that the person giving the feedback is providing it thoughtfully, with minimal judgement and with adequate context. This enables the person receiving the feedback to take it in with a minimum of defensiveness. Let's take a closer look at SBI, beginning with definitions of the terms and then considering a few examples:

Situation
Describe the situation that the observed behavior was a part of. The more specific you can be about where and when it occurred, the better.

Behavior
Describe exactly the behavior you are talking about. Think of playing back a videotape, using words instead of pictures to describe what you saw. Don't talk about what you believe, assume, or think the individual was doing. Simply describe the behavior factually.

Impact
Share with the individual the impact of the behavior on you or others that were present. You are making your internal experience known to the individual. A description of the impact will start with, "I felt..." or "I was..." or "It appeared to me..."

Example

Non-SBI feedback	**SBI feedback**
Patricia, I really hate it when you show up late to our meetings!	Patricia, during our operations meeting last week (*situation*), you walked in 20 minutes late right in the middle of Todd's presentation and discussion (*behavior*). It caused us to interrupt the flow of some very important conversation. What's more, that wasn't the first time you've been late, which really leads me to question your commitment to our project (*impact*).

Once you become comfortable with SBI, an option is to add a fourth letter to this model, "A," which stands for "Alternative." Call this SBI-A feedback. This involves providing your feedback using the SBI format and then adding your thoughts about a different action or behavior that might have provided a more effective outcome. Providing an alternative is especially helpful where the SBI was clear but the person receiving it is unclear about how else they could have approached the situation.

Example

Non-SBI feedback	**SBI-A feedback**
Tom, the way you handled that conversation with Sascha was dreadful. Don't do it again.	Tom, when we were discussing the budget with Sascha last week (*situation*), you raised your voice and told Sascha his work was basically useless (*behavior*). I could see him cringe. After that he completely stopped talking so that we had to postpone the discussion (*impact*). I can understand why

you'd be upset. Perhaps it would have been more productive if you had calmly expressed your disappointment and asked Sascha what ideas he had to address the situation (*alternative*).

The team feedback process

We recommend running team feedback sessions three or four times a year. In these sessions team members offer their views of themselves and how they're doing relative to the commitments they've made to the team. They then invite feedback from the rest of the team.

Note: *This exercise is designed to be conducted without outside facilitation. However, if a team is new to this process, consider seeking support from a facilitator. If there are serious individual performance issues in the team, this exercise is not recommended.*

1. Ask each team member to prepare two self-disclosure statements:
   - Two things I am doing well that I believe add value to our collaboration
   - One or two places where I could add more value by changing my approach
2. Have the team sit in a circle so everyone is visible to everyone else.
3. Ask for a volunteer (or two) to pay attention to the timing of the process (unless you have engaged a facilitator who is doing this for you).
4. Ask another volunteer to begin by reading out their self-disclosure statements.
5. After the first team member self-discloses, other team members respond, one at a time, to what they heard. In not more than two or three minutes, team members provide

feedback that may:

- Be reinforcing, noting positive behaviors and impacts based on the self-disclosure
- Ask for more of the same behavior(s)
- Call out unproductive behaviors, using SBI, that were important but not part of the self-disclosure.

6. The feedback recipient takes notes while receiving feedback, but he or she does not discuss or debate the feedback that is provided. This process is all about gathering data in an open, non-defensive fashion. The aim is to listen actively and ask questions for clarity only.

7. In the event that a piece of feedback necessitates a longer or deeper conversation between the giver and the recipient, ensure that an agreement is made about when and how that will happen.

8. After the first person has received feedback from the entire team, they thank their colleagues.

9. The next person repeats the process until everyone has shared self-disclosure and received feedback.

10. When the process is complete, all team members review what they heard and make specific commitments to the entire team for what they will start doing differently.

A few tips for this feedback process:

- Focus on efficiency: Encourage team members to practice speaking simply and directly to each other, with respect, and without embellishing their feedback with unnecessary details or niceties.
- Practice deep listening: When receiving feedback, listen in silence, and practice the SOLER approach that was discussed in Chapter 11:

S: Sit or stand *squarely* in relation to the person you're with

O: Maintain an *open* body position

L: *Lean* in a little

E: Make *eye* contact

R: Remain physically and emotionally *relaxed*

- Avoid "Yes, but..." statements to explain or justify yourself.
- Keep perspective: If you are struggling with a piece of feedback, remember, feedback is as much about the giver as it is about you. What someone is saying to you, about you, says a great deal about what is important to *them*, what they care about and focus on. We all have filters and biases, and these show up in feedback.

Sustain & Renew Conversation Questions

- How could feedback play a stronger role in our individual and team development?
- How would you define renewal for the team?
- How would you rate our team's level of well-being?
- How viable is our team moving into the future?
- In what areas can our team improve?
- What are the strengths our team has to build on?
- I see the future of our team as...
- What is your greatest fear for our team?
- What are the conversations our team needs to have?
- What is the most positive way we can proceed?
- What do we need to understand better?
- What new perceptions and experiences will be critical to our success?'
- How might the team better measure effectiveness?
- What role does development play in the evolution of our team?
- How good is our team at creating space for learning and growth?
- What would a team development plan look like for us?
- Where have we experienced rapid learning?
- What truths about our team are we afraid to speak?
- What are the implications for our team if nothing changes?

- What new ways of thinking and acting are needed to support our strategy?
- What is holding the team back from its potential?
- What is a key team strength that could also serve as a tragic flaw?
- How effectively does the team keep commitments to itself?
- I want to thank _____ for...
- What do we celebrate?
- The thing our team is best at is...

Appendix F: Clarify Context

Clarify Context is, by definition, a big topic. It deals in strategy, large-scale organization change, and changes in leadership. The number of potential tools is vast. The potential for complicating things is great. So, we keep it simple. Clarity and learning are the desired outcomes of this Practice. So, inquiry is where it begins. The Conversation Questions are the primary tool we recommend to teams engaging in this Practice, along with the "Keep/Enhance/Remove/Add" table from Chapter 13.

There is one other technique that I have found to be useful, especially for teams in transition. I discussed a version of it in Chapter 13—the graphical history map. The process I described there was professionally facilitated but it doesn't need to be.

The exercise yields several benefits:

- It gives the team a broadly shared understanding of how they arrived at who and where they are today.
- It provides newer team members a detailed, historical context they have probably lacked.
- It surfaces previously underappreciated or unknown patterns and lessons from the group's recent past.
- It permits intentional letting go of what was, so a team can move forward.

The exercise takes from 90 minutes to three hours depending on the size of the team and how wide-ranging the conversation becomes.

You'll need:

- A large, bare wall
- Several pages of flip-chart paper or a role of white paper 3–4 feet wide
- A variety of colored markers

- A flip-chart stand with paper.

The process:

1. Create a large, horizontal, blank writing space using several pages of flip-chart paper, side-by-side. If you have a large roll of white paper, that works, too. The final dimensions should be about 40 inches high by 6–8 feet long.
    Note: For steps 2–4 refer to the graphic that follows step 3.
2. Use broad-tip markers to create a timeline on the paper you mounted on the wall. Write the years across the top of your chart. Place the year you want to start with on the left and work towards the right with the current year showing up towards the right edge of your timeline. A time span of three to five years is usually adequate.
3. Under that, create two or three rows to accommodate types of events you want to pay special attention to. For instance, I usually create a row to capture big changes in the business. Below that I create a row for changes in the people or leadership in the team I'm working with. Across the bottom I put a row for events in the outside world that may have affected the business and the team. It looks like this:

	2013	2014	2015	2016
The Business				
Our Team/ Function				
The World				

4. Give team members markers of various colors.

5. Explain to them that you want them to populate the timeline with the events that occurred during the specified time. Instruct them to focus on events that are meaningful to them and that shaped where their team is today. You can have them work individually, though I find having them work in pairs is most engaging and leads to more ideas.

6. Encourage them to use symbols and images as much as possible, limiting the number of words to only the essential ones. Stick figures and rough sketches are ideal. They'll have a chance later to explain what they were trying to represent if it isn't clear.

7. Allow them to interact as they work, so long as they keep adding pertinent information to the timeline.

8. Notice when the conversation and work on the chart start to slow. When there is more talk than drawing and writing, suggest a halt to the process. Before you stop it, check with the group to be sure they're feeling that the timeline is complete.

9. Once you've ended the process, invite the team to step back and silently consider the entirety of what they have created. Give them two or three minutes to do this.

10. Facilitate a conversation about the timeline, starting from the earliest events. Ensure that you stay with a period of time until everyone understands what is meant by the symbols, icons and words that will have filled the chart. As needed, have them add to the timeline, capturing new memories as they surface. Allow for storytelling to clarify and add texture to the unfolding history.

11. Give the group the freedom and time required to make sense of the history they're discussing; resist over-facilitating. Only intervene if their conversation stalls, if you sense that they aren't deepening their understanding and/or aren't continuing to move forward in time at a reasonable pace.

12. On a separate flip chart capture the big ideas and insights

that you hear coming out of their conversation. Don't interrupt the group's conversation as you do this. Simply record what you hear.

13. When they've worked all the way through the timeline, again ask them to step back and consider what they have learned through the process. Ask questions like:
    - What were your insights and "ah-ha"s?
    - What surprised you?
    - What patterns emerged?
    - What excites or concerns you?

If the group is slow to start or engage in your questions, share the flip chart you created from the ideas and insights you overheard.

14. Allow the group to explore and test its conclusions and discoveries. It's likely that individual perceptions and insights will vary. For instance, newer team members will probably be struck by how much context they had been lacking. More tenured team members may see parts of their history in entirely new ways. All of it is valid and useful.

15. As the conversation slows ask the group to summarize what it has learned. Capture this on a flip-chart page.

16. Ask the group what this exercise means for them, what they should be focusing on going forward. Contract for how this work will happen, and capture whatever commitments are made.

17. Photograph and save the timeline for future reference.

18. In cases where it feels important for the team to make a new start, to leave the past behind them, ask the team to remove the timeline from the wall (they may want to photograph it first). Have them fold it until it's as small as possible. Invite as many of them as want to, to carry the folded timeline to a waste receptacle in another room or space and to dispose of it with as much ceremony as feels appropriate. Some teams,

where it was possible to do so safely, have chosen to burn the chart in a fireplace or fire pit. The key is to consciously enact this letting go in a way that all will remember it.

Clarify Context Conversation Questions

Change in leadership:
- As the new leader, what excites or worries me about this opportunity?
- As the new leader, what skills or capabilities will I need or need to develop in order to be successful?
- As the new leader, what do I need to know about this role and this team that will help me to succeed?
- As members of the team, what do we want our new leader to know about us as a team and about our HPC journey so far?
- As members of the team, what are we most worried about as we make this transition?
- What is most exciting to us?

Change in organizational structure:
- What is this team's function in the new organization, broadly?
- Has it changed?
- Have our internal customers or stakeholders changed?
- Is our team set up appropriately to account for the changes in the organization? If not, what needs to change?
- How should our ways-of-working change to deliver value to the business?

Change in strategy:
- What is the shift that has taken place in our business?
- What do key customers think about what is going on in the business?

- What are the business goals, challenges and operational constraints that our business is facing now and how have they changed?
- What does the business want our team to achieve?
- How do we fit in?

Change in team membership:
- How will we effectively on-board our new members and actively integrate them into our team?
- If new members are joining, what are their strengths and needs?
- What is our team's working style and what are its implications for new members?
- Do we have the right capabilities on the team as we move forward for the organization?
- What is each team member's level of readiness and willingness?

Notes

Chapter 3: Research and the First Insights

1. FIRO-B—Fundamental Interpersonal Relationship Orientation-Behaviors. Schutz's work suggested that anyone working within a group has three fundamental needs or concerns that need to be addressed, those being the need for inclusion, for control and for intimacy. Each of these three needs is both wanted from others and also expressed by the person having the needs.

2. Stephen Colbert, when he hosted the *Colbert Report*, coined the term "truthiness" to describe the factual-sounding-but-not-quite-factual tidbits that most politicians traffic in. Truthiness is what keeps websites like Politifact and FactCheck.org in business.

Chapter 4: What Doesn't Work

1. Jon R. Katzenbach and Douglas K. Smith, *The Wisdom of Teams: Creating the High Performance Organization* (HarperCollins, 1993).

2. J. Richard Hackman, *Leading Teams: Setting the Stage for Great Performances* (Harvard Business School, 2002), 60.

3. Ibid.

4. Katzenbach and Smith, *The Wisdom of Teams*.

Chapter 5: The "I" in Team, Part 2

1. Edgar Schein, *Humble Inquiry: The Gentle Art of Asking Instead of Telling* (Berrett-Koehler, 2013).

2. Jon R. Katzenbach and Douglas K. Smith, *The Wisdom of Teams: Creating the High Performance Organization* (HarperCollins, 1993).

3. There are numerical values associated with these ratings but such specificity isn't essential for this discussion.

4.   There are 27 possible combinations or patterns of needs states — three needs states with three possible ratings (H-M-L) yields 27 possible patterns. McClelland and his colleagues did groundbreaking work in identifying how these patterns show up in subsets of the population, like successful entrepreneurs and middle and senior managers.

Chapter 7: The Practices of High Performance Collaboration

1.   Connie J. G. Gersick, "Time and Transition in Work Teams: Toward a New Model of Group Effectiveness," *Academy of Management Journal* (1988) vol. 1, no. 1, 9–41.

Chapter 10: Intentionality and Cultivate Collaboration

1.   Stephen M. R. Covey, *The Speed of Trust: The One Thing That Changes Everything* (Free Press, 2008).
2.   Stephen R. Covey, *The Seven Habits of Highly Effective People: Powerful Lessons in Personal Change* (Simon & Schuster, 2013).
3.   Patrick Lencioni, *The Five Dysfunctions of a Team: A Leadership Fable* (Jossey-Bass, 2002).
4.   Christopher Avery with Meri Aaron Walker and Erin O'Toole Murphy, *Teamwork Is an Individual Skill: Getting Your Work Done When Sharing Responsibility* (Berrett-Koehler, 2001).

Chapter 11: Discipline and Activate Ways-of-Working

1.   Jon Petz, *Boring Meetings Suck: Get More Out of Your Meetings, or Get Out of More Meetings* (Wiley, 2011).

Chapter 14: The Special Practice — Clarify Context

1.   Max DePree, *Leadership Is an Art* (Crown Business, 2004).

Chapter 15: Putting the Framework to Work

1. Jon R. Katzenbach and Douglas K. Smith, *The Wisdom of Teams: Creating the High Performance Organization* (HarperCollins, 1993).

CHANGE
MAKERS
BOOKS

Changemakers Books

TRANSFORMATION

Transform your life, transform your world - Changemakers
Books publishes for individuals committed to transforming
their lives and transforming the world. Our readers seek to
become positive, powerful agents of change. Changemakers
Books inform, inspire, and provide practical wisdom and skills
to empower us to write the next chapter of humanity's future.
If you have enjoyed this book, why not tell other readers by
posting a review on your preferred book site.

Recent bestsellers from Changemakers Books are:

Integration
The Power of Being Co-Active in Work and Life
Ann Betz, Karen Kimsey-House
Integration examines how we came to be polarized in our
dealing with self and other, and what we can do to move from
an either/or state to a more effective and fulfilling way of being.
Paperback: 978-1-78279-865-1 ebook: 978-1-78279-866-8

Lead Yourself First!
Indispensable Lessons in Business and in Life
Michelle Ray
Are you ready to become the leader of your own life? Apply
simple, powerful strategies to take charge of yourself, your
career, your destiny.
Paperback: 978-1-78279-703-6 ebook: 978-1-78279-702-9

Burnout to Brilliance
Strategies for Sustainable Success
Jayne Morris
Routinely running on reserves? This book helps you transform
your life from burnout to brilliance with strategies for
sustainable success.
Paperback: 978-1-78279-439-4 ebook: 978-1-78279-438-7

The Master Communicator's Handbook
Teresa Erickson, Tim Ward
Discover how to have the most communicative impact in this
guide by professional communicators with over 30 years of
experience advising leaders of global organizations.
Paperback: 978-1-78535-153-2 ebook: 978-1-78535-154-9

Future Consciousness
A Path to Purposeful Evolution
Tom Lombardo
How do our unique conscious minds reflect and amplify nature's vast evolutionary process? This book reveals how we can flourish in the flow of evolution and create a prosperous future for ourselves, human society and the planet.
Paperback: 978-1-78099-985-2 ebook: 978-1-78279-070-9

Modern Machiavelli
Troy Bruner and Philip Eager
Modern Machiavelli will teach you smart, social tactics to advance your career and improve your relationships. This book explains how to successfully manage conflict, influence others, and understand the overt and covert dynamics of interpersonal power.
Paperback: 978-1-78535-611-7 ebook: 978-1-78535-612-4

Soccer Thinking for Management Success
Peter Loge
Success used to look like football. Now success looks like soccer. Soccer is 90 minutes of systems thinking in action. This book is by a soccer fan and player who has spent a career building and running teams and organizations. He draws on insights from leaders, known and not-so-well-known, who use soccer thinking to succeed.
Paperback: 978-1-78535-754-1 ebook: 978-1-78535-755-8

Readers of ebooks can buy or view any of these bestsellers by clicking on the live link in the title. Most titles are published in paperback and as an ebook. Paperbacks are available in traditional bookshops. Both print and ebook formats are available online.

Find more titles and sign up to our readers' newsletter at
http://www.johnhuntpublishing.com/transformation
Follow us on Facebook at
https://www.facebook.com/Changemakersbooks